HOW MANY EGGS THEN FOR LADY THATCHER?

A. Vesselo

MINERVA PRESS
LONDON
MONTREUX LOS ANGELES SYDNEY

HOW MANY EGGS THEN FOR LADY THATCHER?

ISBN 1 86106 510 8

First Published 1997 by
MINERVA PRESS
195 Knightsbridge
London SW7 1RE

Printed in Great Britain by
Antony Rowe Ltd, Chippenham, Wiltshire

HOW MANY EGGS THEN FOR LADY THATCHER?

To Rosa,
the best of wives

Contents

One	Sally and the Eggs	9
Two	Women and Men	12
Three	Communities and their Purposes	15
Four	The Community and the Individual – Some Serious Reflections	19
Five	Ambition, Competition and so Forth	23
Six	The Mind and 'Reality'. Of Virtue and of Vice	27
Seven	War and Peace. More on Virtue and Vice	31
Eight	The Theme of the Buccaneer	34
Nine	Whose Benefit? Foretelling the Future	39
Ten	What is History?	43
Eleven	The Synchronic and the Diachronic	48
Twelve	Communism, Capitalism and so Forth. I. Communism	53

Thirteen	Communism and Capitalism. II. A Square Look at Capitalism as Such	60
Fourteen	Capitalism and the 'Social' Question	65
Fifteen	Wealth as Aim; and its Implications	70
Sixteen	The Market, and what Underlies it	75
Seventeen	Democracy	81
Eighteen	The End of History?	87
Nineteen	The Present, the Past and the Future	92
Twenty	A Misty Forward Glance in Time	98
Twenty-one	The Play and the Actors	104
Twenty-two	Two Kinds of People?	108
Twenty-three	Aims and Ends. Personality, and the Irresistible Urge to Personalisation	112
Twenty-four	Simplification; and the Economy	118
Twenty-five	More on Personalisation; and on Public Relations (PR) and the Like	123
Twenty-six	To Consult the People?	127
Twenty-seven	Oversimplification – and Some Thoughts on Monarchy	131
Twenty-eight	Morality?	136
Twenty-nine	Sex and Royalty	142
Thirty	Sex and the Moral Question in General	148

Thirty-one	Morality and the Community	153
Thirty-two	Power and Glory	157
Thirty-three	The Nature of the Ego	164
Thirty-four	How Do Moral Codes Arise?	169
Thirty-five	The Interpretation of 'Community'	173
Thirty-six	Profit in Relation to a World Community – and Competition	178
Thirty-seven	Competition and 'The Common Good'	184
Thirty-eight	The Common Good – and Common Standards	189
Thirty-nine	Leadership and Democracy	195
Forty	The Need for our Threatened Society to Change its Colours, and Rapidly	200
Forty-one	And the Nature of the Change	205
Forty-two	So How Do We See Things Now?	211
Forty-three	The Task to be Faced	216
Forty-four	Good and Bad; Right and Wrong	221
Forty-five	A Discussion of Terminology	226
Forty-six	Morals and Religion	231
Forty-seven	The Life-Process	236
Forty-eight	In Sum and in Conclusion	241
Index		245

One

Sally and the Eggs

My wife had a friend, Sally by name, who ran an excellent guest house in the Lake District. We spent a few days there one summer, together with our young son. On coming down on the first morning, we were presented with a very good breakfast including eggs; but to our surprise, whereas my son and I each had two eggs, my wife had only one. This was no error. It turned out to be Sally's regular practice, and in relation to all her guests. Men two eggs, women one. No differentiation in payment, be it noted, nor any preliminary inquiry made to guests as to how many eggs they might prefer: the law simply laid it down – men two, women one.

My wife was taken aback, and, as one must confess, just a little deflated. We discussed the matter but decided very quickly that it was not something which could be outspokenly aired. If you knew Sally you would know why, without need for further explanation. She is a lady of determined character, with whom one may well differ from time to time in opinion but with whom it is as well, on the whole, not to involve oneself in argument. She knows what she knows, and all her actions are based on the soundest and most incontrovertible principles.

This is really one of the more extraordinary aspects of the case. You would think, from the manner of her egg distribution, if taken on its own, that she ought herself to be a lady of meek and submissive disposition; but not a bit of it. In her own home she certainly rules the roost, and with a firm hand. She has had two husbands, each of them unquestionably her second-in-command, and, so it would appear, selected with that status in view.

I do know, of course, that this matter of the eggs is not something of Sally's invention (she is not, after all, a particularly inventive character). But although my wife and I had certainly heard of this kind of thing in a vague sort of way, we had never ourselves experienced it before. It seemed to be something which belonged to – what shall we say? Some earlier era? The Arabian Nights? Is that far-fetched? One wonders sometimes if anything is far-fetched in this rather odd world of ours.

Of course, one also realises to the full, in favour, as it were, of Sally's discrimination, that women are different from men. Of course they are; and it is really quite unnecessary to list the differences. Apart from anything else, they tend to be physically more delicate, and there is no doubt whatever that they do often have smaller appetites. If my wife and I had been asked how many eggs we wanted for breakfast, it is perfectly possible that she would have opted for one and I two – though I would not guarantee this; it could have gone the other way. This is really the whole point. If there was a choice, we had a right to be asked, both of us.

Sally, believe it or not, is a feminist. She believes very firmly in what used to be called Women's Lib and in all that kind of thing. Is this a paradox? In the abstract, yes, I suppose so. But in concrete terms, no, not really. For her belief in women to the fore means really Sally to the fore, and in that context other women sink back with the men, or even, in some respects, behind them.

May I refer back at this point to the title of this little work. The question it asks introduces into the discussion a lady (now ennobled but whom many may still perhaps prefer to think of as 'Mrs' Thatcher, as she was in the hour of her most resounding exploits) of rather special qualities and who is worthy, I feel, of special consideration in our context. If, then, Lady Thatcher and Sir Dennis, Bart, had been present at one of Sally's breakfasts, should Sally on principle have served them with, respectively, one and two eggs in her usual way? Or should she, without departing from her own assumed theories, have looked deeper into the matter? It will be understood, from all that I have said, that her egg distribution could not, in her mind, be thought to be based on any underlying conception of women as inferior creatures but only, in general, as having smaller appetites. But could a woman of – now as ever – such immense and indeed appalling energy as Lady Thatcher, with little apparent need of sleep or rest, be considered to fall into such a category? Surely, half a dozen eggs could not be too many for such a long-standing and continuing power in the land. No need to ask – just put them on the plate.

I agree that there is a small area of uncertainty here. Sally is not known (as far as I am aware) to have ever made any other differentiation than that between one and two eggs. It is not a matter of careful individual assessment, on whatever precise basis of evaluation, and the awarding of eggs accordingly; it is a simple and limited variation, on a very simple plan. And whereas the question of how much one is actually paying for the breakfast is evidently not, as things stand, allowed to enter into consideration, I feel pretty sure that it would be bound to do so once the present maximum egg-quota were exceeded. This does raise an interesting point. Are we to take the basic quota as one egg or two? If one, then two would seem to represent an unarranged discount in favour of brute physical force; if two, then surely the ladies have obvious grounds of complaint, and should be allowed at least the possibility of taking the spare egg away (suitably wrapped) in their handbags.

But to return to Lady Thatcher. She is an exceptional woman and deserves exceptional treatment. Away with quotas and limits in her case! She must be allowed whatever her vigorous stomach requires; and that can hardly be less than the equivalent of three men's stomachs. Nor do I think that there should be any question of her paying anything more. Once the original differentiation has been accepted, the fact that one must now and then – however rarely – pass beyond its original limits, in highly exceptional circumstances, must be accepted too and without conditions. But I make no claim to exactness: when I say half a dozen eggs for Lady Thatcher, I admit that this is mere intuitive guesswork, and that anyone else may compute things differently; indeed I should be glad to hear from anybody who is able to make a more accurate and authoritative judgement.

Two

Women and Men

I would like, if I may, to take this matter a trifle further – further than Sally and further even than the redoubtable, the world-overshadowing Lady Thatcher; for there are interesting implications. Sally is an example of instinct, convention, or whatever it may be, riding high over rational calculation. She emerges out of a particular human context in which certain attitudes have become apparently immovable, admitting little room for questioning; indeed the very idea of questioning them would, within that sort of context, probably cause much surprise and even possibly a measure of pain. In the specific case of Sally and the eggs, the result would seem of distinctly minor importance; but what it stands for more generally, in human history and experience, is not: there is nothing trivial about it.

Before I leave these two formidable ladies – to whom I shall, however, indubitably require to return, and more than once, before we are through, since together their pulling force on me, I have to admit, is quite extraordinary – I really must go a little deeper into the question of what there is in common between them. For there surely is something there of significance. It is not pure accident that they have come together in my mind in this way, even if it may seem on first glance that any essential link between them is fairly slender. It is not just that they are of the same sex – or gender, if, as some appear to feel, 'sex' has connotations not quite appropriate for certain particular occasions (or perhaps such persons are simply bored with the word, as indeed they have some right to be, and prefer any usable alternative by way of a refreshing change); though the matter of the sex is not altogether irrelevant. The fact is that they are both fighting women, women with whom one would not go willingly into battle without strong incitement, though the grounds in each case for the urge to do so might well be different. And I think, together with this, that the principle of instinct etc. riding high over rational calculation operates very forcibly in both, though the power of articulate and indeed blinding rationalisation (as distinct from reason) is I must agree much stronger and more efficient in Lady Thatcher than it is in Sally, who has in any case had much less practice in that art and would merely defend herself with vigour to the best of her ability.

As to their both being women, is it a fact that women are more likely to be of this overpowering nature than men? That could certainly be so up to a point, and some would hold that this is so precisely *because* women have been subordinate to men for so long that once given their heads, they are unlikely to show the high degree of judicious restraint that we should prefer to see. I doubt if this would be true just of women because they are women. The same sort of phenomenon is observable to an extent in Africa, not of women but of men, where the black man, freed from the white man's bonds, often shows every propensity to let his new freedom run well away with him. This is, again, perhaps as little to do with colour as with sex (or gender, if you prefer). All one may reasonably suggest, on the basis of such observed facts, though it may not take us very far, is that human groups of any kind, when faced with roughly similar situations, react in some respects in roughly the same manner.

What, however, of the vast body of men themselves? Are we able reasonably to maintain that men in general are more rational than women, or, for that matter, that white men are more rational than black – or than any other selected colouring of skin? It must be obvious to the meanest intelligence – and that phrase itself is from one angle an indication – that not all men, of whatever hue, are of the same ilk. Mr A and Mr B, who may be next-door neighbours, may differ markedly from one another in their degree of rationality; and not only in their degree of rationality, but in their general approach to the problems of life and to its aims. It is true, of course, that men live in communities, and that the values of such communities tend to attach themselves to the individuals in those communities and to reflect themselves in the actions of those individuals and to their beliefs, in so far as they may be said to have beliefs in any sort of active sense. But there will be differences, nevertheless, in the actions and reactions of these individuals, and we would be very wrong to ignore them.

Mrs Thatcher – as she was then – had no time for 'society' ("There is no such thing as society. There are only individuals and there are families") but even she recognised communities, as *vide* the community tax. But what is a community, and how and by whom are its values determined? A community is a gathering of living creatures existing and operating together for more or less common purposes, and its values depend upon the nature of those purposes. This answers the questions up to a point only. Up to that point things are fairly clear; beyond it, we begin to have to feel our way with considerable care, and not unnaturally, since the concept of purpose, particularly in relation to a group, is a good deal more difficult to analyse than one might in fact think. How can 'common purpose' arise? And how are we to know with any certainty which individual among the many is fundamentally responsible for its original specification?

Three

Communities and their Purposes

The first thing I have to say is that I am not sure that these new questions have been correctly put. This is the way with questions and answers: in order to achieve answers appropriate to a problematic situation, one has to be quite sure that one has analysed the situation, and the problems involved in it, in such a way that the questions based on the analysis are not so formulated as themselves to lead the answerer astray, or to become what are known as 'leading questions'. We all know the principal example in this kind of field: the popular referendum. Referenda are normally suggested in order to solve problems of some difficulty about which strongly opposing views are held. In such circumstances, how are we to be quite certain that the questions to be put are not biased, however slightly? But it is of absolute importance that they should not be. It is not just a matter of vetting the superficial wording. If the problems to be solved are of such difficulty that they require a referendum to cope with them, then *ipso facto* they need much closer attention than is able to be given to them in the relatively simple forms of words which are all that is humanly available for a referendum. This quite apart, of course, from the separate question of how, when the great minds of State are unable to agree, a mere counting of a multiplicity of heads will help us to do any better: a simple casting of lots would probably be at least as satisfactory. The truth is that these matters sometimes go so deep that it is impossible to set out simple pros and cons about them; and the more the argument continues, the more the fog gathers and bewilders. This is the real case for referenda – that they at least help us to get shot of an intolerable nuisance with a single cut, let the result be what it will.

This is not the way, however, to get at the genuine and irrefragable truth, whether in a large or a small matter. And in any case, in discussing common purpose, what it is and how it comes about, I am not looking for a helping hand out of a difficult corner in deciding what I or anybody else should do, but merely trying to find out how things may conceivably happen in the world, with no consequent action, on my part or anyone else's, in view. The formation of communities is not a process invented, consciously or otherwise, by human beings. There are also animal and insect communities, where invention in our sense can hardly be in question, and where common purpose, while present, can hardly be claimed to arise from any act of conscious or quasi-conscious deliberation or be assignable in its origin to any particular individual. Among animals there are leaders of packs, but they do not create purpose, though they are important in helping to fulfil it. I am not sure how far even such leadership applies to insects – in the case of bees, for instance, the queen may well be correctly claimed as constituting the centre of operations, but in no sense surely is she a 'leader'.

While it is by no means true that common purpose on all levels must necessarily be of the same or a directly similar nature, and must arise in the same manner, yet I think it must give us serious pause to realise that the phenomenon we are discussing is far from limited to humankind. It appears to be natural and basic, and we are probably misconceiving its character if we attempt, on the human level, to detach it in essence from its evolutionary predecessors. I do not mean at all to suggest that it will have undergone no changes in the transition, but I think that we must at the very least recognise that its roots go beyond the human and must be explained in more comprehensive terms.

So, of the two questions posed above – (i) how can common purpose arise? and (ii) how can we ascertain with any accuracy what individual in a community was originally responsible for the articulation of that purpose? – only the first, perhaps rather surprisingly, now remains, because only the first is sufficiently generalised to defy demolition, while the second involves an assumption which is clearly now less than self-evident but without which the question, in that form, loses its meaning. The first question itself is not directly and seriously answerable, with whatever flights of fancy, in the form in which it stands: we first of all have to be a little clearer about what it is that we have under examination. The basic purpose of a community, on whatever level of existence, is to survive

– though for what further purpose is far from plain. (If we talk about 'the survival of the fittest', we tend naturally to ask – 'fittest for what?'; to which the only firm and reliable answer appears to be – 'fittest to survive'.) This basic community purpose is represented in every member of the community as his or her common purpose, and at this point it divides itself into two: on the one hand the aim remains the survival of the community, and on the other it is the survival of the individual in his or her character as part of the community. The second of the two divisions can bulk very large and can quite obscure the first, but it derives from the first and, I suggest, never ceases to represent it, even in the case, let us suppose, of the individual on a desert island, separated physically from the community which begot him but still carrying the community in shadow form with him though he may be entirely unaware of the fact.

This is, of course, the opposite of the famous (notorious?) Thatcher comment on 'society' which I have quoted. Not that the point is of outstanding significance. Politicians' remarks of this kind are never to be taken too seriously, and are liable to be flatly contradicted at any time by the original speaker should the occasion seem to him or her to require it. This is not so much a U-turn as a P-turn ('P' for politician). A politician who knows his or her business will not be primarily concerned with sheer consistency: he or she will say – or declaim, if the opportunity allows – whatever comes in handiest at the moment; and if some pedant should point out that the current statement or demand is in direct conflict with what the same speaker said or implied equally loudly, let us say a week before, the speaker will reply without hesitation that what was earlier said was in a quite different context, and the issue will then, if need be, be deftly diverted into some other appropriate or probably inappropriate channel. These are the kinds of things that a politician must learn at the beginning, before his or her career can get under way.

Such things are common form, and not many, I imagine, will fail to recognise this. In the training sessions which one understands that political parties run for their parliamentary representatives I am told, though I can claim no direct experience, that in these days of high-powered public relations, among the techniques in which instruction is given are not forgotten little items of necessary guile of the kind I have indicated. I am, however, inclined at the same time to believe that to a certain cast of mind, more subject perhaps to the forceful inward pressures of personal ambition than to any profound urge for the exploration of objective truth or for the betterment in same notable way of the community through the amelioration and expansion of its resources, such items of technique come perfectly naturally.

Four

The Community and the Individual – Some Serious Reflections

We are back to what we left only a moment ago, to the community and its relationship to the individual. This is a very curious relationship, resembling a system of inherent paradoxes. For the first thing is that the community's duty above all would seem to be, as we have observed, to survive, but to survive, as we know without having to be told, is something which the individual, in the end, is above all unable to do. The human individual, having inherited a high degree of self-consciousness, does his best, in a manner, by giving himself a name, which he may pass on to his descendants, thus living on by proxy. That name also, in a particular form, serves to mark him out personally, so that it may become famous through his deeds while he is in the land of the living, and, if he is fortunate, may ring down the ages, so perpetuating his memory even when he himself is gone. The fact is that this is all a makeshift; but he may become totally obsessed by it, none the less, and the communal needs out of which it arises may fall back into heavy concealment.

Another common inheritance, and not only by any means among human beings, is the fighting spirit, which can take any number of shapes, some very apt to community requirements, and some on the face of it at loggerheads with them. This strange variability is a feature of every instinctive characteristic which the community or its sources implant in us, such implementation being made ultimately and in intention (if we may use such a word) for the community's own purposes, but with no assurance whatever, in the short term at least, which is after all the term of individual life, that it will effectively be so used.

I spoke earlier of a community as a gathering of living creatures for the pursuit of common purposes, and this general form of words could have readily suggested a certain underlying unexpressed belief as a foundation for the statement. All statements suggest or imply other statements unsaid which are understood and accepted: there is no statement on earth which speaks for itself only, any more than, as they tell us so frequently, there is such a thing as a free lunch. If one concentrates on humankind, and thinks no further beyond this, the suggestion will almost inevitably be of individuals as the prime factor in a community: the individuals first, the community second. Yet what I have been saying since may well appear to have inverted the relationship, in a peculiar way which some might hesitate to countenance. Indeed, whatever one may think of these later remarks of mine, it is difficult to maintain the idea of individuals first, community second, the moment one allows oneself to extend one's gaze to the wider field, and considers that communities do not arise only on the human level, and that on other levels the conscious formation of an active community by individuals with their own prior purposes in mind is, to a greater or lesser extent, inconceivable.

How can a community be prior to its members? It is true, a community cannot physically exist without members; but it is also true, on the other hand, that individuals cannot, as far as we can see, ordinarily exist without acknowledging in some way membership in some community or another. Whatever it is which creates life creates also in the same breath – the word is not inapt – community life, and the two things are and remain inseparable, with the idea of the community in the beginning and throughout leading the way, though later events may, on particular levels, mask this aspect of the relationship.

A community has no limits of size. There are larger communities and smaller communities, and communities embracing communities and communities within communities. There is, at the summit of one's conceptions, the one all-embracing community of all living things, something of which we cannot have any direct experience, but which imposes itself in idea on us none the less. This is the old opposition – or necessary connection – between the one and the many. There is no one without many and no many without one. This is the way we think, and have to think, whatever it represents in reality (what is reality?). I have spoken up to now in mainly outward, physical terms, but we view ourselves also in inward, spiritual terms, something corresponding approximately to the Greek *psyche*. At one end of the spiritual chain stand we ourselves, each of us, looking within us, as the basic one, and at the other extreme end is the supreme One, above all, whose manner of being (supposing that it exists other than in our mode of thinking) is unknown to us and whose relationship to us we endeavour to determine according to our mode of thinking or according to the mode of thinking of the community of which we are a part. We see the One as like ourselves in some ways and quite unlike in others. We are, ourselves, physically mortal - we know this, though it may be difficult for us fully to conceive the notion, and we can hardly help thinking of the spiritual element in us as possibly or probably more than mortal. But as to the One supreme living essence, it is an essence whose fundamental characteristic is immortality.

We live and die in time. But the supreme One of our fancies, who (or which) does not die - and so perhaps does not in our sense live either - is surely beyond time. If it is beyond our conceiving to imagine how this can be, we can at least symbolise it by imagining the One stationed on a conceptual mountain-top, surveying the great field of time as we survey space, seeing it from end to end (whatever this means) as a single vast continuous extension. What, in that case, is the One's relationship to the events which time encompasses? Is he involved in them in any way, other than being in some manner supposedly their source? Or is he truly beyond them as he is beyond their encompassing time, interested, we assume, in their outcome, but otherwise having no involvement in them once (if such a temporal expression as 'once' is permitted in such a context) having set them on foot?

Against this notion of a spiritual supreme entity, there is the physical and natural One of our more material conceptions - the universe, or the Universe of universes, having from its own side no necessarily spiritual element or aspect, even though we have to recognise it as having life within it, if only at the point where we make contact with it; and at the opposite end to the physical encompassing One of our conceptions lies the minimal one, the conceptual irreducible, at first thought to be in actuality the atom (so named from the Greek 'uncuttable', 'indivisible'). But the atom itself has proved to have within it further minute, impalpable worlds of its own, worlds indeed of enormous hidden power, and immensely dangerous for us to handle.

The community, any community, battles to survive; it fights to live – and often, it seems, lives to fight. But since it exists only through the medium of its individual members, they too, as we have seen, must, as individuals, each in his own measure and manner, share the same natural impulse, must partake as individuals in the battle for survival – in part for their own survival, for as long as that is possible in part far the survival of their community. Are these two requirements always, or even for the most part, bound to be in harmony? We have already glimpsed the fact that this is by no means the case. The requirements, as instilled by nature, are in themselves quite blind. They may work together, or they may conflict violently with one another, and in the short term, in such a conflict, when it arises, it is not invariably (indeed it is rarely) the community, as a community, whose needs are likely to be fulfilled. Furthermore, since there is a multitude of communities in the world – let me speak here only of the human world – it is the commonest thing on earth, and we have a superabundance of evidence of it in the appalling century now coming to an end, for one community, small or large, to set itself violently against another, letting the purposes, the needs of the overriding community of all human beings go hang.

Five

Ambition, Competition and so Forth

It was the regular thing in this country in the past to talk of contemporary 'statesmen'; but whereas we still use the expression, it is nowadays customary to limit its application mostly to historical characters, envisaged as existing somehow in an ideal way against a larger-than-life setting (occasionally too, we talk of 'world-statesmen') – otherwise we talk mainly of 'politicians', whose activity is nearer the ground, so to speak, and whose concern is more with personal ambition, with 'high-flying', with 'achieving', than with 'the good of the state'. 'High flying' and 'achieving' are broad terms applicable with others of their kind over a much wider field of operation than in politics only. In fact they have often as much to do with the accumulation of large sums of money as with anything one might, in one's less earth-bound moments, consider to be of a rather loftier nature.

The curious thing is that the accumulation of money, which one might think of naïvely as having essentially utilitarian motives – all effort being thus reduced to that of improving one's basic material situation, to the end, it would seem, of protecting oneself from the pressures of poverty and allowing one to live with comfort and dignity – turns out, ultimately, to be nothing of the kind. We accumulate money primarily in order to vie with other accumulators of money, or so it must at least appear. Otherwise why the yachts, the helicopters, and private jets, the vast mansions scattered over the surface of the globe with appropriate quantities of obeisant staff? Why the extravagant and obviously unhealthy supplies of food and drink? Why the incredible, soaring additions made regularly by those at the helm to their own personal incomes, so often perfectly regardless of the shockingly bad (and ultimately self-defeating) example thus shown to lowly wage-earners near and far? Why the ill-merited golden handshakes for those being in fact ejected from office? 'The good life' would seem to signify not living as well as possible within reason, but demonstrating by conspicuous display, come what may, including total disregard in remarkably many cases for legality, that one is in all obvious material matters outstandingly superior to the next man.

There is nothing fundamentally new about the so much admired 'competitive', combative instinct making itself felt and visible in all this, but the form in which it manifests itself is nevertheless for us, in the near universality of its coverage in these days, a novel one, with its undoubted source in the modes and methods of the American plutocracy, so powerful in the present world. This is a pity, not because our past ways of living have been inevitably so much better than this American style, but because they have been at least distinctively different (as well as ours being temporally rather more deeply rooted, for whatever that may be worth). The point about such difference is that it shows with some clarity that there may after all be more than one approach to life and its multifarious problems, and that the customs and standards to which we have become habituated in our own immediate community are not perhaps so eternal and immutable, so certain in their shape and impact as we may be otherwise tempted to imagine. But it is not an answer to anything to allow one's own community and its customs to be smothered, to be swallowed up entire by the standards and manners of another community: that way all we are doing is losing a valuable comparison and in effect exchanging one dominion, in itself unsatisfactory, for another no less so.

Politics, we have been frequently advised, is about power; but the full force of this affirmation, and of its largely disagreeable implications, will be likely to take quite a while to penetrate one's consciousness. For, whereas it is perfectly possible in the abstract to conceive of power as being exercised with purely beneficent and altruistic motives – 'for the common good' (though the extension of 'common' in this context remains remarkably indefinite) – this, regrettably, is not according to what habitually takes place in the world in which we actually live. The ideal and the actual, it must be said here, require to be kept always well apart in our minds: does this seem a terribly obvious injunction? Yet profound confusion between the two is all too frequent. 'Power' – in Lord Acton's concise observation, never seriously contradicted in the century or since it was first aired, despite its deliberate lapidary brevity – 'tends to corrupt, and absolute power corrupts absolutely.' (His following sentence is perhaps a little less well-known: 'Great men are almost always bad men'. By 'great men' here, he means in respect of material power.) The truth is that the possession of power is essentially the possession of *personal* power, and, without effective and clear external constraints, the personal element here will invariably take the reins into its hands and run away with itself.

Theoretically, this is a strange phenomenon. The individual exists in the first place to promote the survival of the community – what else? – yet in the situation we have described he or she is simply using the community for his or her own personal ends. Whence comes the urge for survival at all? We do not know. What we see, however, is its conversion in these circumstances into purely personal terms, with whatever self-contradictions. Not that the community as such is altogether lost in such a conversion – the usual form is for it to be equated with the all-powerful individual. "I am the Community," says the latter in fact or in effect ("*L'état c'est moi*," said King Louis XIV), "I am your King, your Leader, your deified Emperor, and all you do is for me and for my descendants (for I have unfortunately not yet learnt how to attain, for myself, personal, corporeal immortality): you live for me, you toil for me, you fight for me – you die for me, as needs be." When they are not in actual fact fighting for him, he employs them to build for him enormous palaces or other monuments or memorials, secular or religious, so that in connection with these his name at least, if not he himself, may live for ever.

We have, historically, from the earliest times to the present day, as many examples of this really quite curious phenomenon (much more curious, if we analyse it, than its frequent repetition in one shape or another might make it appear) as we might wish to look for. It is common form, and even where the checks and balances of a relatively liberal type of constitution prevent its full and extreme expression, the principles underlying it may still be seen to operate, if in a slightly less obvious manner. Every government seems to have as its prime objective the perpetuation of its own rule, and every leader of every government visibly concentrates this objective in himself (or equally, or possibly even more so, herself).

How can one *be* many? A good question. But note, if you will, that in 'I am the Community' the last word has been spelt by me with a capital. This indicates that what we are speaking about here is not a mere haphazard grouping of easily isolable individuals, like dots scattered without any enormous degree of meaning over a surface, but an organic formation, made up at its base of individuals, but constituting, in its totality, a greater Unity, a Unity essentially superior to the parts from which it has been put together. This conception has truly much to be said for it, provided, however, one is not led by it too far beyond the realms of reason – a danger, unfortunately, to which one may all too easily succumb. It might seem that the conception I have articulated is primarily of a philosophical nature, somewhat out of the way of thinking of the man in the street; but quite the contrary. It is only the articulation which is in any serious respect philosophical: the conception itself, apart from its analysis, is entirely native to human thinking; though without analysis, and for that matter even with it, it remains open to all sorts of misreadings.

Six

The Mind and 'Reality'. Of Virtue and of Vice

The human mind, as I am not the first to have pointed out, conceives in categories. Categories are ideal formulations. Perception is not possible without such formulations; so that the severe empiricist, who sees experience fundamentally in terms of a process from the particular to the general, is never more than half-right. What we perceive, in effect, is perceived in terms of an ideal form to which the perceived more or less corresponds, though never exactly, and indeed in some notable respects it cannot possibly correspond in so many words, since the form is abstract and the perception concrete. But that is not the only difference between them: their fit-together is never more than approximate, in the very nature of things.

The abstractions of which our ordinary speech and thinking are full, and without which human language and communication would be impossible, are reflections, as it were – or conscious articulations, if the description in preferred – of the basic categories I speak of. We need such explicit abstractions to make connections, to make sense of the world and to understand it, in so far as we ever do understand it. But we had better beware of imagining, or of imagining too soon (usually much too soon) that the world of approximations which we are in the process of building up is yet genuinely near to, or even, on the worst analysis, in any genuine way related to the abstract world which we have set up for ourselves as a model. We need as often to pull down as to put up, and we need to be sure that our vision of the Reality we see as our goal is not dimmed and distorted not just by the inadequacies of our comprehension but by wilfulness, and by an upsurge of irrationality in us which, in the end, is unfailingly destructive.

I have at this point switched my focus, without prior announcement, from the categories governing perception (and conception in its relation to perception) to the categories of ethics and ethical judgement. The two fields are in fact allied to one another and not, as some would like to have it, to be viewed as entirely separate realities, but it is as well nevertheless to distinguish between them. There is one very clear distinction to be made – that whereas in the perceptual world as such there is a link, that of numerical precision and calculation, between the ideal and the actual, from which derive the formidable powers, lately opened up to an unprecedented degree, of the material sciences, there appears to be no such thing on the side of ethical judgement, though in ancient Greece the Pythagorean School would have held, to the contrary, that the rule of numbers extended to ethics too: they assigned to particular numbers particular significances in relation to action and behaviour, attributing a special virtue in this field to the number three (a number which has been awarded mystical significance by other schools of belief in other cultures also).

What are we to make of the *idea* of virtue at all? What has virtue to do with survival, the primary aim for all of us, it seems? In fact, in its origins, in its Latin form, the word means 'manliness', which is hardly what we have primarily or particularly in mind in our normal usage, though one sees a not extravagantly remote connection. In Homer the word we interpret as 'virtue' is related to the Greek concept of 'goodness', but that, in its primary reference, relates to nobility and breeding, rather than to virtue in our sense.

Do these derivations teach us anything? Something, perhaps, but we should avoid jumping to hasty and rash conclusions. The evolution of our idea of virtue in a more specifically ethical sense, and with a broader spread, out of this kind of narrow beginning, where the main *motif* is that of valour, associated with physical strength and with superior status, is no more revealing to us in our search for fundamentals than is the story of any evolution in any such search. What it amounts to is, apparently, that something more emerges out of something less – something more in kind, not merely in degree. How can this be? What it certainly cannot convey is (what some are nevertheless prepared to maintain) that the more can be *reduced* to the less. This is impossible. What has happened is that the more has been superimposed upon the less, producing in effect a curious amalgam.

The point at issue in our case is the question of how and to what end notions of justice, equality, altruism and so forth impose themselves upon the otherwise overriding urge to survival, personal and communal, which appears to be at the root of all our actions and activities. In wars, where one whole community pits itself unrelentingly against another, such notions, it seems, have little place. At all periods of which we have note, the practices of war are based on nothing but brute force and skill in the use of that force. Any 'rules of war' (there are no laws in the applicable sense, only 'rules', if anything at all) are rapidly abandoned, and the glory of the victor is routinely gauged by the number of the enemy he leaves dead upon the field.

As for the means employed to such ends, anything goes, without limit. I refer you, as a most interesting example of the ideas in operation, to the speech of Shakespeare's Henry V at the gates of Harfleur just before its capitulation, where the threats put in Henry's mouth by our great dramatist are at least as blood-curdling (no respect being shown to age or sex) as those of the maniac Saddam Hussein to the United Nations forces at the time of Kuwait. The ethics of this play are incoherent and it is possible to find other passages in it apparently contradicting the tone of the passage I refer to. Some people indeed go so far as to regard the play as in general 'anti-war'; but this is distinctly over-subtle. I cannot help taking my passage at its face value, and I suspect that the speech was greeted by its audience with hearty cheers. I may add, going back in time, that the history of the ancient Greeks, who were in many ways a truly enlightened people, is thick with bloody wars of Greek city-states against one another, often for little or no good reason, resulting frequently if not inevitably not only in great slaughter but in mass enslavements of populations and in razings of cities to the ground. It has been the tendency of modern historians of such events to record them without special comment, as if they were matters to us totally of everyday, as indeed they evidently were to those involved at the time.

Modes of warfare may have changed by an immense amount in the last two and a half millennia but it is difficult to see that the spirit of warfare has itself in essence changed, whatever the considerable difference in details of execution: to make the point I need perhaps refer only to some of the hideous incidents of the last World War, as also of the numerous extraordinarily vicious minor wars which have rumbled menacingly through the decades since it ended. Yet at the same time it is true, whether we act according to what I am about to say or not (and in warfare we do not), that we have also developed across the centuries certain standards for action which, so far as one can see, have little to do with the impulses and requirements affecting warfare, and which, in theory at least, should make some impact even on the standards relevant to the waging of war itself.

Seven

War and Peace. More on Virtue and Vice

The standards of war are the standards of dextrous and compelling force, without restraint, and without, as a rule, more than the thinnest pretence to 'justification' on the part of the aggressor. These other standards to which I refer keep force at arm's length, applying it only, under fixed and agreed forms, to the righting of agreed wrongs, according to a system in which every man's rights, high or low, are held, in pure theory, equal to every other's, and where the invasion of such rights is prohibited and, in its due degree, penalised by superior authority. If one thinks for a moment, the chief thing which stands out here is that in the case of war we are talking about entire communities at one another's throats, in the other what we have primarily in mind is the ideal relationship of one individual to another *within* a community. Here once more I need to emphasise 'ideal', since actual practice is never more than an approximation, sometimes hardly more than the roughest approximation to this conception, a contrast largely irrelevant in thc casc of war. Whether the same sort of standards could be fruitfully applied to communities as to individuals must remain a matter for debate, though one is strongly inclined to ask, in principle at least, 'Why not?' (The answer would appear to be, that where force possessed is overwhelming, principles of 'right' and 'wrong' go without ceremony out of the window; more briefly, that might is right, as they tell us.)

There is, very curiously, a not unreal connection in the world of action between theories of justice and the principles of warfare. When communities go to war with one another they need to act as communities, that is as coordinated entities with a clear end in view, that of overcoming the foe. For this purpose it is necessary for the individuals within the communities to act as allies, to befriend and help one another, and though this still does not equate in practice with justice in the full sense, it is a step in that direction. Justice, as I have said, is in any case an ideal, never properly achieved on any serious scale in actuality; and there are, also, ethical ideals which go further than mathematical justice, where the latter is overridden by ideas of kindness, of sympathy, of helpfulness, refusing even, in the ultimate, in particular appropriate instances, to be put off by impassioned and uncomprehending resistance from the side of the object of attention itself. These last-named ideals and ideas can come into play at any stage in the life of a community, whether expressly recognised (in terms which may at times seem very striking in view of their apparent flat contradiction of ruling values), or, for the most part, not. There is nothing to induce us to believe that they occur, in principle, at a certain point of development only and never before or elsewhere - or, on the other hand, that, having arisen, they show any truly impressive signs of taking the lead. They seem in fact to be on hand at all times to some degree, though mostly, it must seem, in the background, and too often very much in the background.

Such ideas have stubborn powers of persistence within a community but they are never seen to be dominant, and there is usually by the great majority little enough pretence of upholding them or any important part of them at any time when there is no actual enemy battling at the gates. As and when, in these days, they are specifically raised, and publicly aired, the purpose of the airing will mostly be to provide some manner of specious cover, some ostensible 'justification', in the name of altruism, for an action motivated in reality by personal or communal (or a muddy mixture of both) self-interest. The word 'humanitarian' is nowadays much in evidence in such a context for such a claim even when all the facts speak with convincing clarity the other way. Hypocrisy (of which this is a grotesque and obvious example) is, so de Rochefoucauld has told us in his *Maxims*, the homage paid by vice to virtue. His epigram has been frequently repeated; but I do not know of anyone who has looked at all deeply into the question of just *why* vice should feel under any pressing obligation to pay homage to virtue - vice which so often in every period (our own too) has been prepared to make so vainglorious and so loudly trumpeted a boast of its prowess, not merely indeed without apology but with every sign of self-approval. 'Aggression' and 'the killer instinct', copied in basis from this attitude, appear now in most visible quarters to be the order of the day.

The case for a measure of surface self-justification in the above sense might perhaps have been a trifle stronger in the society inhabited by de Rochefoucauld, restricted as that society was in some aspects of its thinking, if not in its behaviour, by the rigidities of certain ecclesiastical demands upon it, than in our own, where in the last few decades typical demands of the kind have grown to be a great deal more loosely felt than ever before. But if, quite possibly, social circumstances gave rather more prompting to a desire for self-justification and so for the resultant epigram at the time of its conception, that is really a good deal smaller matter than one might think, and has relatively little to tell us of the true foundations of the case. Churches and religions and their doctrines are not the only bearers of the 'moral' message, a message that I see, in its source and essence, as independent of any or all religious doctrines, however much the latter may seize upon it and develop it, each according to its own imagining, and press it home upon us – and too often in what some may feel to be a highly distorted and controversial form. I would think that even the most determinedly wayward mind must hold somewhere within it a feeling of some ethical system of standards from elsewhere, perhaps only vaguely and inaccurately imagined in its details but, at root, compelling nevertheless, and in principle more firmly based than even the most presumptuous urgencies of personal self-interest. That this system is more than the individual goes without saying: does it, then, derive from the community as community – or is it more than this too? Who is to say? (Remember that all the aim we have been able so far to attribute to the community is the driving aim to survive: can that system go deeper than this? What of the overriding Community of all communities? Are we to say that that has some superior aim? Of what sort? How are we to know?)

Eight
The Theme of the Buccaneer

I spoke of vice openly flaunting itself, without thought of apology, and I must comment on this. The wild man (forgive me if I include woman too under this appellation) and his ungoverned actions may have a positive place in our lives. They serve at the least as a violent but useful counter for our theoretically more peaceful middle-of-the-road existences, and an outlet in fancy for our hidden emotions and more wilful desires. We glamorise the murderous buccaneer, the vicious hoodlum because they represent a suppressed destructive part of ourselves: it is better, I must suppose, rather than giving way altogether to that fearsome part in us, to give rein to its excesses in small quantities, in exhausting games and sporting exercises and so on, or even in the watching of such things, or otherwise (I return to the theme of the buccaneer) merely to allow ourselves to admire its unrestrained free play remotely in others, distant from us in time and place, or both – provided those others *are* sufficiently distant from us not to intrude their standards (for they have indeed their own if ferocious standards – nobody is without standards) upon ours. Regrettably, such a proviso is impossible to enforce and has been all too frequently overruled in our world's somewhat gruesome history. I have some other associated points to make.

The general broad theme as outlined has a number of typical variations. Sometimes the deeds of some particular outlaw, real or mythical, are elevated to a higher degree of common acceptability by the attachment to them of a fanciful moral aspect. This is the Robin Hood conception: of one who takes it upon himself to right the wrongs of society by, as in that case, robbing the rich in order to give to the poor. At the other extreme, no moral gloss being offered, there is the type of case where open and ghastly villainies are perpetrated, no attempt is made to conceal their character, and there is no too obvious cloak of romanticisation to moderate their effect. This is really the Dr Crippen/Jack the Ripper conception, the subject in its crudest and on the face of it least appealing form: why are we so fascinated by these glimpses of the darker side of the human soul? The phenomenon has no really easy explanation. Our experience here as reader or onlooker has been held to embody a purgation (echoing Aristotle) of some of the more tumultuous elements in our nature, elements from which we need relief. I am sure that here too there is something to be said for such a view, though the situation is rather different from what I had originally posited; but I would doubt, certainly, if it could ever be anything like the whole story, and there is also the fact that what is a relief for some is likely to be an unhappy stimulus for others.

These things go deep and their different varieties are not to be too much interrun with one another in the mind. The excitements they stir in us are different, though evidently allied to each other in some basic way – as are too the excitement of battle (people fight as often for pure excitement as for 'causes' or cash), the excitement of those who once made holiday at a public execution, the excitement of the chase, and the clear excitement evinced (not altogether attractively, one may possibly feel) by the famous and admired television presenter showing us scenes at close quarters of wild animals hunting or ambushing other animals and tearing them to pieces for food.

I throw in here some not altogether irrelevant remarks about the IRA. The main impetus behind the IRA's murderous operations in our times has been, in my opinion, the excitement of the game: nationalist claims, so loudly trumpeted, come actually well behind this. A few moments' rational thought puts a strange twist on the general picture. It should be obvious, I suggest, that any British government would at heart like nothing better than to be able to withdraw itself in a reasonable way from Northern Ireland and its entanglements and without loss of face. There are plenty of quite recent precedents elsewhere for this sort of action, and not least perhaps Britain's own withdrawal from Empire after the war. Of course, the presence in the region of a flourishing Protestant community with strong allegiances to this country presents a problem of no mean order in that context; but in my opinion undoubtedly a major, if not *the* major, factor preventing such an action in Northern Ireland is – the IRA itself. Politically, no government could possibly be seen as agreeing to cave in to violence, or the threat of violence, from an organisation such as the IRA. It is politically out of the question. Do the IRA not see this? But if, in some of their more rational moments, they do see it, I doubt if it matters to them all that much. The excitement of the game is all that really matters to them, and their ostensible concern with Irish nationalism is a useful enough banner for them to wave in our faces but represents something to which they themselves, I suggest (is this a startling notion?), attribute in actuality little more than superficial significance, whether they are themselves fully aware of the fact or not, and, if they won the day here, the result would simply be to turn their violence elsewhere.

There is one respect in which the ideal of the buccaneer and the outlaw – of the bold adventure beyond the law – whatever its confessed ethical deficiencies, has an actively beneficial side (not merely as a compensating or balancing factor), in setting before our eyes an imaginary domain, which, though imaginary, is not necessarily altogether out of our effective reach given sound practical adjustments, where we need no longer be ruled by the conventional routines and stiff and hampering formalities imposed upon us in the world we know, a world in which from cradle to grave we seem to be circumscribed by other men's restrictions upon us, never free, it appears, to think at ease in our own way and strike out our own path. The ideal, from this angle, has great potential value, but – as so often in such cases – its strong spirit cannot be taken neat.

What we have first of all to realise is that to escape from our environment in any full and profound sense is not merely hideously difficult – it is, strictly, impossible. We are born to an environment, we live in it and with it, we are a part of it and it is a part of us, and whether we like it or not (indeed we may very much dislike it) there is no chance of our passing securely beyond it while we live. The most we can do is to make an effort to change our place in it, but if we can do this, we face two opposite threats – on the one hand, if we try to overcome our environment by attempting to ignore it and acting instead according to our own strongly felt criteria (provided we consciously and determinedly have them, which is the first necessity), we are liable to end up isolated, without much consolation, in the short term, from the world we have in effect rejected, and without aid in any misfortunes we may encounter: we can do little more then than shrug our shoulders. On the other hand if we try to change our place in the environment by manipulating it, so far as we can, for our benefit, we are likely to find ourselves throwing off its pressures by creating pressures of our own, freeing ourselves if successful from other people's restrictions upon us by in turn imposing our own restrictions upon others, which may make us feel for a moment 'on top of the world', as they say (not too inappropriately, perhaps), but may, in the long run, have unpleasant implications for everyone, including ourselves, as the turbulent history of mankind has shown on a large and a small scale on innumerable occasions. So the alluring buccaneer model, if not without virtues, needs to be followed with immensely more judgement and restraint than most people are willing or perhaps able to bring to bear upon it, particularly in the second and greatly more frequent of the instances I have quoted.

Some years ago my wife and I, on a short walking-tour in this country, found ourselves, one sunny afternoon, climbing a hill the summit of which was crowned by a well-known monument, I cannot now remember which. We reached the top and sat down on the grass at the foot of the monument. A few moments later a small group, two young women and a young man, came up after us and sat down a few yards below to sun themselves and inhale the breeze. They were chatting gaily to one another when there appeared below them at a small distance a larger group – of fifteen or more – who had now halted on a small shelf to gather their forces and assemble themselves about a man who was evidently their leader. On seeing this, the young man just below us, turning to his female companions, observed to them in what I can only describe as a somewhat disdainful and clearly self-satisfied tone, "Here they come – in their thousands!"

The implications of this curious and quite inane remark are worth dwelling on for a passing moment. In the first place the remark is patently absurd. I do not mean in its obvious exaggeration, which represents the sort of hyperbole which is common enough in speech and which nobody would normally dream of taking literally. I mean, rather, in the contrast being suggested between the speaker and his entourage and those to whom he thus referred. What was there really to differentiate them? The speaker's group, it is true, consisted of three only, the others were five or six times as many; the speaker's group was headed by the speaker himself, or so I assume, from the sound of him, the others were being led by a guide, possibly from within the group, possibly not; the speaker's group, finally, had got there *first*. I have a feeling that the last point was the big one in the speaker's eyes, and that the other points merely added strength to it. The small group having got there first, the speaker felt that the place was now in a sense *their* property (we above them were only two and out of sight, and could easily be ignored), and that this noisy rabble of outsiders had no right interfering in it.

What has this trivial incident to do with the attraction in general, when allowed to work its effect without check or moderation, of the buccaneer ideal? In its rather more than glancing way, it has a good deal to do with it, as I firmly believe. The incident's very triviality emphasises its significance, showing how hidden but persistent inner impulses rise to the surface in all sorts of circumstances, unimportant as well as important, and in all sorts of individuals. The desire to appear superior to the crowd (the 'hoi polloi'), to spurn any such persons as consent to be led by another, and to look down upon them from a more or less lofty eminence (in this case, it happens, a physical one), to claim the semi-proprietary rights of the acknowledged first arrival at a picked spot – these are all symptoms, indeed the most commonplace of symptoms, of the pursued ideal in question and of its epidemic prevalence in all places and, it would seem, at all times.

One last word before I leave this little anecdote. The young man of whom I speak was attired in almost mountain garb – strong, heavy boots; thick, rolled-over socks, with trousers of stout, good quality material tucked into them; appropriate upper garments – for the ascent of our little hillock. Did he have more strenuous operations within his near intentions? I do not, of course, know, but I rather doubt it. I suspect it was all a carefully organised build-up to impress upon the viewer, any viewer, the outstanding nature of his personality, which, it will be observed, left much more of a mark on my wife's mind and mine ('Here they come in their thousands' has since become our watchword in suitable circumstances) than the personality, possibly sweet and delightful, of either of his female companions.

Nine

Whose Benefit? Foretelling the Future

The projection of personality is no side-issue in today's ceaseless struggle for existence. Let us be forthright on this not uninteresting topic. Our world is not – it never was, will it ever be? – a world constructed for the quiet, the unassuming, the self-effacing, the modest, to give undemandingly of their best for the good of the community, awaiting only in return a full and generous consideration of what they have to offer. This is not the way of the world we know, though some in the past may have tried, for reasons with which we are not in tune, to persuade us that it is: this is, rather, a world for the unrestrained and for preference unfeeling self-promoter with the brazen voice and the prime urge, brazenly declared, to hoist himself above the multitude in any manner possible, at all costs, and without limit. Attendant upon the self-promoter is the promoter of others' selves, the image-builder ('image' suggesting something imaginary, something that is not but that is thought fitting for the occasion), the public relations man: they feed one another.

'Feed one another' – a revealing expression, springing naturally to the pen, since this is very much the central characteristic of the communal organism, whose components do in fact feed one another, physically (whether by offering food in some form, on the human level usually at a price, or, if we include all the animal kingdom, by being offered themselves as food) and metaphorically, with among men every kind of (paid-for) assistance imaginable, so that the whole becomes a swarming anthill of scurrying opportunists seizing on every chance of serving their human neighbours' needs – how magnificent! – but primarily, mark the fact, with an eye to their own benefit, to the extent (not always however the greatest extent possible) that they are able to judge that benefit.

How, indeed, does one judge benefit, whether for oneself, or for another, or for the community at large, on whatever scale? What constitutes benefit? It surely is not simply 'good living' on the lines of the multi-millionaire yacht-owner? Different persons would undoubtedly define it differently, and it is reasonable that they should, since we are not all built to the same mould (a horrifying thought if we were). The simplest thing to say is, without being more specific, that one's individual best benefit – if it is not to interfere with that of others (a proviso, I regret to say, which not everybody in our present-day climate of affairs would accept, but it must be stressed) – is the freedom to live out one's life in the way that suits one best and infringes least upon the freedom of one's fellows, and that the community's best benefit is the promotion of the freedoms of its individuals in this sense, together with the effective prolongation of its own existence. This is a fairly neutral solution and I do not pretend it to be adequate: it is not sufficiently positive or explicit; but it is not seriously to be argued with as far as it goes, and it will get us a certain small way. Meanwhile we have to face the great, the outstanding question: even if we consider that we have reasonably well determined what will be to our benefit, how do we work out some reasonably assured scheme to get us there?

There are few actual events in this world which allow themselves to be foretold with anything resembling complete certainty. The death of the individual is, surely, certain, but its manner and time are not – except perhaps where some fatal disease is known to have hold, and an expert calculation can be made of how long it will take to have effect. What I am speaking of, let us be perfectly clear, is thus not some kind of objective certainty, in the sense, actual or (more easily intelligible) hypothetical, of one specific concrete event absolutely and necessarily following on or being otherwise involved in another, irrespective of whether there is anyone to observe the conjunction or not – but subjective certainty, the extent to which an individual or community can foretell with some accuracy any future course of events of a kind such as to affect him or it. The last phrase ('of a kind...etc.') is included because it makes plain what is truly behind the conception – that we are talking in highly concrete terms, and that the surveying or considering subject is the essential centre of the operation in every respect. The circumstance of death and the fatal disease, that I have mentioned, may give some notion of the very narrow limits within which subjective certainty can authentically be seen to work: if the details are small and precise enough and the envisaged future not too relatively far off, we may speak of some kind of future certainty with a measure of confidence, but if the situation is at all more diffuse, it is a different story.

If foretelling a future course of events in order to determine what shall be ultimately to one's benefit as an individual presents plenty of problems and of opportunities for misjudgement, the problems it presents to a community, that is to say to the government of a community, tend to be overwhelming. The truth is that we cannot even foretell the weather in more than the roughest way, but when it comes, for example, to economics, to the economic welfare of a whole community, we are lost in a confusion of speculation, of elaborate guesswork often prinked out as high theory: and our equipment to deal with the situation seems of an extraordinarily primitive kind. I have spoken of certainty, but it is not really just certainty which we lack: a better eye for the genuinely *probable* would help enormously.

One does innocently wonder why, in this day of the all-conquering computer that is able, able through the ingenuity of men's devising, to work out apparently the most complicated of problems in the flash of an instant, it is nevertheless not possible to organise an effective plan to overcome at least some of the difficulties of adequate economic forecasting, so as to make at any rate large-scale, enduring recessions things altogether of the past. Perhaps something is being done about it even at this moment? Or perhaps the network of causes and effects is too intricately involved in this case for even the most skilled of computer programmers to unravel successfully. I confess I am not sufficiently expert in this field to offer any convincing answer, though I am inclined to think that my second alternative is more likely to be correct, and that we are still very far away from undertaking such an enterprise with the hope of reaching anything even remotely resembling a full and satisfactory solution.

There is, however, one singularly obstructive factor also to reckon with. It is impossible, on a general consideration, that any really effective solution could be found which is of anything but a longer-term nature; yet those persons given the task (or giving themselves optimistically and usually with a show of bravado the task) of finding it seem invariably to be searching not for some authentic long-term unwinding of the knotted and resistant tangle, requiring essentially persistence and above all patience from all concerned, but for some short-term cure-all based on some simple or heavily simplified principle recognisably related to party political dogma and offering immediate (or more or less immediate) results. We stand thus perpetually in our own way.

If this seems an exceptionally perverse situation, yet at the same time it is exceptionally easy (sadly) to understand. We are individually all short-term creatures; it is only the community which has any genuine long-term existence. But although, from a long way off, we can see, by the light of reason, of a reason whose rationality is superior, if we allow it to function as it should, to the sub-rational pressures and urges of the individual, that the true ultimate benefit of the individual must lie in the benefit of the community, and the benefit of the community must lie in the benefit of the whole community, not in the benefit of one partial community battling fiercely against others – yet we cannot fail to realise that the situation, thus expressed, has too little in common with the world we ordinarily inhabit. It expresses an ideal state of things, towards which we may strive occasionally in our moments of extreme lucidity, but otherwise and for the most part we are controlled and driven by the pressures and urges to which I have referred, and which demand of us that we fight for ourselves and not for anyone or anything else, so that in that context (since we are short-term creatures) it is the short term which rules our actions, and it is short-term answers, however inappropriate they may eventually turn out to be, and be seen to turn out to be, which we require from government for our needs. We can, naturally, interpret the short term with some small degree of elasticity, taking into account our descendants up to a certain point, but the contrast between the short and the long term still remains and remains strong, and particularly in relation to what we ask for from government.

The difference, in many respects the opposition, between the short and the long term is near the heart of the problems of government, of its essential nature, how it functions and how it should function, its (long-term and short-term) aims, and these are matters near the heart of the problem of man, of the individual and the community and their interpenetration one with another.

Ten

What is History?

The balance needing to be struck in actual operation between the individual and the community is in all circumstances an extremely delicate one, and constantly being overweighted on the one side or the other. If the survival of the community is to be accepted as the major issue, the fact remains that it can survive only through the medium of its individuals, and the neglect of the right of any individual to live out his or her life making the most of it in freedom (without, as I have said, interfering with another's equal rights) is, through that individual, a neglect of and to that extent an assault upon the community and its aims. So it seems, at least, through the eye of any individual seeing without bias; yet this, it would appear, is a highly sophisticated viewpoint, and certainly not one which has appealed strongly at all periods of human history so far – a brief history, and its verdicts, to the extent that we are able to decipher them, are not always necessarily to be taken with ultimate seriousness.

"History is bunk," said Henry Ford. Much more recently, as a result of the sudden collapse of the Soviet Union from internal stress, a voice was raised – as it happens also in America, by a Japanese-American, this time a member of the self-styled intellectual community – to proclaim that the end of the twentieth century of our era signals 'the end of history'. Neither of these typically extravagant-sounding statements ultimately carries much weight in the form in which it stands, though they are well-shaped to attract attention. The latter brought fame and its attendant fortune to its originator through the book in which it was proposed; it was incidentally hailed enthusiastically in a *Times* leader after a public debate on it in whose sponsorship that newspaper had participated. Events have now moved on, and it is perhaps not too much to say that many of the book's hasty conclusions, monumentally successful though they may have been in catching the public eye, have already proved somewhat flawed. For all the outward waywardness of their formulation, the two statements are worth a moment's serious consideration.

Let me say at once that for me Henry Ford comes a good deal nearer the truth than does his successor. Does this startle? Believe me, it is not because of some hidden admiration I have for big-business men; quite the contrary, as these pages will effectively show. It is strictly a matter of interpretation. Ford's words as they stand, unsupported by any context ('context', as I am aware, is a marvellous political cover-word, but I think I can show how it really does apply here), appear extreme and baseless – ignorant or at least wildly overstated. What do they truly mean? They were uttered in 1919 from the witness box, in a case brought by Ford` against the *Chicago Tribune*. I have no record of the case before me, nor have I attempted to obtain one. But a point is nevertheless very clear. He cannot possibly have been speaking in purely general terms – come to think of it, why should he have been? What could have led him, out of the blue, to make such a ponderous and sweeping judgement on things so largely out of his ken? He was speaking of particular matters quite near to him, and specifically, in all probability (I do not, of course, know for certain) of the car industry, in respect to which he was after all something of an authority. He was, it seems, scornfully rejecting the claimed validity of an historical precedent being thrown at him. "History shows ..." they had presumably said. "Hang history!" was what his words meant, or "What your 'history' shows is not relevant"; and in that context, I suggest, the words were by no means entirely unreasonable. Had he known that the reported exclamation would be set down without qualification against his name for ever, he might, I imagine, have been a little more circumspect in his phrasing.

The fact that the words in question, unqualified and quite wild-sounding, are all that remains of the argument in the popular consciousness demonstrates nothing except that popular memory is selective and can be extremely misleading. Even on the broader basis, however, while it is true enough that history in any deep sense is far from bunk, it is also regrettably true that the prejudiced, patchy and simplified version of 'history' which most people, not excluding some specialists, carry with them may after all not be entirely unworthy of the description. As to the specialists, conventional past presentations and interpretations of historical happenings are too often sadly wanting, dwelling as they do far too concentratedly on battles and bloodshed, on the glorification of aggression and of 'great men', with distortions of values on a grand scale, and leaving the development of thought in its various branches, and of modes of living, to be dealt with in the interspaces of the historical narrative, as matters of apparently lesser importance. It is true that it is possible and indeed essential to give extended treatment on their own to the thus compressed (or even entirely omitted) subjects; but this cannot make up for the apparently secondary place already allotted to them in the basic treatment – and the problem is made more confused by the fact that without the basic treatment, despite all the distortions of values to which such a treatment is patently liable, much of what these subjects contain become to some degree one-dimensionalised or even meaningless, certainly at least to the lay reader.

This defective approach represents an attitude now, it must be acknowledged, in many respects old-fashioned but still heavily persistent, and its persistence is partly due to the greater ease with which, in what sets out to be a narrative structure, one can treat of violent events than of ventures into the discursive depths of thinking and analysis. Audiences respond to the presentation of such events very readily: the violence in them arouses emotions which we all continue to carry with us, and the largely surface nature of such emotions helps to encourage rather than divert the flow of a narrative, as we can well enough see from recurring major elements in the TV fare we are daily and nightly offered. Partly also, however, the defect of the approach is due to the perpetuation of a fundamental misunderstanding of the community-individual relationship in what I may call the 'leader' theme: I will go further into this in a while.

As for 'the end of history', the applicability of this conception depends upon a use of the term 'history' in a sense which most of us would have difficulty in recognising. The theory behind the idea is supposedly based on Hegel, or on an interpretation of Hegel – which does not make it necessarily less frankly nonsensical, if one may put it crudely, (since Hegel, like some other nineteenth-century philosophers, was quite capable of talking his own brand of high-sounding nonsense, interpretable in various, often openly contradictory ways, according to choice), though some may find it for this reason more impressive. 'History' as normally understood can hardly come to an 'end', except through the world's or mankind's sudden destruction, which is not at all what either author meant. In any case the present-day author's reading of the consequences following the collapse of the Soviet Union is, to say the least, more than doubtful. We had and have no reason whatever to believe that what faces us now is some kind of march into glory. But the chief reason why I pause on this, to me, peculiar notion is that it has in it an interesting echo of something else – of Winston Churchill's 'broad uplands' of freedom and happiness to which he loved to point the way as our goal in his wartime and immediately post-war speeches and writings. Anyone setting up 'the end of history' beside Churchill's 'broad uplands', however, needs to consider that the latter, in its bold rhetoric, offered its audiences, in practical terms, an ideal very suitable for their ears in moments of extreme stress and danger, to buoy up their spirits and strengthen their moral defences – but not, I fear, to be taken too seriously in the long run as offering a realistically attainable goal in any sort of near future and certainly not to suggest specifically and with assurance the possibility or probability of humanity's proximate arrival, after a long precarious climb from obscure savage origins, to a sunlit civilised plainland where all is bright and beautiful, and to that extent, one must suppose, static, an outcome which surely cannot possibly be. Our present-day coiner of the phrase about the end of history might have been better off, if he thought of Churchill at all, to think of another, more famous saying, when Churchill described a critical moment of victory in the war as being at last not 'the beginning of the end' but, if anything, 'the end of the beginning'. So, the other could have said, modifying the form of the original, if he wished to make a phrase (always a perilous wish), history is not what we have thought up to now; in any true sense it is only just about to begin.

It is, let us agree, at least a fact that our views about history and what it presumes to tell us are changing, even if slowly and, I would say, somewhat lopsidedly; and it is certainly about time that some broad change did take place from the bloody misconceptions of earlier days.

On the other hand this change of viewpoint, long overdue, is not owed to any sudden change in the facts, which, for the past, near or far, remain (down in their hidden or largely hidden essence) essentially what they were, though the spotlight on them has now begun to shift and they are illuminated for some of us in a different way. What *is* affected in the facts in general is in those facts which are now developing or about to develop under the more or less direct if broken influence of the (though partial) change of view. The questions then arising are: how real and whole-hearted is the change? Is everybody likely to be affected by it in the long run or are only a few here and there? How really beneficial is it and to whom, and how lasting is it likely to be? Does it always work in the same direction?

'The end of history', in so far as it seems to be based on a rosy optimism about the future of the USA and its power in the world, and in so far as it sees the collapse of the Soviet Union as standing for an automatic ascent to liberalism and democracy in the world, is a self-deluding simplification, for one thing ignoring the distinct dangers for us all attending the Soviet Union's break-up into internally contending elements, and, in the ideas put forward, not likely to have much influence over precisely some of those individuals and groups most needing to have their actions restrained.

The theory is, as it happens, not a bad example of a well-known phenomenon, the recurrent search for some sort of terrestrial Utopia. Utopia is, literally, 'nowhere' – not, as the popular and frequently repeated misconception has it, 'place of well-being' (in relation to which the absurd antonym 'dystopia' has accordingly been coined) – and, being nowhere, is also in no time. Time, for any utopia, must appear to stand inevitably still. Imaginary Heavens are always essentially static; and so with 'the end of history', which can only be conceived in such terms because it is essentially unhistorical.

Eleven

The Synchronic and the Diachronic

Static Heavens are a curious but easily explicable mirage in a world where in actuality nothing remains still or the same for two half-seconds together, or even for one. Have we not all at some time wished that, if only for a moment (an idea which is itself a curious contradiction), we could hold the fleeting instant at rest, so that we could savour its peace or other pleasure to the full? We breathe out our life entirely in the present, but it is a present which is perpetually becoming the past, never waiting for us. Where has this instant gone? It has receded from us immediately, before we know, and the longer we live, the more speedily it seems to vanish into the endless pile-up of the years that are over and finished and never to be experienced at first hand, in love or hate, pleasure or pain, by anyone again. Time is always on the move, but when we are children it seems to be following its track at a snail's pace, while when we are old the years fly from us like puffs of wind.

When I was quite small, I remember a series of very short stories in a children's comic – I think *Tiny Tim's Weekly* but I could not say for sure, and it is long gone, of course – concerning a character known as Little Bluebell, the Fairy Schoolgirl. It has occurred to me since to wonder what happened to her when she grew up. (Fairies may not, as such, usually grow up but schoolgirls surely do?) Did she, for instance, become first of all a Fairy Teenager (or whatever would then have been the appropriate title, 'teenager' not yet having been invented), before becoming eventually a Fairy Adult, or Mature Fairy, and what happened in between? It is difficult to think of her with her fairyness intact going through all the compulsory alterations of otherwise normal growth. The truth is that the stories were about an essentially stationary character, fairy or not – no less stationary in effect than Barrie's Peter Pan (though with little resemblance to him otherwise), not subject to change - and if they had gone on for twenty years or more (perhaps they did, I cannot say) she would have remained always exactly the same and a schoolgirl.

This is indeed the form not merely for Little Bluebell but for all fictional characters of a certain style, detectives in particular and similar heroic and clever righters of wrongs (Little Bluebell too was a tiny member of this club, a righter of wrongs in her own little fairy way), who exist in a world not of long-range continuity but of isolated and thus in the long run static episodes, in which, from episode to episode, however many and however 'action-packed' they may be, the central character never usually shows any serious signs of ageing from his or her first appearance before us.

We have heard much in the last few decades concerning the concept of the 'synchronic' approach to life and language as contrasted with, and sometimes apparently elevated above, the 'diachronic' approach to the same. The distinction, in this form, is one we owe primarily to Ferdinand de Saussure, a Swiss-born scholar specialising in what we have come to know (partly through him) as linguistics. He flourished at the end of the last century and early years of this, and propounded some original ideas - not always completely thought-out, but that is the way with original ideas, particularly at the hour of their inception. His name, in connection with those ideas, has come again into considerable prominence in recent decades owing to a pronounced partiality shown for his views by the American linguist, Noam Chomsky.

The interesting thing about Saussure in our present context is that he spent most of his teaching career in discoursing on matters of significance relating to the history of language and its development, that is, on what is primarily the 'diachronic' aspect as he called it, and what in fact was up to that time the traditional main subject of study in the field of linguistics. But in his heart he became less and less attuned to this aspect, and more and more came to feel that for him, at least, much of the deeper study of language lay in the 'synchronic' aspect - in the study of language, or of a language, as it stood, in all its variety and extension, at a single moment of time. Since his day the idea has spread widely, even if the diachronic approach has by no means been entirely supplanted (it would be very difficult for it to be so).

The problem we face here, and one which has never been sufficiently considered in the context, even if it has been raised in other contexts, is, as I have just previously indicated, that the 'single moment of time' referred to is something extraordinarily difficult to capture, and, as and when theoretically captured, of highly dubious significance. This statically conceived moment (note that 'static' is Saussure's own chosen word) is both the epitome of reality and, in one and the same breath, the epitome of unreality – of reality, inasmuch as it is indeed the *only* reality with which we can ever have any direct contact, any time before or after being known to us solely by inference (whether using personal memory of events as a base or depending altogether on more general principles) and *spatial objects in time* being known directly to us only through the here and now, all beyond this again being accepted as real through inference and convention only; but of unreality, in that it is by its very nature and innermost essence perceptually ungraspable, being created – as I have said – only to dissolve, immediately and irresistibly, and without the hint of pause, into we do not know what. The Presocratic Greek thinker Heraclitus is reputed to have made the point, two and a half millennia ago, that you could not step into the same river twice – which a slightly later follower did his best to make more emphatic by saying that you could not even do so once.

But supposing that we were actually able to halt a language at a given 'point in time' (as they say), so as to study its structure and elements in detail at that instant, what would be the value of such a study? The answer is very uncertain, and it can be argued that the question itself is of very uncertain meaning. All languages are in perpetual movement, and the movement is intrinsic to them and part of their life. Take the movement away and what is left is, as it stands, not strictly a language at all but a fossilised remnant – it only comes back to life when, in considering it, we breathe its original life back into it, considering how it arises and where it is going. If we are to make any real sense of the situation, we have thus to interpret 'point' quite loosely, as encompassing in fact a period of time (and not excluding comparison with other periods of time and indeed other languages), and there can be no doubt that this is substantially what Saussure had actually in mind. In which case what we have is not so much a new approach as an acute and striking variation on the old approach, starting – and this can be a refreshing novelty – from another angle but using in principle the same techniques, however refurbished.

One further word about the 'synchronic' view of language before I leave the subject. Who is to say which of the unending potential series of synchronic states of a language is the one which most truly represents that language's nature? For example, any native speaker of a language will have found some of the changes taking place in it during his lifetime distasteful to him. To what extent should he treat the feeling as a genuine sign of ineptitude in the change – of the language being 'degraded' by its admission? Or how far should he rather trust that the change is in all probability simply one item, in itself lasting or no, in an entirely natural and necessary process and that his first reaction to it was due merely to its superficial strangeness to him? It requires a highly sensitive judgement to make the needed distinction reasonably effectively on the spot; only over a longer period – 'diachronically' – can a sound judgement be more readily attempted.

Some linguistic features change quite slowly, some as in aspects of vocabulary can change quite rapidly, and not always in the same way (for instance 'stunning', which was to be found in Dickens but has quite recently been resurrected on a large scale, as it were from nowhere – one almost wonders if 'top-hole' and 'topping' will be coming back), some, as in pronunciation, are changing subtly at every single moment, though the differences may reveal themselves with any force only in the quite long term (old voice-renderings, on record or film, can be very striking in this respect – and can sound actually remarkably stilted to a present-day ear). Change of structure and of form in general can take a very considerable while in relation to the human lifespan to show itself, but it is impossible to overlook, and a temporal cross-section taking little proper account of historical development will always be misleading.

What this means is that the synchronic – even interpreted loosely – without the full support of the diachronic has no real status. In a deep sense, what Saussure was wishing in effect to do was to call a halt to the unending forward-wash of time, to survey language, and all about it, in peace and quiet and restfulness, free from all external interference – I fear, an impossible dream.

I must sympathise, and most heartily, with anyone wishing to take a fresh look at the problems of language or anything else and to get well away from the traditional, from the too narrowly academic, or alternatively the too broad and imprecise of popular idea - from the long-standing self-imposed limitations and errors which, once laid down or given entry and by oversight or misplaced intention allowed with too little reservation into the canon, become eventually almost too formidable to overcome. A clean break may then often seem the only way out, but too clean and violent a break may lead, as they say, to getting rid of the baby with the bath-water. This has frequently happened and will no doubt happen again, since to be extreme is part of human nature, showing itself, for example, in day-to-day criticisms and reviews of books or films or other productions, in journals of all kinds (by no means only in tabloid publications), where the tendency to see in terms of sheer black and white is very visible indeed, and a new film, for instance, may be lauded to the skies or damned to the depths with apparently no serious effort made to distinguish separable elements in it analytically for considered approval or otherwise.

Twelve

Communism, Capitalism and so Forth

I. Communism

We have been talking of language. In all the vast field covered by this subject, a subject of such importance to us at almost every moment of our waking hours, there is nothing more important than semantics, the meaning of the words we use, and nothing more intricate. When two persons are in furious argument on a topic, the first thing to decide will very often be whether they are even talking, in reality, about the same thing. The bigger and more pressing the topic, the more necessary and at the same time the more difficult it may well be to make any clear decision of the kind: it may be that the central term relating to the topic has critically altered its significance over time, without many people being sufficiently aware of the fact; or that the term is in any case, as so often happens, a nebulous one and allows at all times of multiple interpretations; or, of course, that both things have come, in a measure, together; and it is not always easy also to tell how far the differences in interpretation, by those concerned to argue on the topic – differences probably largely unsignalled – are deliberate or unintentional. The trained semanticist may feel that these are very obvious problems, but they combine to face us emphatically, none the less, in many circumstances.

Some admirable examples of these unending difficulties are to be found in the circumstances surrounding the birth of the concept, which we have touched on, of 'the end of history'. There is, of course, the question of the meaning of 'history' at all in such a context, but I think this is a fairly evident point, and I do not propose to go into it again. Much more important is the question of what is meant by such phrases as 'the death of communism', 'the final victory of capitalism', and so on, and of what real validity can be attached to such singular, apparently once-for-all and final notions.

Something has collapsed, most certainly, but what? Was it Communism? This is a huge abstraction. What did indubitably collapse upon itself was the unwieldy bulk of the Soviet Union, which, after seventy years of existence and many decades of implicit menace, proved itself unable to hold together, economically and politically, and succumbed to the internal forces pulling it apart. Was this a communist regime? So it proclaimed itself to the world, but what it was, in concrete fact, was primarily yet another species of dictatorship, of authoritarian rule. 'Communism' itself is one of those ideal states of things which, so far as I am aware, has never yet been brought to genuine realisation in any place or time of which one knows, though there have been small groups in the past, before the name itself was invented, with various resemblances to it (say, an early style of what is sometimes called 'primitive communism'; or, as in the middle ages, small religious communities, perhaps; or larger but still comparatively small and self-contained highly militarised communities such as the ancient Spartans, as some have claimed) – and though its name, in modern times, has served to frighten many of those in the West who had built their lives upon a different, more pragmatic foundation, one not too concerned with theoretical moral values, one way or another.

What is communism? I omit the lengthy and involved Marxist account of how it 'inevitably' must arise – based, here again, on Hegel (!) who has much to answer for – as this has little present relevance and I confine myself to the central theme on which the idea rests, that of common ownership, intended to overcome at last the distinction between rich and poor, between the haves and have-nots, a distinction which has bedevilled human society in all its developed forms. But what happens in fact, when the principle in its modern shape is nominally applied, is that a single individual seizes power in its name, constructs a tight court around himself, and sees to it that all other persons carry out his wishes without query, on pain often of death (or worse). This is the well-known 'cult of personality'. The difference between this and fascism is that the latter makes no real pretences: it has thrown off, for the most part, the trappings of civilised behaviour and, from the beginning, is out for nothing less than naked power and conquest by the 'leader' and his kin or close allies, everything and everybody else being entirely subject to his whim, in so far as he can enforce it and by whatever means. He works on his populace entirely by emotion, and the depths of his prejudices can be appalling, as we have seen with Hitler. The patina, at least, of civilised practice in dealing with other nations may be retained to a cautious extent by the communist but far less so by the fascist, who can be and can show himself to be, to those he treats as his enemies (which is everybody he cannot charm or cow) the nearest thing one can imagine to pure evil.

'Communism' is said to be now dead, leaving capitalism the triumphant victor, and for all time, or so the latter's enthusiastic supporters, ignoring its patent inadequacies, proclaim. A main basis of capitalism is the dominance of 'the market', more properly of the free market, where supply and demand and unhampered exchange rule. The trouble is that in the real world there is no such thing as a truly free market, even nationally (ignoring additional complications internationally). Sooner or later, and for the most part sooner rather than later, as we see on all sides, one or two powerful organisations accumulate all the chief forces of the market to themselves, so that a superior regulatory regime is needed to hold them in and restrain their powers; so that in effect, in order to remain 'free', the market has to have its longer-term freedom curtailed. Mrs Thatcher made much of 'the market' as against contemptuously the 'nanny state', but preferred to overlook the point I have just made, a very obvious point nevertheless, which I think even the blind must see. As for 'nannies', she herself was the nanny of all nannies, making sure, for example, that local authorities who did not obey her requirements implicitly were heavily descended upon, or even abolished if need be. And while 'privatising' furiously in all directions, theoretically for greater efficiency, in practice at least as much to give the plutocrat, her own class, more opportunities for gain, and at the same time urgently to replenish emptying government coffers, she was also mercilessly centralising the powers of government (under the necessary, if, it is true, altogether unlikely assumption - shared by her in principle with all authoritarians - of herself personally remaining always at the helm).

One should perhaps look a trifle more closely into the pros and cons of the theory of central planning as against dependence purely upon 'the market'. In central planning the basic principle is for supply to be adjusted by the central authority to the needs of individuals in the community without regard to the monetary or equivalent wealth at the individuals' personal disposal and requiring in return only the individuals' best and most appropriate services to the community for the community's general good – more concisely and epigrammatically put by Marx as "from each according to his abilities, to each according to his needs".

A brilliant theory, a wonderful ideal, but, as usual (I fear) with such ideal but undetailed conceptions, a theory facing overwhelming difficulties in the descent of the ideal into practice. For, in the first place, how are needs to be determined without some clear external indicator? Are we to say that everyone's needs are the same? The quotation's words do not necessarily say this; without further context they could easily be interpreted as meaning the opposite. It is fairly obvious, at any rate, that all needs are not in fact the same; but the degree of variation – and over what sort of range? – is hardly for a bureaucratic centre to determine with any pretence of efficiency. And what, in any case, are needs? Who is there, and where, to give a convincing and reasonably unarguable answer? Some of those scheduled to be at the receiving end may well feel that all they truly need is the opportunity to obtain enough food and shelter to keep body and soul together in all normal circumstances, provided only that they can also at all times think their own thoughts and express them in their own way and pass from place to place at will and without hindrance. But by others this may be felt far from enough – some of whom, particularly if their thoughts do not happen to be of (let us say) the profounder type, might even be willing to give up some of the fundamental provisions here specified, in exchange for some of the more material comforts of existence. Furthermore, do not all human things change with time? Human needs included: whatever the answer to the original question, if answer of some suitable kind there is, it cannot remain fixed, even so, for more than a moment. It will require revision, not once or twice, not now and then, but unremittingly, and the bases of revision will themselves be less than certain, and increase uncertainty.

So much, briefly, for the problems of distribution; but what of the problems of supply itself? The state as principal buyer and seller and central owner has evidently a task of very considerable magnitude before it in the calculation from one moment to another of precisely what is required in order to provide the group needs of its people, and then in the actual provision of those needs. Since this is not an economic treatise, I have no intention of delving into any of the minutiae of how such an economy can be managed; I will only point, once again, to the most obvious, indeed most sensational example of how such an economy can apparently be mismanaged – the example of the Soviet Union and its unpredicted yet (as seen from outside) sudden and total collapse. Of course, the Soviet Union represented central control on a vast scale. Is a smaller-scale operation of this kind more likely to achieve its goal? Personally, I doubt whether relative scale, above at least a certain limited size, is so powerful a determining factor. Very large scale has, for one thing, its positive theoretical advantages, in requiring potentially less in the way of dependence upon an external and, very likely, hostile world – given, to start with, the particular society's own not inadequate internal resources such as can be suitably manipulated whether for direct supply or for not less than equal-partner exchange. I am certainly not saying that scale has no effect, since it is bound to have an effect, of one sort or another, in any kind of operation; but it is, here, it seems to me, a far from simple effect, and I cannot see it as in any meaningful sense the main factor in the collapse of the Soviet Union. In that collapse I see two main factors – on the one hand there are the formidable basic difficulties, such as I have just very briefly set out, of any system of central planning for the comprehensive fulfilment of social needs, however good the intentions, and on the other there is the regrettable but inescapable fact that human intentions are rarely unmixedly good, and in cases of the kind under consideration inevitably and demonstrably impure, to say the least. We started from this point in examining the status of heady views about 'the death of communism', and I now return to it.

When authority is concentrated, without the strictest safeguards, into a single hand the results are in the long run always disastrous because no human being in the history of mankind has ever been able to resist the temptations of uncontrolled power. If this statement should seem to suggest, on the side, the reasonable possibility of an individual arriving at such a position of power full of noble intentions and only later allowing himself to become corrupted, let me qualify the impression. Such a possibility could only conceivably arise where the individual was an inheritor, not the founder or active consolidator of the post. Where he is the founder or consolidator as described, it is commonly only the already corrupted who stand the slightest real chance of arriving at the position, all weaker elements (including any whose drive for the seat of power is in even the smallest degree enfeebled by the intrusion of other aims such as the promotion of lofty ideals) having been eliminated on the way.

The pursuit of absolute power, if it is to be successful, must be absolutely ruthless and without diversions, emotional or otherwise. I have to stress 'absolute'. I am not talking of power and its achievement in a political system with appropriate or more or less appropriate checks and balances – a system which has in many respects very different characteristics from what I am describing, if not all of them entirely innocent ones, since power is still power, under whatever restraints. I will come to this in a moment.

The maintenance of such power, once obtained, has also to be ruthless, remaining firmly committed to itself primarily, and allowing admission to itself of other things and other interests only in so far as they positively assist it or (at least) in no way interfere with it. Any eventual weakening, for whatever reasons, of this thoroughly egotistical self-concern must lead without fail to a weakening of the central structure and in due course to collapse.

Naturally, a regime of the kind in question, which managed at the same time adequately to satisfy the needs of its subjected populace, would be less likely to suffer in this way – but that does not happen in fact because in essence it is a contradiction in terms. A suppressed and repressed populace cannot also be a populace of individuals and groups living out their lives in ways which feel to be truly fitting for them: some few will no doubt accumulate considerable material wealth and delegated power in courting the Master, but they will always be in a relatively small minority, and the populace at large will tend to be in a perpetual state – even if only a passive state – of waiting to break free.

The theory, however, that a thoroughly downtrodden populace will in due course somehow break free of its own accord, however heavy the weight of the oppressor's foot upon its neck, is a romantic illusion. If the oppressor is sufficiently well-organised and sufficiently determined, and ready to commit any crimes, without limit of type or number, to retain his seat, the chances of internal resistance against him succeeding or even coming to the point of being seriously visible to the outer world are slim indeed. This is not pessimism: it is brutal fact, as many experiences in our sad century have clearly shown. Stalinism is but one example. It is only when the 'great leader' dies – as he must, however great his leadership – and is succeeded eventually by others a good deal less simply and wholeheartedly devoted to the pure maintenance of themselves in power (including, for preference, the extension of that power) that stirrings from below may begin at last to be heard and felt. It was not oppression which caused the collapse of the Soviet Union – it was the relaxation of oppression, with all that that brought in its train. The lid having been removed, as one might otherwise put it, the contents bubbled and shot up in the air.

Thirteen

Communism and Capitalism

II. A First Glance at Capitalism

Communism is dead, capitalism is triumphant, so we are told. Before we allow ourselves to accept the total accuracy of this assessment, we had better be sure we know at least what the words signify, or are intended to signify, and what will be left of them when the facts and concepts they are intended to encapsulate are, as far as possible, isolated and examined in themselves, and set against one another. We have been to some small extent into the matter of communism; it is time to look, as adequately as we can in the brief space at our disposal (but perhaps a little more closely as is befitting to the victorious party), into capitalism. It may make sense if we keep 'communism' in mind at the same time, since the explicit opposition as conceived between the two, for present purposes, is vital.

Capitalism is in basis a name for an economic system, communism for a social ideology. The difference, from this point of view, is that the first concentrates on one aspect only – however avowedly important – of what goes on in a community, while the other in its ideal origins (never mind how far the execution diverges from it) has an appearance of total comprehensiveness, comprehending economics, that is to say, which could not be overlooked, to such an extent indeed that the theoretical Marxist version (so often considered as if it were the only version possible) seems never to get beyond it, but, properly speaking, treating it, rather, as a vital step in progress towards an ultimate goal beyond itself. If communism cannot possibly overlook economics, so capitalism, though basically an economic doctrine and pattern of practice, cannot in all seriousness overlook the social factor, which exists whether the capitalist likes it or not, and without which capitalism itself could not come into being.

The authentic honest-to-God capitalist with his eye above all on personal profitability will do all he can to fight against the implications of these last remarks and will endeavour, as far as he is able, stoutly to refuse all acknowledgement to the social factor. Mrs Thatcher, we recall, went so far as to assert bluntly that there was "no such thing as society". And what of her party's bitter resistance at all costs to the European Community's (now European Union's) Social Chapter? With this school of thought any reminder of an underlying social reality is unreservedly to be combated and any findings allied to it to be rejected outright.

Capitalism is not economics; it is a popular, catch-all name for a particular type of economic system which can be seen in a number of places in active operation. As such, while claiming on the face of it no regard for anything outside itself, it starts off, nevertheless, from certain clearly specifiable assumptions about the social factor, a factor which the upholders of the system may be unwilling objectively to analyse or even, as we have seen, in some of their major moods, recognise, but on which the system's views are nevertheless definite. They may be summarised, crudely but I think realistically, as 'The devil take the hindmost'.

According to the system the chief aim in life is the accumulation of personal wealth (a British prime minister, as we remember, not long ago gave enthusiastic promises, to a party audience, of "cascades of wealth" to be forthcoming to ambitious individuals through the agency of his government). In a normal and non-totalitarian capitalist society there is however no question of activities of other kinds being in any way prohibited: anyone who wishes can carry on any activity he wishes, within certain legal limits; but if it is an activity not to do with the making of money, that must be his concern. He cannot, if the society is truly capitalist, expect the state to 'look after' him: he must 'stand on his own feet'. If he has inherited money, that will give him a delightful freedom. If not, he must learn to turn his talents and inclinations to the provision for himself of at least sufficient wealth to keep him going; and if he should be seduced in the long run through this process into subordinating what he has to offer to the more casual requirements of a more superficial, more throwaway public taste than his own, that is in the nature of how things are, and must be borne.

This particular point perhaps takes us away somewhat from the broad central theme of the social factor and capitalism's attempt to ignore it. The point, however, is a very interesting one and perhaps therefore I may pursue it a little way before returning to the broader theme. Suppose, then, that an artist, it may be, arises who is, as we say, 'before his time' – whose work is not generally appreciated at the moment when he produces it since it diverges from the traditionally acceptable, but which will be appreciated in due course, when the public eye has accustomed itself to a new and unusually illuminating viewpoint. He, himself, is not willing nor even able to adjust himself to his current public's preferences and prejudices, when his own vision is so profound and clear. Suppose, in short, that we have a Van Gogh, who dies leaving a house full of paintings, unsold and unsaleable, yet any one of which only a century later (and what is a century?) can fetch easily a million pounds or more at auction. What are we to make of this, in the context of an outlook such as the one we have just been describing? I think that the convinced capitalist would probably say, "Very sad, but it is not possible to cater for such extraordinary cases – after all, there cannot be many of them."

If I have the capitalist's answer right, and I do not easily see what else it could be, short of an overturning of the basic principle on which he operates, then it can shed considerable light on the principle in general. The essence of that principle is very generalised, very sweeping, obviously unwilling to take account of special cases which might in any way interfere with it. Let us see what the answer at root involves.

First, let us agree that the case of Van Gogh is an extraordinary one. But may its extraordinariness not rest rather on the fact that it is extreme, and therefore extremely visible, than that it is in every way singular? May there not be other cases, who can say how many, of the same kind but lesser in degree, which remain hidden, which have not the same exposure as that of Van Gogh? Who is to deny the possibility – I think the probability – of the existence of a variety of such cases, largely or totally stifled by an unfriendly environment, needing but failing to receive the stimulus of an encouragement not, in the social climate we are considering, available to them for their fulfilment?

It is a matter of values. It is not a question of how or whether one should attempt to cater for extreme and totally unforeseeable cases: under that light, indeed, one can expect no more than a host of ready clichés, such as that 'genius must work out its own salvation', 'it is the destiny of artistic genius to starve in a garret', and so forth. The question is, rather, whether it is reasonable that *the* great priority in a state should be to open up every possible opportunity for the making of money, leaving all else, whatever it is – according, that is, to the unadulterated capitalist canon – to care for itself. Is this, then, to be exalted as the end of life? What is the true end of life? We do not know, it has to be admitted; but not everybody, surely, is bound to agree that our main aim in all circumstances must be to wax fat if only we can discover in ourselves the astuteness necessary for that accomplishment – to get ahead of the other fellow at all costs (not always, maybe, with the closest regard to legality), to tread heavily on his face if need be, at any rate not to worry overmuch about him if he is left far behind in the race. This, after all, is 'competition', also known to some in the past, more disparagingly, as 'the rat race'.

In this world, it is true enough, we are thoroughly dependent upon physical resources, and we require to make the most of them. It would hardly do if we all universally aimed at being brilliant artists, at any rate if we aimed at something of the kind as our first endeavour. Most of us, as it happens, have no such wish. Most persons who need in their lives a degree of external financial support (that is to say, most persons) are content to join the struggle for existence on a normal footing, exercising their faculties in the most monetarily profitable way open to them, without any exotic urges after aesthetic or intellectual self-expression unrelated to monetary gain. In this environment, it is to be noted, 'art' of various kinds and 'ideas' do have their part to play, but under a capitalist regime it is a part in principle subordinated to the acquisition and accumulation of wealth, towards which they have to be directed if they and their creators are to have any chance of keeping their heads above water.

It is to be understood that the system I have been describing is capitalism in its pristine purity, not the sort of misleading mixture we commonly encounter, a mixture flaunting itself no doubt as the genuine article but admitting alien elements at various points here and there to modify its pressures. We in this country today have certainly never experienced the rule of pure capitalism, despite the Thatcher (and succeeding) years, during which every effort appeared to be being made to squeeze and crush out every item of method of an alternative nature. Nevertheless, 'profit' and 'success' (the latter meaning in this context profit again, and in superabundance) were the watchwords, room continued to be left, albeit grudgingly, for certain interests and services not directly connected with these notions but tacitly if often unwillingly accepted as having, in their own name, a certain public value. I spoke just now of mixtures, and it will be evident that it was this type of thing I had then in mind; but, having used the word, I must emphasise here that capitalism itself is in its own essence an inextricable mixture in a quite different way. The pursuit of profit, beyond a very limited point, has little significance in relation to the material benefits it brings: beyond that point, as I have said before, profit is pursued above all as a cover for self-aggrandisement – a pile of material goods being no more than the visible sign that 'I am much better than anybody else in sight'.

Fourteen

Capitalism and the 'Social' Question

Let us at this point take a look a little more directly at the 'social question'. Very roughly speaking, the social question is concerned with the relationship both as it is and as it should be (whatever 'should' properly means here) between the rich and the poor – or rather, as the leaders of capitalism tend to see it, between the 'successful' and the 'unsuccessful'. How does it come about that there is this division at all? Is there any obligation on the successful to give support to the unsuccessful? Whose fault is it that the unsuccessful are as they are?

The first thing to note is that the existence of success would seem necessarily to involve the existence of its opposite, since success and failure tend to be relative terms to one another both in conception and in practical outcome, and to an extent it must be true that the successful are successful precisely because they are 'better' than the unsuccessful. Can we imagine a state of things where everybody is or becomes successful? The concept of 'competition', an aspect of the battle of the strong, suggests the impossibility, from the capitalist point of view, of such an evenly-balanced state of things. Or, if not totally impossible, it is not something seen as in essence desirable. The whole idea of competition is to get ahead of the others . What, then, happens to the others?

A capitalist system bases itself on the principle of an economy in vigorous and efficient *movement*. It can have nothing to do with the static, and this is reasonable enough, since the world is in perpetual movement, and a static economy will inevitably fall behind in the long run – which in the present-day world, where everything appears to be accelerating at a great pace, is not likely to be a very long run. Life in general has never stood still, though in the past it may in its beginnings and in parts of its development have been so slow in its movement that it could have seemed, even to some hypothetical outside observer, to be standing quite still. Once upon a time the dinosaurs, as we are frequently told, ruled the world, but now they are long gone and have become a byword for the old and obsolete. Though on this last point an opposite comment has also occasionally been made. Obsolete they may now be, but we need to be reminded that they are reputed to have held their position for some 140-150 million years, while we, the present-day masters of the earth, have under a million years to show in all from our very first and most primitive emergence, at least with any certainty. (Considerably larger conjectures have been made – but the maximum is no more than five million). Does our pride, our huge over-confidence in our abilities, lead us to scoff at such a comparison?

Perhaps we should think of the great human empires which, at the time of their greatness, have seemed capable of going on for ever and ever, but which now, in their monstrous character as overpowering imperial regimes, are quite dead and done with, surpassed if not forgotten. What of the once-great British Empire itself – now hardly more real, I think, than the more recently defunct Soviet Union, though having dissipated its strengths and broken up its parts in a rather different way? I think the lesson is, not to be too sure. Movement is life; but over-rapid movement, careless of how and where it drives itself or allows itself to be driven, may be death.

I have asked what happens in a capitalist type of economy to the others, those left behind (and fully intended to be left behind) in the race. On a strict capitalist basis, their fate is in principle simply to be held up to all and sundry as examples to be avoided. They have, in principle, no rights, no claims to maintenance from the goods of those more successful than themselves. (From where else? There is nowhere else.) They have failed, and must suffer for their failure. The only qualification of this apparently extreme situation is that success and failure are not two absolutes; there are a variety of degrees of both, and there will be many of those who fail in their own eyes, or in the eyes of some at least of their fellows, or both, who are nevertheless, in the event, not without means to maintain themselves and their dependants, and who may still, according to the rules of the game, look down with appropriate arrogance upon those lower in the scale than themselves.

I have also asked whose fault it is that the person viewed as a failure under this system fails. There will be various answers, ranging from a consideration of those men or women who join the race straightforwardly to win but are defeated, to those who, for whatever reason, have decided not to join the race at all. In the midst of the course, however, there will also be a number of individuals who have joined a sector of the race where the greatest material rewards are not normally on offer (no more than a limited degree of 'success' in this sense is therefore ever possible to them) but where a greater personal satisfaction is available for them through the work to be done in itself than in the pure pursuit of physical gain. These individuals are not classifiable as failures unless they are unable to meet the requirements of their own particular sector - or unless, it must be added, the sector itself is so precariously balanced at the edge of the capitalist economy that the fundamental requirements of that economy become at times very difficult indeed to meet. I instance again in this connection Van Gogh (cf. page 62)

Whose fault is it that the failure fails? I doubt whether the true capitalist would in fact show much interest in this general question, or even find it particularly meaningful. The failure fails because - short of some totally unpredictable accident interfering with the natural trend of events - he is not 'good' enough to succeed. Those who have opted out of the race completely have obviously only themselves to blame; but as to the others, they have tried and lost, and there is really nothing much more to be said. They have no claim on the goods of those who have been more successful than they are, a thing which would surely be contrary to nature.

This highly simplistic attitude is based ultimately on a curious metaphysical theory relating itself to every part of the human scene, as will become more evident as we go on. (Do not tell me that capitalism has nothing to do with metaphysics - of course it has, and the more so because the point is unacknowledged). There is thought to be an order of nature, which it would be almost a sin to contradict, and which naturally favours the astute and the predatory, the 'hard-working' (along a particular channel) and those who (from a particular aspect) are generally 'better' than others. There is an interesting resemblance between this and the Aristotelian view that individuals fall into certain 'natural' slots, according to which an individual becomes, for example, a slave because his character is naturally slavish. That example may seem to us outrageous, but this is because we no longer treat slavery and serfdom as essential elements in our economy: we do, however, tend very much to treat those who are underdogs in our society as being so because that is what their characters somehow deserve. And as to slavery, it may be as well to remember that it is not so much more than a century ago that a great civil war was fought over, at root, the very institution of slavery: this was in what today we think of as probably the capitalist society *par excellence*. (The Northern United States, which won the war, and had abolished slavery, was fundamentally capitalist and growingly so and had no need of slavery, which could even be regarded as an impediment; in the South, which clung fiercely to slavery, slaves were felt to be an essential part of what was still largely an agrarian economy: the Northern decision – like so many political decisions – was thus practical in origin rather than in any deep sense humanitarian.)

Harking back to Aristotle, we may observe that the society in which he lived and taught and wrote was not a capitalist society in anything like our present sense, and that the ideals which he promoted were in no way aimed primarily at the accumulation of as much wealth as possible (which is clearly the present idea). He believed that the 'blessèd' man (the translation 'happy', frequently found, can give a misleading impression, suggesting a subjective approach, which is not in question here) should have an adequate sufficiency of worldly goods, enough never to feel want, but this was to be very far from his end in life: rather, it was to enable him to carry out what were his true ends without the pressure of anxiety. Aristotle was a philosopher, and had the thinking man very much in mind; others in later ages found other ideals to dwell on and to magnify, but even though in all ages of civilisation from the beginnings we are aware of prominent individuals accumulating vast quantities of wealth – as a rule much more for display than for utility (an approach we can never get away from) – the idea of such accumulation being striven for by all individuals in a society as their prime aim has been a fairly recent innovation.

As I have said and must re-emphasise, we do not live under a pure capitalist regime, despite all the vigorous apparent moves made recently in that direction; and nor do the Americans. I have attempted to draw a picture of what capitalism in theory stands for, but it is not a picture of what actually is, nor even perhaps could be without at least some quite startling (and damaging) changes in the human mind and outlook, changes which it is difficult even to envisage with any clarity. Capitalism is not really about money; it is about status, about being and showing oneself to be 'the best' (so the ancient Greek nobles were the *aristoi*, 'the best', and their rule was the rule of 'the best', aristocracy), and money is here the symbol, the token of superiority. Men, in organising for themselves states in which their communities may flourish, have done so through the establishment of hierarchies, and the capitalist state is essentially yet another kind of hierarchy, differing from some of its predecessors in being a good deal more fluid than they, allowing plenty of room for movement within its orbit, but movement which, as many have found, can be down as well as up (an echo here of a frequently repeated public warning to the rash investor), and taking little account of any who cannot easily accept its decidedly harsh and restrictive values.

The social factor, whose idea the capitalist dislikes with intensity, but which he is fated to have to deal with, requires of him that he divert some of his riches to the support of those in his community who have either fallen behind in the race, or who need a modicum of assistance in entering the race, or who are in some other way disadvantaged. Why should he give such help? If he has to meet such requirements, he would much rather do so by distributing charitable largesse which he could treat as being of his own free will, and which could afford him also some not inconvenient publicity, than by being compelled by law, through the undesirable anonymity of taxation, to give up some of his gains for other persons to redistribute. But why should he help at all? A very good, very sound question, which cannot be answered adequately without delving into matters of morality, a thing I regret I cannot undertake at this particular juncture on any serious scale, since it would open the gates at once on far too wide and deep a subject. Yet I must say straight away just a very few simple words on the matter, leaving the rest for the moment to the imagination.

Fifteen

Wealth as Aim; and its Implications

To propose the accumulation of 'cascades of wealth' as a first priority for the State and for its constituent individuals has certain critical dangers which experience has well demonstrated. If wealth is an acknowledged main aim, the means to achieve it will become in practice relatively unimportant. Laws to restrain 'unfair' activities can never have more than limited effect, because legislation can never cover all possibilities, and ingenious persons can, with a little effort, find their way round many legal obstructions put in their path. Questions of 'fairness' and 'rightness' are thought pretty irrelevant: if the law allows it (whether altogether intentionally or no) that is good enough. This is what may be called the problem of legal loopholes. But there are other problems, worse ones. Not everybody is anxious in all circumstances to stay within the law. The buccaneering instinct, to which reference has been made above, remains strong, and is at base specifically lawless; and, the aim having been set, with effusive blessing from the capitalist state, the wily and the increasingly powerful will use every means, legal or otherwise, to attain it. Now the problem is not to avoid outward illegality but simply to avoid being caught; in the course of which continued effort bribery and corruption in the highest places are not eschewed and are often welcomed or even invited. The undermining of a government through these processes is not unknown. We should perhaps not be too complacent if we have not seen this last consequence visibly taking effect in our own country: it could happen here too – it has certainly happened elsewhere. It has also happened that gangster fraternities, though they may derive in their origins from other sources, have found the sort of atmosphere I speak of an admirably stimulating one in which to thrive, and to be able to infect their surroundings, in return, with their own virus.

"Come, come," says the defender, "but no human system is perfect." Personally, I find this answer a feeble one in regard to a system lending itself so easily to abuse, casting itself so readily into the lap of the miscreant, but let us pass on – to the point I have been edging towards, to the opposite end of the scale, to those who are unable to stand up to the race, who have perhaps fallen by the wayside at an early stage. "You mean the incompetents, the losers, the *layabouts*?" says Mr Moneybags. No, I will not agree that I mean the 'layabouts'; but let us look into that term: it is worth a glance.

'Layabout' is, of course, an emotive word. It begs all questions in advance, with a brief, sweeping, derogatory description of a broad group of people of the widest variety of kinds. Their limits are unspecified except that they comprise, lumped together, all those, at the bottom end of the scale, whom the capitalist would far rather forget. Why – however much he is inclined to repeat, "Am I my brother's keeper?" – is he unable to forget them? It is because, I suggest, he feels uncomfortably that there are those among them to whom he owes, obscurely but irresistibly, some kind of genuine moral duty, those who have fallen behind through no fault of their own, perhaps through some physical or mental inadequacy not of their causing, and it is because he does not like this feeling that he tries, as a salve to his conscience, to assimilate such individuals to the undesirable class of layabouts. The 'layabout' is, properly speaking, an idler, a loafer, a good-for-nothing. In the usage referred to, it has the extended, vaguer significance of any such person who obtains goods to which he is not entitled, having done nothing to earn them. From here it is an unnoticed step to its use as a term of general disparagement, throwing together disparate types having little in common except, as I say, that they inhabit the bottom of the scale and that the capitalist would much prefer to forget them: the truth is however that the nearer the individuals concerned actually come to the extended definition of 'layabout' above quoted (of one, that is, who obtains goods beyond his entitlement), the less is the capitalist able effectively to ignore them.

Others in the wide, blurred class created by his terminology he might, if things were different, succeed in forgetting about except as objects for occasional and lordly benefaction; but these thrust themselves upon his notice precisely because they do not wait for the crumbs to fall from his table but take whatever they can get, from wherever they can get it, by whatever means. This is very uncivil of them; but they could, after all, claim that they were merely carrying out the lesson taught them by their masters: to take what you can get and not be too nice about how. In their open disrespect for law and order they are nearer in character to the gangster than to, let us say, the manipulative financier, but, as we have seen, the gangster can flourish very well in a capitalist society, and one might add that the border between the official capitalist and the gangster may not always be entirely clear. In the party of the layabouts is also the pure vandal, the defacer and destroyer for their own sakes. The nihilistic attitude so represented would appear to be an inevitable concomitant of the 'free-for-all' society where, in principle, anything goes, so long as it provides personal satisfaction - profit above all, but otherwise whatever gives one any kind of satisfaction, and hang the community or any individuals in it other than oneself. I am not advocating oppressive laws to deal with such a phenomenon: I am suggesting, rather, that in a better-tuned society the phenomenon might be in less haste to show itself.

I do not wish to defend the actual layabout any more than I would wish to defend the gangster. The truth is that I heartily abhor them both, but I only wish to point out that both are elements, unhappily, congenial to the type of society I describe. They occur as outgrowths of it, and they have somehow to be coped with: this is not in the first place a matter of morals but of expediency - which is not to say, however, that moral matters are not for consideration. The capitalist knows full well that he must indeed face moral issues at some moment or another, however little he relishes such an encounter, however much he pretends that moral issues are not for him, that they are inventions foisted upon him by religion, or socialism, or what have you. The truth is that he may push morality out by the front door but it will come in again at the back (hence 'the back door' of which he so often apprehensively speaks). What place have morals in such a society? It is astonishing that they should have any place - but still they have. It is a point in favour of something; I am not sure what.

Here I can perhaps draw attention to a movement which has grown in recent years, under the auspices of an organisation known as Business in the Community - whose aim is to induce businesses, large and small, to take an active part in promoting the welfare (though this word itself, tending as it does to call up socialist ideals, through its use in the past by socialist regimes, is inclined to be treated as taboo – 'prosperity' is usually preferred) of their local communities. It is claimed that companies can improve their own image and prospects by involving themselves in the community at large and helping to meet the community's needs. A very important part of the effort is directed at involvement in education, and here certain potential material benefits for business, such as the recruitment of useful staff, are very evident, but the net nevertheless goes wider.

I can sum up the general attitude behind the movement by two recent quotes from statements by officers of the Business in the Community organisation:

> (i) ...companies were beginning [by 1985] to sense that they were really contributing to the long-term viability of local communities, often developing their own customer base
>
> (ii) *(referring to small businesses in particular)* We explain that by looking at local needs they can expand their customer base and perhaps improve relations with their suppliers.

It is clear that the primary inducement rests in showing that 'community involvement' is not based on altruism (in the current climate an unappreciated virtue) but rather on a keen-eyed (optics three-quarter closed) perception of what is good for profits. There is a marked difference here from the Quaker ethic of Victorian times, when firms such as Cadburys, Rowntrees and Boots provided free housing and education for employees, no doubt not without an eye to the firms' own prospective and in due course evident benefit but not solely for such self-centred motives: the idea of a modicum of altruism was certainly not spurned but rather proclaimed.

What do we make of this? Which way are we to look – at what appears to be the ethical guiding spirit, in this connection, of nineteenth century Quakerism or at the seemingly straightforward profit-directed approach of today? Shall we say that the mask has now been removed, that the clear-sighted, no-pretences, end-of-the-twentieth-century attitude at length and at last says it all, and that self can be declared freely and finally to be the centre of all and all that really matters, that now at any rate honesty rules and that if we help others in any way it is primarily in order that we may help ourselves rather more? That 'morals' in such a context are a mere hypocritical figment?

Frankly, I doubt it. Human beings are a great deal more confused than this in their motivations and aspirations; and whereas the Quakers – bless them! – may not have been quite so single-mindedly and unaffectedly moral and philanthropic in all their excursions into community-help as might sometimes be thought, on the other side the present-day organisers of the efforts and enterprises here in question may not be quite so free from the more purely ethical considerations as they perhaps like to tell themselves (and tell others). Perhaps it might even embarrass some of them a little to think or talk about such things in today's prevailing atmosphere. Who shall say? Perhaps, indeed, the common cliché of 'enlightened self-interest' could be applied fairly literally, or in a measure at least, to both parties, though the degree of applicability of the two contributory elements in the expression may still differ somewhat between the parties.

I have been dealing so far only with domestic problems, and I did say in so many words a while back that I must ignore the complexities of international issues – since these jottings are not intended as a treatise on world economics, or on global ethics, or the like – but I do feel it difficult to forgo just one small passing mention of the impact of the capitalist system on the economy of the less privileged nations. I quote from a *Times* summary of Easter 1992 relating to a BBC popular programme on why Africa is poor. Here is its closing sentence:

> Using a jocular style for a serious purpose, the programme explains the effects of unfair trade, the debt burden, environmental damage and bad government, all compounding the vulnerability of powerless people.

I do not propose to analyse this or expand upon it, and, for simplicity's sake, I propose to continue keeping as far away as I can from international issues, even if it is impossible to edge them out entirely and in every respect. But I could not abstain from this passing quote.

As to the 'losers' at the bottom end of the domestic scale, I will come back to them again. They are too important to leave alone with the very limited comments I have so far been able to make. But in the meantime I would like to go on to something else.

Sixteen

The Market, and what Underlies it

The heart of capitalism, we have many times been told, is 'the market', more fully and more correctly 'the free market', and I have already pointed out that this freedom is – perforce – nothing like so unrestrictedly free as is sometimes pretended. But let me go further into what 'the market' signifies. It rests upon the equation of supply with demand, without pressure; the theory being that if demand is strong enough and can make itself adequately known, supply will inevitably follow it, without state intervention, and by this means a balance will ultimately be achieved in which all reasonable wants will be satisfied and nobody left in the lurch. This is another of those marvellous theories that certainly seem to be effective enough up to a point, but up to a point only, beyond which is a no-man's-land of darkness and – I fear – confusion. I do not think my statement of the basic equation is unfair as a nutshell description of what is generally thought; but apart from the fact that the equation, despite its appearance of dynamism, is conceived, at root, in too static terms (tending to take too little account of considerable changes perpetually proceeding in society's background conditions, and particularly swiftly in modern times), the truth is that it has, in the form stated, two fundamental weaknesses.

The first is the lack of any specific reference to money, which is a vital element in the equation. Money is the medium of exchange, a neutral factor as far as value goes – not itself, that is to say, of any direct value, or not necessarily so, but of value primarily or essentially for the goods of every kind into which it can be converted by exchange. Of course, money or something like it is known or assumed to be *involved*, but that is not really good enough, for the point is that without it this particular equation simply disintegrates. It is money that makes the equation work, and this must raise the serious and basic question of how individuals obtain the money and how far they are able to put it to the service of the equation. The fact is, however, that the equation, in so far as it is real, has very little to do with individuals directly but rests upon a mass statistical principle, and the relationship of the individual here to such a principle is as highly variable as the relationship of any single individual to any covering mass statistics of any kind. In the actual world affected by our equation, some will no doubt get everything they want, some nothing or almost nothing.

The other weakness is that the second half of the statement does not logically follow on the first. Since we have already had to admit, as the result of a slightly closer look, that the equation in no way lays it down that every particular individual will at any stage necessarily be affected in the same manner as every or indeed any other, it is straight away and automatically clear that the ultimate balance, if there is one (and I have already urged that the implications of the theory are too static in this respect in relation to the facts and their constant mobility), cannot possibly guarantee that all reasonable wants will in all cases be satisfied. What, in any case, is 'reasonable'? The equation could only guarantee the ultimate fulfilment of all reasonable wants – even totally ignoring our previous point – on a sharply restrictive interpretation of 'reasonable', one having the requirements of the theory primarily in mind (that is to say, by begging the question); and as to there being eventually nobody left in the lurch, this must, of course, depend, whatever way you look at it, on there being nobody with insufficient funds to purchase enough to satisfy at least minimal human needs, there being nothing in fact to show conclusively that this will be so. There is much to suggest the opposite.

In regard to the matter of what is 'reasonable', we face here the same sort of problem as with the Marxist 'needs'; except that in the latter case we have a human authority (however inadequate for the task) to whom the problem is laid down as specifically referable, in the former the answer to the question is – well, really and truly, I suppose, whatever anybody with some kind of axe to grind (and with no human control to whom he is responsible) chooses to make of it. This is more than a casual difference: it leads us on to something fundamental.

The difference is between an (ineffectual, no doubt) attempt to make things work on a more or less rational human level and, on the other side, the determination to leave things in the end to the Great Decider, to Fate, and to the gods. The motto implied in the second option could well be, "All's for the best in the best of all possible worlds". Since the latter part of this motto is obviously untrue, let us forget it and dwell for a moment instead on the first part.

"All's for the best" is founded on faith. It is not demonstrable fact. It is not even quite certain what it means. Is it supposed to take effect in the immediate present, or over the extent of a particular, given activity, or over the span of a human life? Or simply in the long run; but how long a run? The issue is what is known as clouded by doubt: it begins to look like the triumph, as they say, of hope over experience. On one level the notion is reminiscent of the popular mythology given form in so many magnificent Western films of the old days, in which the handsome stranger comes out of the East to put things to rights in a small community growingly at odds with itself. Having overcome the local villains, he departs as silently and enigmatically as he came. This is admirable and heartening and possibly not entirely out of touch with reality at all points, but at any rate it does not reflect things as we know them in everyday and it is at the opposite end from the events of, let us say, Greek tragedy.

Greek tragedy may not, then, seem to have anything much in common with the idea of "all's for the best"; but, oddly enough, it was the most rational-minded and orderly and comprehensive in range of all ancient Greek thinkers, no other than Aristotle himself, who based himself on a concept not unlike it: 'Nature does or makes nothing in vain... but everything with a view to the best'. This occurs in his work *On the Heavens*, but it is not singular to that work, and it is a concept which follows about with him wherever he goes. Nature, he holds, does everything for an end – a well-conceived end. This is not something arrived at by him as a result of detailed argument but is a governing preconception on which reasoned arguments can themselves be founded. It may be remarked that this is not a totally unusual type of situation at any period of human thought or, for that matter, with any thinker: under the best worked-out, most elaborate and accurately (often perhaps defiantly) argued of demonstrations, look always for the fundamental assumption, itself not rationally argued (frequently, for that matter, not even stated), but on which all else nevertheless is dependent, on which all else stands balanced. Once the assumption is revealed and itself subjected to serious examination, the rest of the argument may, very likely, begin to fade, extensive uncertainty to reign – and it may continue to reign for an interminable time, since such underlying assumptions are very often basic and troublesome, and next to impossible to get out of the way, though one debate them furiously 'till the cows come home'.

Aristotle's belief in Nature's rightness shares, I must say, an important part of its outlook with, implicitly, that of modern Darwinism; at the same time it is quite characteristic of a leading aspect of the classical Greek attitude, however much it might seem to conflict with some of the attitudes of the great Greek tragedians (there is nothing strange in the fact that these two types of attitude seem to run side by side: such apparent psychological and behavioural contradictions are a commonplace in human history). Note that I do not speak of attitudes, poetic or popular, and variable in place and time, to anthropomorphised divinity, to the multiplicity of gods and goddesses, heroes and heroines and sprites, whose asserted governance of, or at least interference with human affairs is at best wayward and unsure and who, as often as not, are not even in the closest harmony with one another. What I speak of is something more deeply underlying, less obvious but in the end more powerful, a belief in an undefined, impersonal destiny to which it is often felt wise to leave ultimate decisions.

I draw attention to the persistent use, in the appointment of officials in the developed Greek democracy, of which Athens is the type, of the casting of lots; and lest I seem to be wishing to place disproportionate emphasis on one angle of what is after all a fairly complex situation, let me quote a single sentence from the writing of an impartial commentator – from the Scandinavian scholar Hansen's work on *The Athenian Democracy*, a work not long ago published over here. "The vast majority of magistrates", he says (p.229), "were selected by lot". This may seem to us "crazy", he also says, but "it is the fact". – What, then, are we to read into it?

I daresay, in passing, that some of *our* methods might seem crazy to *them*. How about our insistence, in this country, on awarding the full powers of government to the political party with a majority of seats in the House, though it may be with a minority of the votes? The consequent disfranchisement, in these circumstances, of the larger part of the population, and it may be for years, is accepted as a necessity to achieve 'strong government'. Maybe it is worth the price, though I doubt it (is it impossible for the subtle mind of man to find a better solution?), but the least it does is to make our version of 'democracy' look, at this point, surprisingly feeble. The Greek method was very different. We owe the word and the idea to the Greeks, but the conditions under which they operated, as we have, of course, to remember, were very different from ours. Nevertheless the difference between their and our attitudes is rather remarkable. The number of citizens, of persons accordingly qualified to take part in public affairs (no further qualification being considered necessary), in the Greek city-state was small enough for direct (as distinct from representative) democracy to be practicable, and on this basis all efforts were made in a democratic state such as Athens at her peak to give every so-qualified individual the opportunity to serve the state directly in an official capacity: if this meant adding to the normal processes of voting also appointment by casting of lots (as above indicated), together with rapid turnover of magistracies (basically annual), this was thought to be entirely fitting.

The Athenians did not find such procedures peculiar because, as I am bound to hold, they did not find it altogether contrary to reason to leave things, in the last resort, to the (unnamed) gods to determine. If they were not all that far from some aspects of Aristotle's personally expressed views in this respect, nor are they indeed all that far – let me say it and brave your reaction – from some aspects of our own thinking; not, it may be, in the plain political field, but how about 'the market'?

I have pointed out some pretty clear difficulties in the concept of the market and the theory of its somehow unaidedly effecting a perfect balance, in the most efficient manner possible, between all kinds of demand and all kinds of supply; but, in the face of everything there is to show against the theory as anything more than the roughest and most approximate and generalised presentation of what actually takes place, ignoring all the most obvious and most pressing problems resulting, we still go on to proclaim our belief in it as the great and complete solution, under a capitalist system (assumed to be the best of all systems), to all our needs and questions – which can only be because in our hearts we take at last the same attitude to the acknowledged complexity of human affairs, and to the problem of its disentanglement, as did the ancient Greeks when they used the casting of lots to appoint magistrates. In the last resort we too are content to leave things to the gods to determine, and we seem satisfied that what they determine will be 'for the best'.

I must add, of course, that this is by no means the whole story, whether for us or for the Greeks, who were in very many ways far indeed from passively lying down under anything that the gods might wish to throw at them. So we too, while hailing 'the market' as the great and ultimate deliverer, have, in the West, learnt to make as sure as we conveniently can that the market's worst defects do not overwhelm us. We know the virtue of 'checks and balances', even if we do not seem always to be terribly good at passing on the lesson learnt to others – so that the nations of the East recently freed from Soviet shackles have been liable to find themselves plunged head first into the whirlpool of 'the market' without adequate protection and without having had time or opportunity to build up an adequate 'infrastructure' (as it is nowadays called) on the basis of which a capitalist-type economy can be made to function without too severe a strain.

Seventeen

Democracy

We hear a good deal these days in exaltation of the virtues of democracy as against the manifold vices of tyranny; and who indeed in his senses (apart from the tyrant or would-be tyrant himself and his entourage) is there who could honestly deny the emphatic superiority of the former in most ways that come readily to mind? Almost the only at all weighty argument that can be proposed in favour of tyranny, even forgetting the automatically pejorative implications of the name itself (for which, therefore, one should perhaps substitute the term 'dictatorship', embodying an idea still not without vociferous and often violent support in various parts, if primarily, it must be acknowledged, among the emotionally unstable, with whom our uneasy, imperfectly balanced world remains extremely well supplied) is the argument that one lone single-minded leader is bound to have a tremendous advantage in action over a leader or leaders restrained and restricted by a compulsion to consultation. True enough, if one does not mind being led by the single-minded leader down into the pit, a not infrequent dénouement.

But what exactly is this modern 'democracy' that we make so much of, and why do we – or some of us, at least – sing its praises quite so loudly, as if it were the very best of all systems that man could ever devise for himself and for the organisation of his societies? Certainly, it is far better than a worse thing, as I am among the very first to admit, but is that to be the end of the story? Have we, in this, reached the climax, the height and apex of our development? Is that likely? The word 'democracy' itself has grown with emphatic repetition into so much of a catchword that one becomes slightly fearful of asking any questions about it, as if to do so would be to show oneself a traitor to the Flag. Indeed, it is for this very reason that it demands urgently and coolly to be examined, for its significance to be made clear, or as clear as possible, before we sink into a stupor at the word's mere sound.

Democracy, we are told, equates with freedom, and this is really, as it is insisted, the whole basis of its tremendous superiority over any other class of regime. The democracies are 'the free peoples'. A typical democracy is a multi-party state, in which anyone is free to support whichever of the parties he or she prefers (though if it is not one of the traditional main parties the supporter's influence on affairs may tend to be small) and as actively as he or she likes. We are free also in speech, within the technical limits of slander and libel – that is, provided we do not overstep certain legitimate and understandable marks – and we are free to carry out activities of any kind, with the proviso in principle that one person's freedom in this way does not encroach too far on another's, though this may not always be an easy thing to determine. Democracy also, we are asked to believe, necessarily involves a capitalistic ethic (if 'ethic' is quite the right word ?).

The fundamental idea of democracy has in fact nothing to do with capitalism. As we well know, it means simply 'government by the people' – or, rather, a little more accurately, 'people government', which implies not only government by the people but (presumably) for the people. The word would therefore do very well as an alternative for what has hitherto been known to us as 'communism', a term which has been regrettably spoilt for future use through its capricious adoption as a banner by a variety of self-seeking and self-promoting dictators: plainly, therefore, I refer not to anything in the manner of this last but to that pure and untainted ideal of the communist state which nobody, to one's knowledge, has ever yet made any serious and conscious attempt to carry into practical effect (and it does not seriously look, from here and at this moment, in view of the immense and self-consuming rapacity of the human race, as if they ever will).

It will be worth our while to take a slightly nearer glance at the origins of the democratic idea. The big obvious difference that strikes the eye, and one to which I have already alluded, is that the Greek state was small enough and, in general terms, compact enough to give all citizens in a democracy the chance of a direct share in government and even, too, in the dispensation of justice in the courts; and that the physical climate was benevolent enough to assist in this by allowing a gathering of thousands of people in the open air to carry out the necessary operations. This very obvious difference is popularly dwelt upon as if it were all that mattered – but, basic and important though it undoubtedly is, it is far from all that matters, and the notion that it is so is or can be desperately misleading. The truth is that the Greek attitude was different from ours in a number of deep-seated ways. I have already drawn attention to the method of appointing magistrates by the casting of lots. (Let us not make too much of this. Leading officials could be directly elected by ordinary vote, and the famous Pericles, who was chief minister in Athens in the latter part of the 5th century BC, was elected year by year over many years in this way. But the lot was a very significant element in the system none the less.)

As indicative as anything, however, is the background of Greek political thought against which the democratic state stands and from which it cannot be divorced. The leading emphasis is not on 'freedom', nor is democracy seen as one pole of a straight opposition with, at the other end, 'tyranny' (I use the latter word here in our present-day sense) – an opposition between the good and high-minded on the one hand and the bad and totally undesirable on the other, as with Reagan's description of the late USSR as an "evil empire". The main emphasis was not on 'freedom', according to our notion, because that concept had other connotations to the Greeks, actual slavery being as normal in a democracy as in any other kind of state: democratic voters were 'free' men but that is because slaves had no right to be included among them. Nor was democracy considered as one end of a moral opposition between two directly antagonistic types of entity, being seen, rather, as one of a series of three possible types of state, of which democrats would naturally think of their own as the best but not because either of the other two was simply to be condemned out of hand. The three were: monarchy – or alternatively (in the Greek sense) tyranny, the rule of one man; aristocracy or oligarchy, two sub-types, the one denoting the rule of 'the best' (the nobility), the other of 'the few' (a group of the wealthy), the two not to be thought of as entirely mutually exclusive; and then democracy, the rule of 'the people', meaning of the citizen-community as a whole, some thousands of them. This breakdown presents us with a somewhat different picture from our own accustomed conception, and one alien in many ways from our own mode of thinking. If we wished to compare our conception closely with the Greek and bring the two views as far as possible together – not admittedly a particularly easy thing to do – it is reasonable to suggest that what we today call 'democracy' finds its most intimate parallel with the Greek idea of oligarchy rather than strictly with their reading of democracy, the name notwithstanding.

So in sum it is obvious that the concept of democracy and what is meant by it has changed a very great deal since the idea's first invention, owing to the fact that what applied to Greek conditions no longer in large part applies to us, not only because of the considerable difference in size between their states and ours but also because of significant changes in our ways of thinking. The one thing we appear still to share in is a belief in the virtues of majority choice, though the Greeks will very likely have believed in divine inspiration somehow guiding such choice, while we, with our notably more secular outlook, are denied any underlying comfort of this sort. And while every effort was made by the Greeks to fulfil the idea of 'people rule' by offering every citizen the opportunity to participate actively in such rule, we for our part are content to leave the effective rule in the hands of a few, giving others the opportunity merely to participate in the selection of those few. Further, we leave the few, once selected, to enjoy the fullest authority for four to five years, as against the much more rapid turnover (annual in principle) favoured by the democratic model, Athens. Not that so rapid a turnover would have any real practicality with us – even a period of four to five years is in many ways quite inadequate for the size of some of our present-day tasks, but it has nevertheless also the (opposite) disadvantage of restricting too tightly the voter's power to correct mistakes. That such mistakes are made no thinking person will surely deny.

The truth is that in choosing a mode of rule, if we can imagine ourselves deliberately doing such a thing, we face difficult decisions whichever way we turn. A gain on one side can be a distinct loss on another. We had better be clear that for most of the time we can do little more than make the best of a bad job. 'Democracy' is no panacea for all the ills of the world. Democracy may not be merely submission to mob rule, as some élitist thinkers, including Plato, did not hesitate to maintain it to be in Greek times, but no more is it the answer to all problems. It is a makeshift. It avoids a worse thing – for which we must be grateful. But there is no proof, nor even any profound likelihood, that democracies are always highly likely to come to the right electoral decisions, or that the governments they elect are highly likely to make the right judgements in their conduct of affairs. Electorates are notoriously open to be swayed by campaign rhetoric (and by clever public relations), and a campaign in advance of a general election can take up nearly a third of the life of a government, not without considerable hampering effect upon the governors. What is more, the least scrupulous of campaigns is liable to be the most effective.

There was much involved argument at the time about why the Tories so surprisingly won the 1992 General Election, but I think the answer is really quite simple – the Tories are, in short, far better con-men (forgive the pun) than are the Labour Party, and I doubt whether there is any need to be a passionate left-winger to accept this. Labour is at a great disadvantage in this respect, remaining in principle saddled with some *beliefs* beyond pure self-seeking, however much the party in recent years may have had to reshape some of those beliefs and bring certain of the items in them down from the skies in order to make them more rationally fitted to cope with the severe practicalities of a wayward and difficult world. (I should, however, make it clear at this point that what I am basically talking about are the general ideas behind the Labour Party's existence, not, certainly, about 'New Labour', whose advent has, frankly, greatly confused the issues.) Beliefs are a heavy load for a political party to carry. The Tories are to a large extent happily free from them. What they pursue primarily is power, together with the provision of conditions offering 'cascades of wealth', as they pleasingly put it, for themselves and their cronies in and out of office: these aims, however specifically determined, and however little in essence concealed, do not constitute beliefs in any weighty political sense, certainly not in such a sense as to shackle, more than very lightly, declarations of public policy. They do not prevent promises being made in all directions to satisfy 'customers' (one of the more recent in-words) of all kinds. Bland political promises, as everyone knows very well, were made to be broken, with or without full intention (that is, they usually mean very little one way or another) – "Read my lips," said President Bush, promising, in his own picturesque manner, no additional taxes, but without subsequent fulfilment – yet, though everyone knows the truth, it is remarkable how often, hopefully or fearfully (for fear, it may be, of some nebulous and possibly unbelievable alternative), people will pretend to themselves that it is not so.

It is even perfectly possible for a democratic state to succumb to a type of mass-madness in which the people are seduced by siren voices into abdicating their powers in favour of some gruesome but emotion-stirring dictator: since there will always in such circumstances be a sizeable rational element in the population who are not susceptible to authoritarian charms, the brutal application of force is usually necessary to overcome their resistance, but it is true nevertheless that without a degree of 'democratic' cooperation in the first place the end cannot be reached. Only some dictatorships are founded in precisely this way but those that are show plainly enough that democracy is not necessarily and in all its modes an unshakeable defence against tyranny: indeed what they show also is that one need not posit the extreme case in order to make evident some of the fundamental weaknesses in the democratic method. *Any* democratic majority runs the risk of being seduced into a faulty choice, given the appropriate conditions, though the choice may not lead to absolute disaster except in the most unfortunate circumstances – this we can assert at least in the short run, though in the long run who can say what will be the ultimate effect of a series of partially or completely ill-judged choices among a variety of nations having the mutual interdependence that modern nations do?

I have sometimes wondered what Baroness Thatcher truly makes of the idea of 'democracy'. Since she does not believe in 'society', presumably she can have little truck, either, with the idea of 'the people', surely at least as amorphous a notion, from her point of view, as the other, or indeed, I would think, much more so, seeing that 'society' has at least in it the positive implication of structure, whereas 'the people' might well suggest merely a human mass, without distinction of individual or type – a Lowry world. But perhaps, being an instinctive authoritarian, she actually prefers to think in terms of 'the people', the sunken mass, well below the level of the capitalistic individuals and their families whom she envisages as sitting on top of the dung-heap, and from whom little half-chewed fragments of benefit 'trickle down' to the others as crumbs do to pigeons from a park-bench.

Eighteen

The End of History?

In any political and social state of affairs, seen from within, if it has lasted long enough without too much or too violent apparent alteration – and I set no specific limits to 'long enough', which may mean decades or more (even much more) but need, on the other hand, mean in some not exceptional cases a very few years only – there is a powerful tendency for an aura of permanent stability to fall over everything, so that it seems as if this, now, must be the ultimate, the goal of all things, however desperately and obviously imperfect it may be clearly seen to be by the at all discerning eye – the 'end of history' indeed, than which, in some of its major aspects at least, it seems possible to proceed no further, to progress no higher. This appearance, extraordinarily forceful though it may often be, is never more than illusion. It has, if anything, less virtue than, say, a long sequence of wins in the University Boat Race, which may, at times, lead the thoughtless to believe that Oxford will never again have a chance of being the winner – at times, on the contrary, Cambridge.

Is it necessary to produce examples? What of all the great European empires which have over the centuries come and gone, but in their day seemed as if they could never be shaken? Not the least of these, perhaps, was our own mighty British Empire, still commemorated in our medals; once, not so long ago, appearing to be so firmly rooted that it would last for ever, but since 1945 – after a war we won! – a melted dream. But there is no need to think in terms of physical empires: this is merely a way of making the point. The dominance of a political party, of left or right, at a particular moment, may seem settled and perpetual; but, even though it may have continued for years, there is a time when it will end, in one way or another. It is as well to remember that everything changes, nothing stands still, and that time, itself, has yet a very long way to go.

We have been presented frequently in fiction with portrayals, some more imaginative than others, of what the future is likely to hold for us; but it is interesting that such prognostications, whether supposedly serious or no, rarely take us more than a few decades or possibly (with what one can assume to be a certain daring) a few centuries ahead of ourselves. Why is this? Time itself is not so limited. The existence of the universe, it seems, on whatever scientific principle we calculate it, can be taken back for thousands of millions of years – and this may or may not record the life of time itself. One knows of no sufficient reason why one should not be able to measure the universe's existence forward on the same sort of scale – and will time then go on afterwards? These are what are known as imponderables (or should one not rather say 'ponderables'? – ponderable, indeed, one may well imagine, until, as they say, the cows come home).

Can time be thought of as beginning or ending? Perhaps not, but perhaps there is a transparent reason for this, and perhaps time can, if I may so phrase it, be thought away. If space and time are no more than the necessary framework of our perceptions and conceptions, and these themselves are no more, as it were, than the stuff of our encompassing dream (representing what?), then time has no ultimate reality anyway, and to that extent it becomes meaningless to talk of it as having either beginning or end. However, within the human dream, as I have described it, there is no easy way of seeing an end to time, and there is no reason at all why we should not think of human life in, say, twenty thousand years' time, and wonder how it will be. In terms of the development of civilisation as we know it, or know of it, this may seem a very long time; but in terms of the being of the universe, or even of the much, much shorter span of man's existence in the universe, it is a moment only. We should have no difficulty in conceiving of it; why do we then not think fit to talk about it, to make some conjectures about it, however slight?

I ask these questions not because I think there is some essential fault in us in this connection, but because I think the questions as such are of the greatest interest and because the answers, when we look into them, may be more than a little revealing of ourselves and our natures and of where we stand in the evolutionary scheme. Our marked hesitation to look more than the shortest way ahead (other than, very occasionally perhaps, in conscious and invariably unimpressive caricature, which for our present purposes may readily be ignored – and it is reasonable also to ignore Messianic predictions, basically non-specific in the forms they assume) may be put down in part to a fear of making too obviously oversimplified projections into the future; but I think this is a very small element in the picture. What is a great deal more important is the way in which the attitude reflects our overruling tendency to tie ourselves as closely as possible to the passing moment, to the 'now' of our lives – incorporating in this 'now' personal memories of past 'nows', to the extent of sometimes clinging to certain of these memories as a lost 'golden time', a 'now' which has somehow slipped away from us against our wills, against our frustrated resolve to hang on to it if we can: it is not at all surprising, in this context, that so many memories of the kind relate to childhood, to a time in our lives when the 'now' seemed hardly changing, and, in that form, never-ending. And it is not only individuals who may carry this image – not always perhaps entirely without validity – of a lost golden time. Whole societies and whole civilisations have enshrined what is in effect the same thought in mythologies opening from a Golden Age of Mankind, systematised, it may be, to form the first age of a progressive descent to ourselves at the foot.

Our conception of the present time embraces in principle all our lives from our first memory; plus what our parents have told us of theirs; and plus, then, anything we may have learnt from elsewhere, about current lives and activities. This is a nebulous 'present', with no firm edges, merging, in the early days of a nation's history, into a 'past' mainly of myth and legend; in later days, into a past looking back more clearly, with the aid of a more specific, notionally more reliable written record of 'actual' bygone events; and, in due course, through the advance of scientific method, into a long prehistory based not on any written record, true or partly true, but on the study and analysis of human and non-human remains and of the soil and the rocks – and so out from here into space and the galaxies and the humming universe, and whatever we may gather wonderingly about these from our astronomical observations and their interpretation.

But this is the present, a present extending itself backwards into a nearer and remoter and remotest past. What of the future? However uncertainly we may read some aspects of the present or past, we cannot, it seems, read the future at all. Why, indeed, should we concern ourselves with it? "Peace in our time", as some will say.

Yet we *must* concern ourselves with it – we have no option. We are proceeding into it without interruption at every instant of our lives, and have essentially, at the very least, to take account of its immediate possibilities, basing ourselves upon our past experience, and guarding against any ill chances which we could conceivably encounter. We have to do more than this. It is not only the immediate future which we have to allow for, but our own longer-term future too – and then there is that of our dependants. At this point we throw overboard entirely the idea, so loudly preached, of each individual's need to be self-dependent, and we make it our business to leave as large piles of property as possible to our personal inheritors, so that the latter can be guarded against all manner of want and material difficulty and can live their lives (as far as we can arrange things – as far as we can 'foresee') in whatever way they please. 'Stand on your own feet' is very much a message for others, not, regularly and in clear principle, for our families. Is there some small hint of a self-contradiction here? Maybe there is, but people have not been widely known to do everything they can, in all purity of intention, to avoid self-contradiction at all costs. When it suits them to do so, they will readily contradict themselves and occasionally delight in it.

But there is more to it again. We are all mortal – even the longest of our lives is extremely short. Nevertheless we most of us strive for some semblance of immortality. The striving is a species of blind urge implanted in us by the Community of which we are a part, of which we would appear indeed to a hypothetical outsider to be hardly more than a particular embodiment, and the workings of this urge are of no rational kind, seeming as often to run counter in their effects to the community's own central urge for survival as to further that urge. We have explored these matters in a measure before: here the point I wish to make is that this bears on our relationship to the future, since it appears that in greater or lesser degree our fundamental wish is to live on through the future, whether through the memory of our name or through our descendants, or both; and from this aspect our face is to the future, whatever its uncertainties, much more than to the past (as it is also for the child, from his own point of view, looking forward with excitement to growing up).

We cannot avoid the future; we cannot pretend it is nothing to do with us; we are tied tight to it, like it or no; we are actually in some respects avid for it, greedy for its hoped-for benefits, quite unwilling to consider its less attractive potentialities. Why, then, if we today in the West are likely to have on the whole so welcoming an attitude towards it rather than otherwise, are we apparently yet so unready to think of it in more than the short, the very short term? Is this out of some sort of fear of what we might find awaiting us in the longer term? Or is it simply due to a want of imagination? Or what could it be?

Perhaps the answers to such questions are not in the end so entirely difficult to extract . Before going on to them, or to my suggestions of what they might be, I should like to make a short preliminary comment of a basic nature, a sort of summing-up of what I have just been saying.

Nineteen

The Present, the Past and the Future

We are never in reality far away from the present time in all its perpetually changing shape and colours. We see the past from its viewpoint: our attention centres itself primarily on the moving moment about us and everything else is seen in its terms. We look back through the spectacles of the surrounding present, whose transforming and, in many ways, contrastive effect we have to make a determined effort to counter if we wish to perceive our intended object with appropriate clarity. (Yet even this effort must not go too far: true enough that if we are clear-headed, and serious about it, we wish, as far as humanly possible, to see things dressed in their own clothes, not grotesquely attired in the garments of an alien age; but we have somehow to achieve this without at the same time descending from what purports at least to be the potentially superior – in standards, in mode of analysis – vantage-point of our own later day.)

So how does this affect our notion of future time? Here equally we have to guard against casting in our image a period or periods other than ours, but the order of the problem is very different, and the temptation to erect empty mental constructs on a faulty basis is much stronger, since we have only the present, and the past as seen in the subtly or not so subtly distorting mirror of the present, to build on: there are otherwise no outlines, however dim, to fill in, there is nothing in essence but a monstrous blank filling itself in in great detail, and often in quite unforeseen ways, as we proceed steadily into it. If this should make it sound as if I view the future as undetermined, or only in negligible part determined, I do not mean that. On the contrary, the future is surely to be thought of, in line with what I see as the more reasonable current conceptions, as fully determined in every way imaginable (some persons, it is true, continue to believe firmly in 'chance', but I see no room for it in the complete picture): this is in fact the whole point, that it is determined in such a vast multitude of ways, from such a huge variety of causes and sources, many hardly if at all known to us, that some of the results to our limited penetration are almost as if the total opposite were the case, as if it were the undetermined, the indeterminable, which ruled.

There was, I suppose, a time, not so very long ago, when it might still have seemed safe enough to forecast a future not essentially different from what was then the present; a time when intelligent citizens of leading nations were prepared to accept the thesis that a high point of culture had been reached (in their environment, at least), which could not easily be surpassed, and which made vast changes as such unlikely. In those days there was apparently no pressing urge to look physically forward in so many words; and imagination, if it concerned itself with reconstructions of the circumstances of living, was content, rather, to portray ideal worlds – in past, present or conceivably future or without reference to time – utopias of one kind or another, which would do away with the more obvious imperfections of human existence in favour of a more equitable general mode of living where more just and happier conditions on the whole prevailed. Only relatively recently, in a less stable-seeming world, with great technological advances observable in all directions, and accelerating change everywhere in evidence about us, has the desire manifested itself to peer, in fictional representation, into what might actually lie ahead. Yet this sort of fictional forecasting tends to have a narrow, indeed a very narrow temporal range.

I think the situation may make itself more readily understandable if one considers that fictional and imaginative writers, whatever their precise field, are concerned primarily to throw their own intended special kind of light on the world in which their readers, or potential readers, actually live. This opens up a much wider area of possibility than may appear. It by no means implies that the writer is or should be bound in his subject-matter and approach to the suburban hearth. The reader's world is not limited to his own immediate circumstances; on the contrary, his adventurous and romantic soul looks out often to much wider, in some if not in all respects more stimulating horizons: the only important thing is that he should not be taken so far away from what he knows directly as to lose contact, to become befogged and bemused. So much briefly for the reader's requirements – how about the writer's possibilities in the context? If one considers that a writer endeavouring to recreate a past period has to convince that he has some fairly reasonable knowledge of the world at that period (involving also in some degree a sound knowledge of events between that period and his own), and needs to assume at the same time some basic elements of knowledge about the period from his audience, it will become plain that the further forward in time a writer about the future wishes to go, the more difficult will his problems be, with nothing to go on beyond his knowledge, for what it is worth, of the present and the past, which may be (is very likely to be) in many ways grossly misleading. And what can he count on from his audience?

It should be obvious thus that a fictional portrayal of a remote future provides too formidable a task for a writer in his normal senses to be willing voluntarily to undertake. The ground offered him to proceed over is much too slippery – if, indeed, there is any genuine ground at all beyond a certain very limited point – and it is not at all surprising that the world of fiction remains for the most part well within the borders of what we (including, of course, the writers themselves) recognise and comprehend in general without too much trouble. It is not, I suggest, that the writers are to be thought of as having an option held out to them which they then shy away from; such an option, as I see it, is never ordinarily within their sights: they have other, for them much more interesting and pressing and more attractive possibilities in view, not to speak of more potentially lucrative ones, which in the present climate of affairs must be a very strong deciding factor.

I have not, however, raised the subject of the distant future purely in order to ask why fiction writers do not write about it. Rather, it was in order to show that, however unreal it may seem to us, however little, as it were, to do with us, however far from the pattern of current thought, it nevertheless is an integral part of our existence in a total sense – in the sense, at least, of our existence as an element in the community as a whole – and, if we are thinking seriously about ourselves, not easily to be ignored. By this I do not mean that we ought to try to work out what it will be like. I do not see how we could attempt to do this. In a way it is well beyond our grasp. But what is not beyond our grasp is to see just what it is in it which puts it so decisively beyond our grasp and, to an extent, why. And also, if it is quite hopeless for us to try to imagine the far future in any kind of living and convincing detail, it may nevertheless not be altogether impossible for us to think of it in terms of certain very wide and yet not totally uninformative generalities, such as to throw back a curious gleam of revealing and unaccustomed light on to the confused, obscure surfaces of our present time – not perhaps an entirely useless outcome. Let us pursue these matters a trifle further.

Just as every individual perceives the world outwards from his own personal ego as the centre, so, as I have said and repeat, do we, all of us, see the whole of time, in so far as we are able to envisage it, from the constant perspective of the present – perpetually and ineluctably changing at every moment though that present may be, whether we actively so recognise it or not. In this context the typical member of a primitive society, untampered with by the intrusion of civilisation, will feel no doubt that his group goes back in its existence, in its manners and practices, into the dimness of the long-ago past (for ever, perhaps, or at least into an imagined Adam-and-Eve beginning of all things), and that it will continue on its way in like style into the remote future; while a member of a certain type of advanced society – say, of eighteenth-century England – will feel, on the contrary, as I suggested a few pages back, that his own group has thrown off past barbarism in the most satisfactory and lasting way, and must now be able to rule the roost, stably, for a long time to come. Both of these very different societies, each in its very different way, is dominated by its idea of the present, the governing present.

There was a view in ancient Greece that the progress of events in time was cyclic, that is to say that after a longish period everything repeated itself. This was not a basic dogma, universally held: it was related to the type of philosophic speculation for which the Greeks have become rightly famous, and which was grounded as far as possible in independent rational-style thinking, yet which could not fail in the same breath to be affected in one way or another by some aspect of current and in part religious-type preconceptions. This particular belief, a very grim one in certain ways, happy though it might appear for a chosen few, provides an excellent illustration of the immense power of the concept of the present over human thought. In this case the present was seen as simply never-ending, coming back again and again simply to where it started. That view connects itself with the other, generally-held, ancient view of space as geocentric – time, seen as a perpetual 'now', seeming thus to ally itself quite closely to the world seen as heart and centre of the universe ('world without end', as we may well say).

Today, if our minds are at all open to the declared results of scientific discovery, we are prohibited from holding any of the above views. We no longer take the world we live in, as did the Greeks and others, as the great centre around which the universe as a whole revolves. In complete contrast we are asked to think of ourselves as dwelling on the surface of a mere minor planet circling a minor star, within an immense galaxy, itself one only of innumerable galaxies, in a total universe dwarfing us to almost nothing. As to time, not only are we required to envisage our universe as going back for a multiplicity of aeons, in which all human existence is no more than the briefest instant, barely even conceivable from the longer aspect, but the idea of a process of never-pausing change tends now to be pressed upon our minds by on the one hand a rearward look at the course of human and pre-human development and by on the other a conception of a radically altered and altering future towards which the perceived contemporary speed of technological advance hurries us on at what seems an ever-increasing pace.

Appearances may, we know, be intensely deceptive, and it could be that the current evidence of rapid and accelerating and apparently unstoppable human progression in material matters is just appearance and no more, but this is hard to believe: the long flow of events, as we see them from our little present eminence, looking behind and (mistily) before, gives too strong an impression, and seems on the whole to offer little in the way of logical alternative. There is, however, one distinct and not by any means impossible alternative: that all the fantastic material advances of which we are aware are due to end quite shortly in a tremendous destructive climax, leaving us in a state of disruption and chaos such as would at the least take ages to overcome. It is true that even this need suggest no more in the long run than a hitch, a break in continuity (there have been plenty of others in history) to be painfully made good so that the forward march can be once more eventually resumed – unless, of course, the catastrophe is in the end so complete and utter that nothing of the human race is left behind to proceed with the march. In view of the immensely destructive and self-destructive elements so palpable in human nature, this doomsday possibility is regrettably in no way out of the question, or even seriously against the odds.

Supposing, however, that man does not in due course destroy himself (I offer no speculative prognostications as to whether he will or not), there are, without the slightest attempt to particularise, certain undeniable facts we can state about the future which stand out in the boldest fashion and require to be taken firmly into account. Suppose we look ahead for a specific and limited period, for, say, the twenty thousand years I have mentioned earlier – a brief enough period in relation to the life of the universe, and, indeed, not a very long one even in proportion to man's own existence, even if we take the latter from its very first beginnings; but although the period is not really so very long as seen against the background of human development as a whole, it takes on a quite different aspect in relation to the rise of human civilisation, which we can trace back in any semi-precise manner for hardly more than five or five and a half thousand years or so altogether, during which the society of mankind has undergone vast and remarkable changes, with more apparently to come, and at an increasing rate. It is all a matter of perspective: from the perspective point of view, what do we make of it?

Twenty

A Misty Forward Glance in Time

For one thing, by the time I speak of, the mass of recorded material will be simply enormous, impossible for us now to envisage with any clarity. No doubt there will have been developed magnificent methods of instantaneous analysis, so that effective ways of handling the material and of sorting it out and *using* it will not be lacking; but I am thinking not of practical handling of information but of literary and artistic endeavour and how the individual gains access, for instance, to an adequate supply of its examples. There will simply be too much for the human mind to cope with – certainly much too much if one wishes to be able in any realistic sense to survey the heritage of the past. Even at the present time it cannot be said that knowledge and understanding of our cultural past are very extensive with most people; and there may even be some scholars who are quietly grateful that so much of ancient writing is now known to us in fragments only and is otherwise lost – so much the less for them to have to grapple with, and this is undoubtedly likely to be a relief to some, since scholars are liable, for all their learning, to have as many human flaws as any of their neighbours (they are certainly not a shade less egotistical or less quarrelsome than others).

I have referred to the human mind, and of course it is true that what I have been saying assumes the capacity of the human mind to be little altered from today. I now have to admit that there is no reason to believe the assumption to be at all a necessary one. In even so little, relatively, as twenty thousand years, man's brain could have undergone a natural development so as to be able to take in more, and more rapidly, than we can at present easily conceive; alternatively, human work on the brain could possibly have achieved the same sort of results. The point that has to be made is that without some such clear general advance in the powers of human comprehension and mental adaptability and agility, the huge, almost unthinkable volume of material with which the human mind will then be faced will be, without qualification, overwhelming.

The implications of this fact are important, and throw light on the present, or at least on what should be our attitude to the present and to its place for us in the stream of time. We have seen already that to regard ourselves as being somehow at 'the end of history' is at best a freakish notion, hardly to be taken with any seriousness unless we are prepared, with the author of the phrase, to interpret 'history' in an esoteric, far from normal sense, and to take also for granted all manner of things which are frankly far from self-evident; and the point that I have just made surely reinforces such a feeling. Even without considering the question, on however general a basis, of what we are likely to find in twenty thousand years' time, the mere fact that we are able to look forward that distance (indeed, that we are quite unable not to, unless we very determinedly turn our heads away, since time, whether we like it or no, runs irresistibly on) suggests strongly that, rather than being at 'the end of history' we are barely at the beginning of it. Cast the mind twenty thousand years forward, see the tremendous accumulation of cultural as well as other material that I have hypothesised, together with what needs to be accomplished in order to cope with it, and compare and contrast this, on the other side, with what we see looking five thousand or more years back.

In those few millennia, as I must repeat, we have built up from apparently next to nothing, in present-day terms, the whole structure of what we now call 'civilisation' (literally, for what it is worth, 'the culture of city living'). I say 'apparently' because the much longer preceding period, retreating from us into obscurity, is quite evidently no sheer whirlpool of meaningless events: however inadequately we are able to discern the shape of what was taking place, it must be plain that the movement then, however slow, however unclear in its tendencies to the generations living and dying within it, was itself no less than, in the long run, a steady if presumably (on the shorter view) interrupted preparation for what was in due course to follow.

The fact remains that what we normally call 'history', if I may retain the word – like all the words we use inconstant in its application and therefore open to abuse by those wishing to make a point – goes back for us no further, from man's first emergence into the daylight of our genuine historical knowledge, than five or not greatly more thousand years, since when what seem to us monumental changes have occurred. If we attempt to look forward, as I have suggested, for something like four times that length of time again, the potential changes to come are simply too much to conceive of rationally. I have limited myself to the contemplation of such a period ahead only because anything more seemed altogether too bold a venture. Yet even twenty thousand years is itself no more, as we have seen, than the tiniest drop in the ocean of time.

I think we may have dealt sufficiently for current purposes with the bottomless difficulties (for they are like Bottom's Dream; they have no bottom) of long-term prognostication. If some feel that such difficulties are in any case irrelevant to the practical problems we face, I would reply that, quite apart from any special matters I have been concerned to consider, all problems of prognostication hang together, and that the practical problems we face today and at all times are essentially problems of prognostication, though in the vastly shorter term. In the long term the difficulties involved are exaggerated and extreme, and ultimately in most ways (certainly in any detail) beyond our grasp, but they are still only greatly extended versions of what we face in the short term, and are nothing less than the direct long-term consequence of the latter; and, when all is said and done, what we face in the short term only enters, in the main, within our grasp in so far as we *have* to grasp it or sink. No one can say that we are skilled in clarifying to ourselves what immediately lies ahead for us, or in working out, with or without computers, how best to cope with it. At the sad grey end of this twentieth century of appalling disorder, devastation and disaster, of man-inflicted mass death in some of its most brutal and hideous forms, while we continue to struggle helplessly, as we still do at this moment of my writing, with, among many other things, the far-spread disintegratory effects of the unexpected implosion of the Soviet Union, it cannot be claimed that our expertise in forecasting even the shortest-term consequences of group action, so that we may be prepared to afford them a modicum of suitable handling, is more than, I am sorry to say, puerile.

So we arm a Saddam Hussein and not much later have to go to war with the man we ourselves have armed. This is a quite typical case, in the broken-glass-strewn international field, of judgement gone wrong on a grotesque scale. Big and bloody wars are a normal result of human fumbling and uncertainty, arising from a confusion of mistakenly conceived goals, too concerned with self-regarding and short-term interests, and combined with that blind desire for struggle and excitement which inspires men's endeavours on every level and which seems frequently to go well beyond any rational control. It would appear fairly obvious that if everybody is all the while striving primarily with all his might to achieve the greatest possible immediate profit for himself and his close cronies, with the perpetual assumption that such profit can only be achieved at the expense of other groups who, even though they, or some of them, may be definable as 'friends' or 'allies', are outside the charmed circle, then a happy outcome for all involved is far from likely, while a more or less unhappy outcome for all is by no means out of the question.

I have used the epithet 'puerile' of our straining and misguided efforts to forecast possible consequences of such group action as is at our disposal, or in which we may participate; and I must emphasise here that this was not a vain choice of words in the attempt merely to find a striking image. On the contrary, my positive feeling is that 'puerile' hits very much the right note, in so far as it is able to suggest a childish game played as much as anything for the simple excitement of the game (including, it is true, the conceived triumph of winning if one should be so fortunate, but I am sure that this does not for the most part constitute the only, nor even in all probability the major impetus in this kind of context, however totally paradoxical the statement may from one angle appear – it serves, rather, as a factitious concrete goal to give some specific apparent point to the efforts and risks involved, with the overriding urge to win at all costs developing out of this as an exaggerated, ultimately 'adult' propensity) for any more basic good or gain that might come out of it at least. We cannot gauge with anything like precision what the future, even the very near future, may hold for us, but the truth is that we do not seem always to be trying very hard to survey the ground rationally in an appropriate direction: we are much too concerned to frustrate the 'knavish tricks', real or imaginary, of our next-door neighbours, who are themselves deeply engaged in playing the same super-childish and at the same time very highly dangerous game and in a similar manner, to worry about attempting coolly, from the right objective distance, to assess the situation as a whole, with an eye to securing some wider and more solid (and more enduring) benefit.

If one wishes for a demonstration, there is one very close at hand, in the shape of the long underground battle, after the Second World War – in what became known as the Cold War – between the Western Powers on the one side, with the American CIA in the forefront, and the East, under the lead of the Russian KGB, on the other. The CIA was perfectly unscrupulous in recruiting even the most villainous ex-Nazis to further its aims – much has been revealed on this as time has gone by – and the Russians, we may be sure, were not backward on their own behalf. (If I put the CIA first, it is because these are 'our' side, and it is thus more necessary to make the point with regard to them.) Past criminal activities of the most vicious kind, that is to say, and on the widest and most unforgivable scale, were deliberately ignored if it was felt that the perpetrators, owing to their training and sinister experience in a field unencumbered by any pressure of moral restraint, together with their readiness now to serve the victors in any capacity, to 'collaborate', made them of possible usefulness as practical instruments in the nefarious game being enthusiastically undertaken. In America in the time soon after the War reaction ruled the day: any signs of a 'liberal' outlook became officially suspect, and this led to the short but distinctly unpleasant period of McCarthyism. Altogether, the true significance of these in principle subterranean but yet in the event only partially and imperfectly concealed manoeuvrings is brought out in the spate of spy-story narratives circulating as novels and films and so forth – as romantic adventure dramatisations of the underlying reality – during the four decades or more in question.

Does this seem a curious inversion – to say that it is the fictional representation which shows us, though not in genuine detail yet in essential form, what was actually taking place in reality? And when I speak in this way I do not mean to imply that there is some conscious near-documentary element in the fiction. Not so, and that is obvious: the heart of the intention is romanticisation, to the extent not infrequently of sheer absurdity; but the fact is that this is actually a reflection, an authentic and vivid reflection, of the model, which in its own turn has about it a strong aura of self-romanticisation, again often even to the point of absurdity. This may not be the only field in which such things happen, where sometimes it may not be always particularly clear which is the 'real' and which the distorting mirror image; but there is nowhere else where it will be truer.

We live by idealisations – I do not say here 'ideals', in as far as this may have overtones suggesting some specifically virtuous aim, and in the present context what is wanted is as far as possible a neutral word covering every variety of moral (and immoral) ground. The Cold War ran itself on the basis of such an idealisation, with, at its centre, what I have called, here and earlier, 'the game' (the term seems to me fitting: it is not in fact unusual in this manner of context). The spy-story gives us the Game in its purity, with every emphasis on the excitement which makes the players in it so ready and eager apparently to further the cause they are alleged to embody, and without the ragged ends, the all-too-frequent off-route diversions leading nowhere in particular, which confuse the reality. Fiction can throw its light on fact in this way, by eliminating the uncertainties and inadequacies of real life and giving us instead a complete and (superficially, at any rate) coherent picture with its own dramatic beginning, middle and end – tragic, comic, or romantic. In the case I speak of the point is particularly strong, since here it is not, as it may be in numerous other relationships, a matter of fictionally injecting artificial rounded meaning of a sort into something in itself in many ways seemingly (as far as we can see, at any rate) only patchily meaningful if at all but – strikingly – of eliciting their own actual inner meaning from the facts themselves. Part consciously, part unconsciously, the Cold War operation as such was played out, in the main, in heavily fictional terms, and it was this significant characteristic that the spy-story brought to the surface and, in so doing, reinforced. (In this way it was very largely different from the common or garden detective story or the thriller.) Had it not been thus fictionally ballasted, the operation could hardly, in its essential inward emptiness, have in the first place constructed itself in any semblance of concreteness and solidity at all; or, having done so, have lasted as long as it did without internal, very probably violent collapse – a fate which, fortunately for mankind, in the end overtook one side only, without physical assault from the other, in the long-drawn struggle (and so even with a modicum of initial restraint at the collapsed side's centre, if not invariably elsewhere), shaking the combatants' world instead of, as it might have done, shattering it to smithereens.

Twenty-one
The Play and the Actors

The whole of life is, of course, in some degree or other a game, though perhaps with some elements in it more distinctively so than others. "All the world's a stage", said Shakespeare, "And all the men and women merely players". This is no mere graphic metaphor, though it may read so, superficially. In the profoundest sense, it – or at least the second part of it – is no less than the truth. We are all actors, at every or nearly every moment of our waking lives, from the first conscious gasp to the last, from the cradle to the grave. Aristotle described playwriting and acting as 'imitation' (*mimesis*): so, as small children, we imitate our elders, and, later, we idealise and imitate whatever model has set itself up most impressively before us, taking into account whatever are our particular requirements (relative to whatever is the particular period we are living in) for both fulfilment and pretence, the latter to cover felt defects, which we none of us lack. The range of such models is strictly limited: it is based on a very few, highly recognisable stereotypes. For if they were not few, they would not be so highly recognisable, and if they were not so highly recognisable, they would be a good deal less alluring as models, since the essence of the matter is that everybody should see at once who and what we are, or imagine we are, or would like people to think we are. The last of these alternatives is evidently the one that comes nearest the mark, and it not only relates to the private individual presenting his or her face to the world (and, I have to add, to himself or herself no less) but relates also to the great public art, so prominent at the present day, of 'public relations'.

Of these two arts, of acting and PR together, both, – overlapping in the instance I am about to quote and intermingled with one another, as often – one of the finest latter-day practitioners is indubitably Our Lady Thatcher, whose expert performance at a latish stage during her premiership in picking up from the ground small items of neatly disposed rubbish cast before her for the purpose, with cameras suitably placed all about to catch every movement, in order to demonstrate to the populace the desirability of maintaining a clean ('green' according to the latest catchword) environment, is well-known and will no doubt be long remembered. As acting, it may be remarked, her customary performances are in general of the 'ham' variety, heavily underlined and, from the purist's point of view, somewhat over-dramatised, but this, it must be added, is really very well conceived for its end, since excessive subtlety, too 'natural' an appearance, is not at all what is required to achieve the broad but telling effect basically intended to be evoked, over all levels of society, with the most impressionable members (this goes, however, a remarkably long way) particularly in mind. Not surprisingly, the then Mrs Thatcher discovered a kindred spirit in her contemporary President of the United States, Ronald Reagan, himself previously for many years a professional actor – confessedly not of the highest acting class – and well accustomed to 'hamming' it on the screen to a wide circle of undemanding audiences, before eventually extending his range to cover the whole American nation.

This is an age, if ever there was one, of exhibitionism. Not that the urge to exhibitionism was noticeably lacking in previous ages, but the opportunities for its expression were far fewer and less convenient. With still and motion picture photography, today, with printing and newspapers and television and the like, with the so-called 'media', never before have there been such tremendously expanded possibilities for the eagerly self-promoting individual, who, once having manoeuvred himself or herself somehow into the public eye or a corner of it, is able to broadcast his or her preferred version of himself or herself far and wide and, in time, into almost every nook and cranny of the surroundings – and the surroundings too can in these days of rapid intercommunication spread very far afield.

Most of us, I suppose, having in our earlier adulthood constructed for ourselves a personality façade with which more or less adequately to confront our often felt to be somewhat awe-inspiring environment, may be inclined in later years to sink behind that façade and at times even almost to forget that it is something we have indeed, however imperfectly, fashioned for ourselves and not simply something with which God in his bounty has provided us. But we are not all content so to rest. The more ambitious among us, the more competitive, as the words go – the get-rich-quick 'achiever', as popularly conceived, the fly-by-night 'high flyer' – have, as they see it, loftier aims, and their self-building must determinedly go on, is never perhaps consciously quite complete. Their wish is to soar above the multitude – their contempt for whom is not always securely concealed – and to reign ultimately among the very gods, like the divine Augustus, once upon a time, two millennia ago. There are surprisingly many of these, and their facial representations, in black and white or colour, and their epigrammatic recorded utterances, meet us every day.

Though they are many individually, their types, as I have said, are few. I have no wish, even so, to go through them one by one or in any detail, but a word or two on the most outstanding may be at least worth letting fall, and may help to stir the memory – there is, for example, the sublime and thoroughly successful intellectual, in lofty self-assurance casting before us from time to time, with conscious generosity, his glittering, well-manicured pearls of portentous wisdom; and then again, not so very far away in the portrait-gallery, if displayed to us in a somewhat different manner, the bulky tycoon or (in couples, it may be) tycoons, swelling with unspeakable self-importance in the midst of their countless riches, such figures to be seen in the business supplements of the leading newspapers in two main styles: on the one hand, bursting with obese grins and huge unrestrained laughter at having done down the suckers (you and me), and apparently not realising or, much more probably, not particularly caring (why should they?) that a rather less uninhibited response to the photographer's "Look happy!" might induce in the masses of those left lagging behind them in the race perhaps a little more sympathy for their – the tycoons' – brilliant (and excellently remunerated) qualities; or, on the other hand, more concerned to demonstrate to all and sundry their steely, stop-at-nothing, ruthless and decisive character than to roll about with vast complacent glee at their success to date (time goes on, it may not after all be quite the same tomorrow, if not forgetting the considerable and well-protected cushioning afforded by yesterday's gains) – the 'loners', seen leaning powerfully forward in their seats with tightly compressed lips and near-closed eyes, the picture of quiet, unyielding, irresistible determination: so they are presented to us, for our admiration and wonder.

So they are presented to us; so they themselves present themselves to us, and to themselves. They are, in their imaginations, the lords of the world – or, at least, of their special worlds, large or small, long-lasting or (more probably, it must be confessed) quite fleeting. They have, by all the means at their disposal, and mostly with not too fine a regard for the ethics of the matter, levered themselves with tremendous energy to the top of their chosen corner, from where they are able to look down in overweening superiority upon the scrabbling mites of humanity below. They feel themselves to be controllers of destiny, no longer subject to the whims of the gods, but rather now to be thought of themselves as gods, by virtue of the white-hot genius which they sense, imperatively, to be within them (and of which they are happy to give us an account through some properly obsequious 'media'-correspondent, if we allow them) and also by virtue of the continuing inspiration of their tightly attached personal Fortune, their Lady Luck, who, they are content to believe, will never desert them: totally governed by these sentiments, they have no hesitation in treating other individuals, few or in their multitudes, as trivial instruments, with only a reflected and second-instance reality. In the apparent certainty of their own unassailable eminence, they are not accustomed to concealing or in any serious way soft-pedalling their views about their fellows and mostly (for them) inferiors.

It will be observed that this last paragraph of description, arising from a consideration of the types of personality briefly outlined just before, and of the spirit that governs them, applies also at the same time to a much wider field, characterising in fact the authoritarian in general, not excluding the political dictators of our time. Indeed this is to say, reversing our perspective, that the authoritarian germ is not to be found only in political dictators, or those aspiring to such demonic heights, but in numerous other persons and places and activities too, everywhere about us, in a general atmosphere where every man, once having achieved a certain relative eminence, can become his own overpowering and awful Messiah, calling to be attended, as his well-displayed charisma requires, by an adoring crowd, many or few, of lesser beings, who will accompany him wherever he goes, until the skies fall or he does. I need not say that 'man' here includes 'woman'.

Twenty-two

Two Kinds of People?

Men (and women) fall at any moment – not sharply but on the whole – into two general classes, those who underrate themselves and those who afford to the shrewd eye every appearance of overrating themselves. The former constitute the majority – if it were not so, it would be much less easy for self-appointed 'leaders' to find followers, people, that is to say, who are eager to make up for their own lack of self-esteem by attaching themselves as closely as possible to others who will guarantee, with high presumption, to guide them successfully through life's complicated and forbidding maze; but the latter grouping, the self-overraters, are by no means as small a number as one might innocently think, and it would appear, though reliable statistics are naturally wanting (but are they ever otherwise?), rapidly on the increase.

The two classes cannot simply be recategorised under other, more usual headings: it is not possible, for example, to equate the self-underraters simply with the *hoi polloi*, the mob, the unintelligent (I would not call them, otherwise, by precisely the name that I do), for there are many in the self-underrating class extending into quite different categories; in particular, there will be many highly intelligent persons whose self-esteem is nevertheless relatively low for (according to their own lights) the best of reasons, seeing that they are able more clearly than some others to contrast their own insignificance and insubstantiality with the overwhelming might, going well beyond human understanding, of the infinite and everlasting universe. It is at the same time true, on the other side, that the self-overraters, as I have described them, may very well themselves be thought also, on a Freudian analysis, low in underlying self-esteem, for which their contrary public showing is compensation, according to the theory of the 'inferiority complex' – thus belonging properly in the outcome with what I have named as their opposite class. I am far from denying all probability to such an analysis (even though Freudianism may be slightly out of fashion in these days) and there is indeed good evidence available on its behalf.

The big executive, unexpectedly made redundant, is liable to undergo the severest of shocks to his self-esteem, irrespective of whether or not he is left with enough (even much more than enough) to live on, and in some well-attested cases this has led to suicide. Possession of piles of money or otherwise does not seem in such cases to matter very much: it is as though the subject's hidden self-doubts are suddenly revealed and found, by contrast with the high position from which he has suddenly descended, unbearable. This does not conflict with my proposition, which is not that the two classes are to be thought of as somehow fundamentally different in kind, but that in practical effect they are at any given moment clearly distinguishable from one another and that the self-overraters would not in the normal way be readily conscious of what lies beneath the surface of their thinking, making the shock of revelation greater when it occurs. Somewhere there is perhaps a third class, mediating between them, but it is not very visible.

The separation between the two classes is in fact never likely to be complete, even in the most extreme form which they can take. Even the authoritarian leader of his people at the height of his glory, bearing, as he firmly avows and no doubt believes, an all-conquering message direct from God Himself (with Whom no other has equivalent contact) and applauded blindly to the skies by his hosts of devoted followers, is not, I strongly suspect, without his moment or moments of even shattering self-doubt, however swiftly he may seek to expunge them from his consciousness. On the other hand even the lowliest of the low – as seen, at least, from the elevated vantage-point of the well-nourished businessman, striding on his superior way – must surely have, even he, his fleeting, perhaps not always so fleeting instants when he not merely feels himself to be the unnoticed, unvalued instrument of a community apparently in most ways careless of his wants and unfulfilled desires but is able, momentarily, to go so far as to identify himself quite unexpectedly with a greater Community, to feel himself in spirit one with an immensely larger and more enduring whole, though the meaning of the feeling may be obscure and uninterpretable. It will have at any rate the virtue of restoring to him temporarily something of his lost dignity and even giving him some tiny feeling, if, maybe, alas, soon gone, of self-importance in the world.

These can be no more than passing conjectures, though reasonable enough, as I believe them to be. More generally, however, from another and broader point of view, it seems to me highly unlikely that many persons are ever directly born, by the predominance, immediately, of a certain ineradicable quality of temperament and attitude, immutably into one of the two eventual classes. The situation in anyone's first years is always, I suggest, comparatively fluid, with development dependent to a degree upon environment and the course of events. It is natural, in youth, given the absence of insuperable obstacles, to feel to an extent that the world is at one's feet and that one has only to press forward in order to achieve one's ends, however (and however confusedly, perhaps) conceived. But we all have our tendencies in one or other direction, some more strongly than others, and these tendencies, and what evolves from them, have little necessarily to do with the condition of an individual's innate intelligence. A highly intelligent man may feel, as I have said, through the very intensity and relative clarity of his vision, that he is hopelessly dwarfed by the world about him and by its incomprehensibility beyond a certain restricted range, and he may be overridden by those with a narrower and, in the same breath, more determined approach; whereas a man of no special intellectual gifts, but endowed with plenty of push and bravado, and observant of those about him and their aims and mistakes and more long-term weaknesses, can thrust himself vigorously to the fore and begin to view himself and cause others to view him as a being of vastly superior quality and faculties within his greater or lesser sphere. Self-promoting shrewdness of this kind need certainly be no sign of outstanding intellect: it can be the very opposite, though it may seem strange in some ways to say it.

There are, of course, innumerably more of the self-underraters than of their visible opposite class, and most of those included are, it must be said, not of the highest intellectual calibre. For the self-selected few, on the other hand, for those regarding themselves as unquestionably more enterprising than their fellows, more penetrating in worldly judgement and much readier to effective action at the appropriate moment, there is thus plenty of opportunity available for the achievement of some passing measure of dominion, or of the outward appearance of dominion, over events larger or smaller, and for indulgence in the sweet satisfaction of self-aggrandisement: once these persons have made one or two positive steps in the approved direction, they will always find eager recruits, among those feeling themselves to have been left behind in the unrelenting race for earthly rewards (left behind for reasons they are unable more than dimly to understand), to flock to their extended banner.

Twenty-three

Aims and Ends. Personality, and the Irresistible Urge to Personalisation

What becomes of 'democracy' in the circumstances described? It is not the first time this problem has presented itself to us. First of all it is necessary to observe that the picture I have just drawn, if considered without care, may too easily lead us back into the oversimplification which is the perennial danger of such generalised accounts. What I have said in the preceding section I hold to be perfectly true in what it maintains, but one has to appreciate, nevertheless, that the items which are placed by it in the forefront are not, and are not claimed by it to be, the whole of the story. What is to be the ultimate balance between the items, who shall say? Just as self-underrating does not by any means need to be equated with lowliness of intellect, so it is true that not by any means all of those individuals who do not particularly seek dominion over others are in that position because they are, in some way, to be thought lacking: it may well be – may it not? – that some of them have consciously and seriously other aims in view, that they hold this short life to open up for them, in however complicated and difficult and obscure a manner, other avenues for exploration, other mountains to climb, other deeper problems to solve. The present-day stampede is for the accumulation of wealth and power, as much of these as possible in the shortest possible time, for oneself and one's close relatives, and hoarded for one's descendants – and let the rest of the world go hang. But how about those who would still agree with Aristotle (and, let it be added, with many thinkers of both intellectual and social standing in classical and later times who would have taken much the same line, whether or not in precisely the same words) that all that the reasoning man requires in the way of wealth is enough to keep him free from need, while he carries on with the true business of life (which for Aristotle meant the expansion of thought)? Many of these individuals may not seek at all in principle to dominate others, but that will not be because of incapacity. Their purposes lie in different – and for them indeed greatly superior – directions.

It must be admitted that the attitude adopted by such individuals is not always likely in itself and as such to have results fruitful in any deeply beneficial way for the community in the short term, even if in the longer term (if that is ever allowed to arrive) things may well be very different – possibly very different indeed. In the meantime one is forced to cope somehow with the insistent and perilous short term, a short term dominated, it would seem, by the crafty, by crooks and fraudsters of a variety of descriptions, by budding megalomaniacs, and by dictators – otherwise inhabited by in varying degree submerged and dependent masses, of potentially unlimited extent. Many members of these masses are held down by main force; but others, it appears, go willingly like lambs to the (often literal) slaughter. What is it that drives them on, or that draws them? The profound unsatisfied craving for a personal saviour, for a seen light in a dark world, combined with a considerable lack of judgement and an endless capability to be seduced by razzmatazz, by rhetoric and fireworks can, I suggest, supply an answer.

I speak of the craving for a personal saviour. The epithet 'personal' here is of fundamental significance, since to the untutored many – I am sorry if I sound deprecatory, I have no wish to be – personality is of the essence. The classical gods were human beings writ large, with virtues and failings and general attributes derived directly from human qualities but greatly magnified, and in as far as the gods may be thought of as superhuman this need not mean much more to us in the context than that they were of super-humanity. Before the days of the classical gods there was, it is clear, animal and, for that matter, vegetation worship, or even worship of impressive-seeming but totally subanimate natural features – fairly manifest traces of which type of worship still remained in classical times – so that the classical gods were in this sense an advance, from our angle (much as the explicit 'an eye for an eye' in another canon is an advance on the previously held claim to vengeance unrestrained and unlimited). From this conception the advance was then to the notion which eventually took over of a single all-embracing and invisible

God, not to be represented in man-made images – but how to be thought of? It was difficult for common men to think of Him as other than another man – an age-old man with a long beard (as a natural symbol of age), brooding contemplatively on high, and with an uncertain temper (the world about us being extremely uncertain in very many respects), whom it was best not to offend. This is not infinitely less anthropomorphic, in the last resort – even though the idea I thus briefly outline was not in quite such specific terms encouraged – than the classical pantheon, if more concentrated. It is worth noting that there is an undeclared approach to the monotheistic conception perceptible in the classical Greek world too, in the references, in Plato and elsewhere, to *ho theos* ('the divinity', 'the deity', with no particular god actually named). What unqualified monotheism, in avowing itself, lost in direct anthropomorphic personalisation of the godhead it made up for by the introduction, alongside it, of outstanding human representatives of the divine in the shape of individual Prophets and the like (who themselves might come close to deification in some cases) continuing to be well-known to us today by name and through their characters and reputed activity, with whatever myths may have grown up about certain of them. We evidently cannot do without some clearly human-style personalities as at least intermediaries for the more remote divine notion.

The dependence of the popular imagination upon the concept of personality can have some curious side-effects. I was reading lately a well-circulated book by an eminent mathematician on the quantum theory, a work addressed to the general public. In order to give the book the broadest possible appeal the writer had attempted to convey the progress of development of the theory, by means of the emphatic personalisation of every issue that arose: thus the wave-versus-particle issue was set forth as though each of the two theoretical possibilities was itself a personal party to the dispute, propagating its own case animatedly against the other. The idea of presenting so abstract and complex a theory as that of the quantum in such terms may seem – it does to me – very odd, but note that the presenter is not any sort of innumerate and barely scientific-minded novice but an eminent mathematician, himself clearly *au fait* with the details of what he describes, on their own ground, and using this device, for what it may be worth, to bring those details close to the public he is wishing to instruct and edify. His task was a difficult one, and I am not prepared to assert that he could have undoubtedly done it much more effectively in some specifically different way, though I do say fervently that his chosen way was not a good one (to me nothing but irritating); but the fact that he chose this way is a remarkable reflection nevertheless of how common thinking runs (not only on the very lowest levels of thought), and of the powerful resulting attraction, justifiably or otherwise, of personalisation as a basis for explanation of even the most abstruse of subjects.

Let me give here now another modern example of unhappy personalisation of the non-personal - a case in this instance hitting us quite hard in its consequences since it involves a misconstruction of basic elements relating to a public issue of great importance. The field is that of economics, concerning which we have fairly recently been regaled from on high, at moments of stress (I refer particularly to some outstanding events of, say, 1991–2, leading up to the day when we were forced out of the Exchange Rate Mechanism), with accounts of how the economy is in a painful state but is due to recover eventually through the application of certain severe measures, which must be borne. The image here is plainly that of a living body suffering from a stomach-ache or perhaps something rather worse, from which it is about to be delivered by the use of some strong and obviously unpleasant medicine. The fact is, however, that the economy is no more able to undergo pain than is the Rock of Gibraltar. Neither the one nor the other has the capacity for feeling pain or any other sensation, the one because it is a totally inanimate mass without room in its existence for feeling or perception or emotion of any kind, the other - the economy - because it is an entirely abstract entity, conceived of by the human mind as an umbrella-notion to cover a variety of factors, in a context of great practical importance, but itself with no sort of actual individual existence. Is this all perhaps terribly obvious? But look at the implications. A living body, having once recovered from a painful illness, is to that extent well again and can continue its life more or less as before - the clear suggestion in this case was that the economy could indeed look forward to an eventually thriving future - but an 'economy' in the quite concrete sense here evidently intended is in fact made up of a multitude of individuals, for many of whom the economy's 'pain' means unhappily no less than personal disaster, from which no proper recovery is likely to be possible: if and when the economy itself 'recovers', such individuals will not magically recover with it but will need to start again with the greatest difficulty from scratch, if in the meantime they have not already gone completely under. The politician who speaks in these terms of the economy and its temporary 'pain' is not unlike Napoleon who spoke of having an annual income of so many tens of thousands of men: he is showing absolutely no regard for the actual individuals concerned. At best, by dwelling so narrowly on his personalised metaphor, our politician is simply deluding himself. (When he says, "It is worth the pain to achieve the end", or words to that effect, one wonders if he really knows what he is talking about.)

Mrs Thatcher, as she then was, no doubt had a glimpse of this sort of situation when she said, "There is no such thing as society", for certainly there is no such thing as society in the shape of an animated individual like you or me. But the precise form of words she used, and the crude meaning she chose to attach to it, distorted the reality into the proposition that the idea of society had no significance whatever and that we had best forget about it. This is, of course, nonsense. As to the economy, I am far indeed from wishing to allege that it does not exist or that the concept has no value, if primarily of a statistical nature; but its personalisation by a Chancellor of the Exchequer, in the way we have seen, is a severe misrepresentation of the facts and of no service to anybody.

I have one more instance which I cannot help quoting since it is so curious and requires a certain amount of disentanglement. After the French referendum on the Maastricht Treaty in September 1992, with a very narrow result in favour, there was much talk about what exactly the verdict was to be taken to mean, seeing that it was a long way from the decisive 'yes' that had been hoped for. But one French politician, at least, offered a highly simplistic view of the result: he held, he told us, that a 'yes' was a 'yes' irrespective of by what proportion of the votes, and that this was the way in which democracy worked, as *vide* the results of government elections, so that the narrowness of the outcome could thus be splendidly ignored.

What we appear to have here is a half-concealed personalisation of 'democracy' as a superior figure – female, no doubt?, like the goddess Athena – of a characteristic and readily recognisable style of behaviour, a style eccentric possibly in some of its manifestations but nevertheless not to be questioned since that is, after all, how the figure clearly carries out her lofty business, and we had better learn to accept it. This is surely patently ridiculous, but it is as well to ask oneself why. Democracy is not only not an individual being but as a concept it is not even as well-defined as the economy: it is, if the truth be told, and we have already been given some inkling of the fact, a distinctly woolly conception or expression which has not always shown itself to actual effect in the same way, and which is indeed hardly more, it must be admitted, than a verbally condensed offshoot for practical purposes of a theory based on the generalised notion, 'let the people speak'. How it operates is in whatever way men and women (the personal bearers of the democratic standard) feel and in principle accept that it should operate in given circumstances. The circumstances of a general or local government election (for strictly temporary posts) and of a national referendum are very different from one another. In the case of such an election men have laid down that for simplicity's sake and for the sake of a decisive result a victory even by a solitary vote is good enough (though large-scale results on such a basis may be considerably less than ideal – hence the arguments in favour of proportional representation and such-like); but in the case of a referendum of this sort nothing of the kind has been laid down nor could it have been. What value ultimately a referendum has or has not I have discussed briefly elsewhere in these pages and do not mean to go into the matter again here; but the general theory behind the holding of a referendum is that by this means the nation's will shall be directly tested on a particular action-point – not for the election of a representative – and in these circumstances a tiny majority is remarkably unrevealing, and should call for serious second thoughts by the referrers, even though their proposal be technically 'accepted'.

Twenty-four

Simplification; and the Economy

Since I have been talking so much of personalisation as a major determinant of public error, I had better say plainly that I would not by any means suggest that it is the only thing of importance needing to be taken into account in the context. Yes, it is of major importance, and I propose to return to it and to some of its most damaging aspects very shortly, but I would like nevertheless to turn aside from it here for just a moment to take into account certain other fundamental causes of significant misconception. Not wishing to travel too far from my original theme, I will limit myself chiefly to one remarkable case which will do for all, the basis of all such misconceptions being in fact the same, simplification on the grand scale.

I go back, then, to the subject of the economy, which I treated just now in relation to personalisation. The economy is singularly ill-understood, even by those specially allocated to deal with it – I refer above all to Chancellors of the Exchequer, theoretically in supreme charge of its handling. It has been the habit of Chancellors in recent years to put forward one particular item, such as the rate of interest, as the instrument of policy to be manipulated before and beyond all others (at times almost to the exclusion of all others) to meet all problems. In the face of so complex a system as a public economy, it is difficult to see how any one-weapon attack of such a kind can possibly work in more than the roughest way, if ever. But more striking still was the aim which a British Prime Minister and his Chancellor not so long ago set before themselves – for a time at least – and before their country, as the one supreme aim to be achieved, overriding, it might often seem, all others – that of 'zero inflation'. Whatever the method employed, the aim itself, the pursuit of 'zero inflation' as the highest priority was and is, it seems to me, quite crazy. Inflation as such is neither good nor bad, certainly not, *as such*, the immense evil it is often portrayed to be. It is primarily a symptom, symptomatic of different things at different times; and everything depends upon its particular nature at a particular time, and what, at that time, it particularly symptomatises. High and rapid inflation is always highly undesirable, because it signifies instability (a key word in the context, frequently to be met with, and here indeed much to the point), and instability is almost invariably an undesirable phenomenon against whatever human background. In practical terms, violently experienced inflation of this kind can have unpleasant and even devastating effects on members of the population who are compelled to suffer it: there can be little need to illustrate the point. But on the other hand a modest rate of inflation is not only compatible with a genuinely progressive economy, it is actually inseparable from it, as a glance over past events in the last century or two will very clearly show. It is natural enough, when the economy is flourishing, and people have money and are prepared to part with it, that providers of goods and services should take the opportunity of increasing their profit-margins as far as they are able, though technological progress may at the same time help to reduce some of the effects of this tendency. Judicious steering at the higher levels of responsibility – assuredly not excepting government levels – will help to maintain a reasonable balance, but there is no doubt, and economic history demonstrates it without question, that there will be a continuing tendency for both prices and incomes to rise, not steeply at any given moment but in a regular upward pattern. If upward price-adjustment is smooth and quite gradual, individuals will have, in general, no serious difficulty in accommodating themselves to it – no more than in accommodating themselves to the other normal changes in their lives with which they have in common experience to learn to cope – and even may not notice directly that it is happening unless it is drawn specifically to their attention. Over the longer term, it is true, the accumulated results are likely to become very noticeable, but they represent in basis factors which are likely to be of positive value, rather than otherwise, to the community at large, and which offer fruitful ground for research by the social-historical analyst.

I should make it very plain, in so far as such a caution is needed, that my comments are related in principle to our modern post-industrial system and are not intended to apply similarly to any pre-industrial society, which will have its own modifying characteristics. However, in our modern world what I have been describing is very much the order of the day. The call for inflation to be kept within reasonable bounds is indubitably itself very reasonable – provided, however, one bears in mind that the aim cannot be treated as a thing on its own, as if monetary inflation were somehow a primary reality unrelated to other matters, many of them indeed matters of more fundamental importance, and having profounder effects on the lives and living-basis of individuals, on their employment or prospects of employment, their housing, their business activities, and so on – these are the things which require, domestically, the first consideration, and to talk loudly of 'zero inflation' in the context shows extraordinary lack of understanding of what life is and means, and of how in fact an economy operates. It is to set up a will-o'-the-wisp to pursue, an illusion: it is as much as to ask that economic progress be halted in its tracks – to ask, in effect, for a static economy (not at all the same thing as a stable one), which is not only quite different from the 'growth' which is constantly being clamoured for but is actually, in our present-day industrialised and technologically developed and developing world, an impossibility, since, on the face of things, nothing stands still in it: the movement, if it is not forwards, is backwards.

The claim, in explanation of the kind of extreme simplification of ends we have just been discussing, is that it provides a 'clear strategy'. But whether it is, strictly speaking, either clear or indeed any kind of serious 'strategy' is surely more than doubtful. It is 'clear' only in the sense that it looks on the surface easy to understand; but its underlying intentions, if one attempts to follow them, are very far from clear, and it looks easy to understand only because the ends and aims that may be thought to be in view have been robbed of their inherent and unavoidable complexity by the manner of formulation of what is actually stated. As to 'strategy' it is questionable how far such a description applies at all in such a case: a strategy, properly conceived, is a long-term approach, moving, maybe, through a more or less involved series of detailed tactics not always, every one in its own right, giving a clear sight of the ultimate aim. But the sort of approach we have before us is essentially short-term; as such it is barely more than a tactic, and what it is seriously after in the long run – if anything more, ultimately, than the maintenance of a particular political party and its leading personnel in power – is quite obscure.

We have come back yet again, it will be seen, to the contrast (or even contradiction) between the short and the long term, which dogs our footsteps wherever we go. We cannot escape from it here because we continue within the world of the politician; and the fully functioning politician, while many of the problems he faces are undeniably, whether he likes it or not, of a long-term – some of them of the longest-term – nature, is himself by nature a short-term phenomenon. Ideally, this would not altogether prevent his taking a long view; but his is not an ideal world, though he may pretend that it is. He has become a politician because he is ambitious, because he means to 'get on'; and when he rises to a position of some power, he feels it his need, for the sake of his personal ambitions, to make himself felt as quickly as possible, since he has no guarantee of remaining in such a position for more than a brief, perhaps very brief period.

He may be technically a Conservative, and he may be in fact succeeding fellow-Conservatives in his post, but his aim is in this connection necessarily far less to 'conserve' whatever may have been the accomplishments of his predecessors, nearer or more remote, than to revolutionise, to be 'radical' – if one may descend into the Thatcher vocabulary – and to display, for all unmistakably to see and marvel at, the sparkle and glitter of his own brilliance.

Oversimplification of issues and of corresponding methods is the standing temptation of the politician. It is bound to be a temptation for anyone wishing to make a name fast for himself, but for no one can it be more so than for the politician, and particularly for the politician approaching or at the seat of power. For who, for example, in such a position would set out willingly to unfold to the unlearned multitude the root secrets and problems of economics in all their genuine complexity? (Who even knows them sufficiently well to be even half-sure of his ground to begin with?) How much easier, more apparently straightforward, vastly more fruitful, to pick on a single idea, a single resonant word even, that everyone can at once recognise – if not, precisely, define – and hammer it home time and again as the answer to all our problems.

This is the way, one may add, to build up an enduring dogma, a dogma indeed which, once set up, may prove extraordinarily difficult to detach oneself from. One reason for the difficulty is that the creator or transmitter of such a dogma is not necessarily to be thought of as merely acting to deceive his public; the first person he acts to deceive may very well be himself.

Twenty-five

More on Personalisation; and on Public Relations (PR) and the Like

I return to the discussion of personalisation: it is the insistent demand for this, coupled with the helpless feeling of so many men and women that the world in which they live is growingly too overwhelming for them to cope with, which produces the phenomenon, of which we have seen so much in this dark century, of unscrupulous domination by tyrants and egomaniacal dictators: by individuals arising, often enough in these days, from nowhere but distinguished always by their loud voices, by their strident, simplistic messages, repeatedly declaimed, by what seems to be their absolute and unfailing certainty in all circumstances, and by their ability above all to lay on a tremendous show for the delectation of the populace. 'Democracy' is no ultimate unassailable bulwark against the assault of such an individual, who presents himself frequently in principle if not necessarily in explicit assertion as a god on earth and who becomes an object of near-worship as such by those who need some visible and palpable divinity of the kind to adore. An unusually clear illustration of this latter syndrome is provided by the instance not so long ago of the elderly German who spoke publicly, in tones almost of disbelief at himself, of how, when young, he was spellbound by Hitler, and looking at him on the podium had felt that he was 'looking into the eyes of God'. Democracy is unhappily capable under these conditions of operating as the active agent of its own destruction; and until men in general acquire a little more judgement and lose a little of their painful and perpetual yearning after a self-appointed 'leader' to show them the way, dangers will continue to beset us and sheer catastrophe never be far off.

I think I can more easily understand the evil fascination exercised over the ignorant or unstable (or frequently both) by Hitler than by Mussolini . Old newsreels bring us closer to the reality of the two dictators than to that of earlier historical figures of any kind of equivalent significance. Seeing Mussolini screaming and gesticulating on high one wonders, at this distance, how anyone could ever have been duped by such ridiculous antics into joining his train; reconsidering his inexcusable attack upon the weak state of Abyssinia, solely and obviously, as he himself did not hide, for the purpose of carving out for himself as easily as possible an 'empire', without which he felt that he would remain of negligible international status, one wonders how anyone could have found even the crudest justification for so plainly egotistical and criminal an act. But whereas the unpleasant posturing of Mussolini strike one in retrospect as mainly absurd, those of Hitler, viewed on the screen, can produce, even now, the authentic chill of doom in waiting.

Hitler's greatest talent – his genius, if you will, for the Devil too has genius – was for black drama, on a monstrous and forbidding scale; forbidding, that is, inevitably, for those clearly threatened by it, but to those, and they were very many (not only, sad to say, within the borders of Germany alone), who were caught up in the web of its however meretricious allurements, it was brutally heartening, its romantic sentimentality was marvellously satisfying, it was emotionally uplifting beyond the reach of reason. (The race of those liable to be so affected still lives on, regrettably, in corners, always ready, given the opportunity, to emerge.) The endless night-marching columns of uniformed men moving forward at a smart military pace to stirring martial music, under carefully directed searchlights, moving with their right arms outstretched, fists clenched, in heavenward greeting for their magnificent hero standing dauntless above them, fearlessly challenging the world, his right arm, too, raised in a curious kind of semi-careless response – arm upright from the elbow, hand thrown back (one presumes that an exact return of the salute would have been an infringement of his superior dignity; or perhaps it would simply have been too fatiguing, even for so divine a figure, so far in theory from human frailty) – such a scene, viewed in newsreel form now long afterwards, with most of the participants probably dead and the destruction which, wittingly or unwittingly, they brought upon their own and others' heads now long past, if not, in its terrible shape and frightful magnitude, forgotten, can still evoke an irresistible thrill of horror in the hearts of many, whether of those having themselves lived, in Germany or elsewhere, through the nightmare of that appalling period – the hour before the storm – or whether of those with sufficient imagination and feeling to react humanly without the need for the reawakening of some actual experience personally undergone.

Beware the perfect PR-man! It seems, at times, as if he could persuade anyone of anything; though this is not in fact true so long as we do not allow ourselves to be hypnotised out of our senses – or, rather, out of our reason. Nevertheless, though some of us will always resist his blandishments, there will always be many who will succumb to them even on the lowest level of their attack – and sometimes the lower the level the more likely it is that the attack will find a response, in the lowest, least rational (but potentially perhaps in many persons most powerful) part of the human soul.

Fortunately there are few perfect PR-men, able to exploit to the full the immensely expanded possibilities open to them in this age of all manner of unceasing propaganda from every quarter, cultivated with intensity on behalf of every conceivable cause (such cause liable often, indeed, to awaken little or no response without its aid in liberal quantity). The inability of some of the highest paid (and therefore, it is true, no doubt most anxious for self-promotion above all) among PR-practitioners to gauge accurately the authentic ground and purpose of their efforts is seen to plainest effect in a number of examples of commercial advertising on TV, where exposure time is short and it should be obvious that the advertiser's best line is to attempt no more than to take the opportunity of implanting his brand name firmly in the memory, but where, often, the opportunity is lost or only weakly taken through the desire of the scriptwriter and those otherwise responsible to show how extremely witty they can be, even though this may obscure what should have been a straightforward and unmistakable message.

There are times, one sees, when simplicity and straightforwardness are of the essence – in public relations it is so without denial. So, also, with certain reservations, in the production of dramatic effect in general; contrary, it must appear, to the opinion of those who have devised for current television-drama, even on the small scale of the brief half-hour programme (the regulation length until quite recently –

there is now an evident move to expand the time markedly for at least the most popular items), a complicated technique, put constantly into operation, based on the introduction of as many themes or plot-strands as possible – a technique by no means limited to the detective story or associated 'mystery' tale, where the theory is to mislead the viewer in various respects, for obvious reasons – with the result, however, quite as often as not, not merely of misleading the viewer but, in the upshot, of thoroughly confusing him. If it is comfortably thought, by those who use it, that this multiple-stranded approach will be interpreted in terms of richness of invention, I would suggest, rather, that its true cause (and also effect) lies in thinness in powers and quality of development; and I would contrast it with the fundamental simplicities of the best of the old Hollywood Westerns, where a single strong theme is followed through with tremendous effectiveness from the opening shots to the climax. (I quote, as a passing example, the old James Stewart film, *The Man from Laramie*.)

It is obvious that the errors of technique I have outlined were not easily fallen into by the elaborate Hitler propaganda-machine, operating under the direction of its sinister but at the same time highly-skilled chief, Dr Goebbels, who brought to his task a clear appreciation of the weaknesses of human nature and of the best and most efficient methods of exploiting them. He knew well, and we have also in our wisdom to recognise that truly effective PR stands upon a necessary basis of dramatic simplicity – indeed, simplification; so that we have in consequence to recognise that the use of any highly-developed form, whatever form, of PR for the presumed purpose of promoting understanding of some subject of inherent and unavoidable complexity, such as economics or political relations in their authentic inward significance, is self-contradictory. It may be objected that this, if it is true, presents politicians (and will always have presented them) with an intolerable dilemma: whether to concentrate on the – regrettably unpractical – ideal of attempting, in a matter known to be of great importance, to convey the difficult truth in all its subtlety, or whether, rather, to attempt to use all convenient means of normal persuasion, while realising that *what* one is trying to persuade people of must fall far short of the truth by its very nature. Is this a serious objection? If so, it is an objection not to my mode of statement but to the facts that my statement covers. We live in an imperfect world.

Twenty-six

To Consult the People?

What I have said is not, of course, quite the end of this particular story, whose inner intricacies are considerable. The would-be purveyor of essential truth must first be sure that he himself knows it as well as it can be known; and, for his part, the purveyor of what may be described as well-intentioned propaganda (for that is what, at best, the alternative approach most reduce itself to) must, if he retains any honesty, be very certain in his heart that behind his persuasively-meant utterances lies a concatenation of true facts in which he himself can sincerely believe, though they are too complex to express clearly in the given situation – but this, again, means that unless he himself is a victim of similar propaganda to that of which he is the agent (or unless, of course, he is to be considered less an agent than an active originator of such propaganda, for purposes not strictly related to basic truth, making him thus doubtfully honest and my epithet 'well-intentioned' hardly correct), then he too must be deeply sure of the root facts which he is claiming, in his discreetly simplified way, to present: he must know the truth even in order, in his measure, to distort it for mass consumption.

But who, in Heaven's name, can know so surely the truth of such matters? In order to be entirely honest, with oneself as well as with one's hearers, one should say to them at the critical moment not, "Do as I demand of you", but, rather, "Consider with me what is the best way". To what extent, indeed, could this be a practical proposition? In a democratic state of the present day it is understood in principle that decisions should be based on consultation, and avenues for consultation are purpose-built into the constitution. Parliaments, Upper and Lower Houses, Cabinets, official Oppositions, Councils and Committees and so forth, are all intended for the furtherance of consultation, on the broadest basis, among groups of theoretical equals (or almost equals) ranged on various hierarchical levels with a single elected individual at the top. This is consultation in government, with allowance made, in the structure so established, for checks and balances in order to prevent the swing of bias, always plentifully in evidence for whatever reason, from falling too much and too unguardedly in one direction.

All this is admirable in idea, if not invariably in functioning, but it is not quite what I had been talking of hitherto. Between government, with all its deliberately-created opportunities for debate and consultation, and the popular mass whom government is supposed in theory to represent, there is still a gap, a wide gap which consultation in any true sense cannot cover. The politician cannot really say to the people, "Consider with me what is the best way", for there is no genuine method by which a consultation of the kind so proposed can be brought into effect – the best the politician can strictly do in the ordinary way is to put forward his preferred recipe to the public, in whatever form he may think most fruitful and forceful, and hope that the public may bend towards it. If he wishes to go further, there is only one way – the way, as we know, of a referendum; and it may not even be in his power to bring such a referendum about.

A referendum is very much a method of last resort. It is not normally written into constitutions as an essential element, and a prime minister can in general refuse to call one if he does not like the idea of it. He may claim proudly that he has been elected to *lead* his people, not to throw back to them any particularly difficult problem for them themselves to resolve. In practical fact his refusal may derive, of course, from a concealed suspicion by him that the result might not go the way he personally would prefer. In any case, it is generally speaking fully in his power to reject the idea when it is put before him. The referendum is not seriously to be thought of as a method of consultation, though that word is, all too freely, utilised in the context: so we speak of 'consulting the people'; but note that we do not speak of consulting *with* the people, a totally unrealistic conception. If the problems facing politicians are frequently a good deal more complicated than is allowed to appear on the surface, those problems leading to loud outcries for a referendum are usually among the most complicated of all, or at least among those whose ultimate and extreme complexities refuse to remain hidden, amid the tooth-and-nail battle being fought over them between parliamentary opponents. 'Let the people decide' becomes the watchword, without however anyone attempting to explain in a convincing manner how a problem of such magnitude as to have arrived at this critical point can be solved through the medium of a simple voting paper, requiring in principle to be answered simply "Yes" or "No", by a populace whose millions of members will undoubtedly include many who will have little enough idea of what precisely it is that they are being asked to answer, however cunningly it is set out for them. – Some of this I have said before. I will only comment, that what we seem to have here, viewed from a certain angle is in some respects, at least, another curious example of the 'free market' or 'leave it to the gods' syndrome – not all that far, that is, from some ancient beliefs and practices which I quoted earlier for Greece but which in fact go much wider and are traceable far back – according to which the most efficient way of solving an otherwise apparently insoluble problem is the equivalent, if I may return here to a modern image, of tossing a coin. It is also true, to continue with the same image, that a little sleight of hand with a double-headed coin in this operation, in order, as it were, to assist the gods in their deliberations, may not be entirely unheard-of.

Government and its structures are odd things, much under discussion at all times, normally starting from the assumption that some mode or other of government is an absolute necessity. Anarchy, though it has had its advocates, would appear to offer no practical solution to anything very much, the freedom from tyrannical or bureaucratic interference which has been claimed in its favour by proponents being evidently more than countered by the freedom of opportunity it presents to all sorts of undesirable interferences of other kinds. An anarchic system – in any case, a contradiction in terms – which seeks to avoid such an open door to conflict cannot be in any true sense anarchic, depending at the very least upon an unwritten group consensus, which means nothing less than self-government, involving attainment by individuals in the group to moral heights patently beyond the reach of most of us today at the best of times.

The Thatcherite theory of minimal government has a superficial – but only very superficial – relationship to the theory of anarchy. 'As little government as possible' is a very different motto from the demand for no government at all, and in any case the motivation behind it is totally different. The Thatcherite and similar aims are not for the removal of all obstacles to freedom of any kind but for the removal of all conceivable obstacles from the path of the seeker after self-enrichment. This involves the abolition of a number of controls and controlling institutions but also the reshaping or reaffirmation of others and, where appropriate for the purpose, the creation of new ones. Since everything has to be paid for, it involves too the diversion of money and effort from other pre-existing ventures (the provision of welfare, for example) to the main aim – which would in fact be very likely the sole aim if it were not for electoral requirements. This is very far indeed from the removal of all controls on everything, and it ends up in many respects with more emphasis on government – central government – than one may be deemed to have set out with.

Twenty-seven

Oversimplification – and Some Thoughts on Monarchy

Having said so much about simplicity and simplification and about oversimplification, I had better make it very clear that what I am presenting as a great threat is the last of the three, not, in principle, either of the other two. Simplicity in itself, far from being a fault or a vice, can be a great virtue, a goal to aim at among the highest, and if simplification can bring about a degree of ultimate simplicity in exposition, it thereby is able also itself to serve an admirable purpose. But it is here that the problem arises, of distinguishing between appropriate simplification, which genuinely leads the way to elucidation, and the kind of popular *over*simplification which by the use of brassy and specious but fundamentally ill-fitting metaphors and by images raising fallacious and misleading ideas in the name of simplicity do nothing in the end but obscure the reality. It is right to make every effort to be simple, for the sake of one's own better understanding as well as that of an audience, but it is all too easy to slip from this into the state of ignoring or even denying the true issues.

Simplicity, it is necessary to add, is not just a matter of clarity in exposition, it is basic to analysis. The specialist starts from as simple as possible a conceptual division, which he can proceed to vary and modify and build up and alter as need be, to fit the complexity of the facts he has under examination. This has nothing much to do with the requirements of exposition or, at least, it has nothing to do with exposition in the sense of transmission to an unspecialised external audience, one having, it is probably to be assumed, a limited attention-span – of exposition, that is to say, of the essentials of a specialised picture previously fully formulated and not intended to be changed in the transmission. In primary analysis, simplicity of approach and method is a necessity: the exposition to which it relates in this context is exposition to one's own internal audience, for the sake of root-clarification of the essentials of a case, a case still unexplored or only in part explored. Simplicity is a means to clarification, seeking a clarity not merely of outward exposition but of exploration, exploration in every way, a clarity which in the end is at the heart of discovery, as well as of the dissemination of knowledge and understanding. But simplification is not in itself simplicity; and, through a sort of pseudo-clarity, can indeed lend itself instead to the opposite end, of obfuscation – often, regrettably, with intent.

We derive the idea of democracy from the Greeks, but our ideas and theirs about it, as I have shown, are very far from coinciding at all points, or even at all main points. Moreover, the claim that democracy (in whatever shape we conceive it) represents an ideal form of government is one that we may make but not one that the Greeks would have made quite so readily. There were many not altogether unintelligent persons living under a democratic system in Greece who were perfectly prepared to enjoy its privileges and at the same time to pour active scorn on the underlying principle, referring to the *demos*, the 'people', as 'the mob'; and it is well to remember that these were not all by any means what we would nowadays call reactionaries. Plato, in his *Republic*, proposed that in his ideal state the ruler should be not the *demos* or some direct representative of that body but a 'philosopher-king', someone entirely above the *mêlée*, free from the constraints put upon an elected officer, constraints of which we today are well aware (including the need for almost ceaseless campaigning, even though the type of campaigning varies according to whether it is pre- or post-election). The solitary recorded attempt by Plato to carry his theory into effect and to create, in Sicily, an actual philosopher-king was, not surprisingly, a dismal failure, since the proposal in the *Republic* is indeed ideal in the sense of being in practicality unattainable. It would not be difficult in fact to maintain that 'philosopher-king' is, in this world, a contradiction in terms; yet it is a matter of some significance that it is for that notion that Plato is popularly best remembered in this context, and not for any subtler rethinking that might have gone on in his mind and for which we are not altogether without evidence. Some of his other analyses were, philosophically, immeasurably more profound; but these, I fear, have left, popularly, considerably less impression.

There have been in recent years in this country calls for the abolition of that on the face of it outdated institution, the hereditary monarchy, and for its replacement by an elective presidency. From a rational point of view, superficially at least, there would appear to be much in favour of such proposals. Only they ignore certain key factors. By an accident – if you like – of history, what we now have in Britain is an hereditary monarchy able to draw upon itself all the curious reverence for a 'superior' personality or personalities which, as I have pointed out, popular need demands, yet the personality in question in this case (whoever he or she turns out in practice to be) happens at the same time to be bereft of any genuine constitutional power. The very fact that the British monarchy continues to be hereditary frees it from the necessity to campaign for its perpetuation, but effective power over our lives lies elsewhere, and we can, as we wish, 'adore' it, or not, together with the pomp and ceremony which are its regular accompaniments, without any tremors. That individual members of the royal family are obviously subject to the same sort of human weaknesses as anyone else is not really an argument against the institution, as some would maintain; on the contrary, it is in its odd way a healthy sign.

We can, without tearing ourselves apart, divide our loyalties, as between, on the one hand, the monarchy, the lofty symbol of state – a kind of symbol which apparently we cannot do without, though it is no part of a strictly rational outlook (so *The Times*, with its own brand of sweet irony, observed, in a leader of 23 October 1992, "People live by symbolism more than by subsidiarity") and, on the other hand, a political party, an active participant in the Parliamentary battle of wits and wiles, of the incessant hue and cry, a party at one moment ruling over our everyday existence, at another not, but even when defeated leaving the human symbol of state, unchanging, still holding the sceptre unaffectedly and peacefully above it, the behavioural vicissitudes of those who actually bear the sceptre notwithstanding. To the man or woman of sense the human frailties so clearly displayed by royalty do not really spoil the picture. They are nothing new in themselves, as anyone must realise if he stops to think – I have a word or two more to say on this a little further on; they show also, comfortingly, I suggest, that royalty is far from godlike, that it is, rather, well-endowed with its share of down-to-earth human failings; and what is indeed to some degree new in the present circumstances is that royalty is as open these days to being lampooned and gaped over and ridiculed in the 'media' as any politician, and with a great deal less opportunity for successfully striking back. Royalty's alleged snobberies and claimed remoteness may be unattractive if not entirely surprising; the actions of royal personages in regard to one another may not always be all that they should be; and undoubtedly it is reasonable, for instance, that some of their immense unearned riches should be returned to the state through taxes, as appears at length to have been agreed; but still – make no mistake – they do us incalculable service by remaining perched above us, as they do, in quaint and somewhat archaic dignity, having no serious power from their lofty eminence to inflict on us any harm, and without our having had to put ourselves to any test in order to set them in such a position of outward grandeur. We surely would not, as I most fervently hope, be prepared willingly to replace their innocuous rule by that of an elected president, one heavily conscious of having fought his way with bitter efforts to the heights of overriding authority (a good deal more than purely nominal) and determined above all to retain that authority by hook or by crook, come otherwise what will, and suffer who may. (There are echoes of this in John Major's symptomatic public declaration, made gleefully and unashamedly on an occasion early in his somewhat ineffectual premiership: "I've got it; I like it; and I'm going to keep it".)

In these – as they say – 'permissive' times, when sexual promiscuity of a broad variety of kinds is countenanced or even actively approved, when marital infidelity in high places is occasionally thought hardly any bar to elevation in office or, certainly, to acclamation by the multitude, when many major and, it was once imagined, immutable shibboleths of the past, for whatever they may have actually been worth, have been scattered to the winds, just why, one asks oneself in some modest perplexity, should the relatively minor miseries of ill-judged royal unions be the object of so much malicious discussion and self-righteous condemnation? Is it that the theoretically ideal royal status is shaken by open revelation of royalty's underlying humanity after all, in this respect as no doubt in others, and its liability to common human error? But was not this liability to error (to put it qualitatively at its least and most neutral) perfectly patent on all too many and often vastly more significant occasions also with past monarchs (Henry VIII? Some of the earlier Georges? I quote very obvious cases, not too far off), in days when such rulers not merely inaugurated ceremonies and official functions or handed out prearranged honours, or, otherwise, sat passively, as it were, on their luxurious thrones, but when often perhaps they in active practice wielded immense authoritarian power, with the full force of the state ("*L'état c'est moi*", as Louis XIV said) behind them? Of course it is true that not by any means all conceived 'moral' limits of the past have been breached at the present day, and indeed it is not so very long since it was possible for a high public official to be propelled headlong into the outer darkness (with tragic personal consequences) because he was unfortunately discovered to be seeking out prostitutes – but what I point to is, of course, on another and altogether much less blatant level, and the question must remain.

Twenty-eight
Morality?

The question of royalty and its marital and sexual relations, and the general situation which the raising of that question helps in some degree to reveal, if not exactly to illuminate, are nothing if not confused, confusion being a hallmark of popular attitudes, of which what we have here provides a very respectable (if I may use the word) example. It is not at all clear what the matter has actually to do with fundamental morality, or with any other kind of absolutes: if we turn aside for a moment from our particular royal question, what does appear to be signified by the general situation behind it, out of which, so to speak, it emerges, is the continued existence of a steady if far from well-defined process of change in mass outlook – part of a constant movement, more emphatic since the Second World War (and more emphatic still since the Sixties), and continuing without noticeable pause to develop and expand its field, as a result of the shaking-up, of the loosening of established traditions and ties, beginning already to advertise itself after the First World War and increasing in effect with the Second and with the succession of devastating human calamities following in its train all over the globe, through the decades, with never any sign of coming to an even temporary halt.

To someone stationed at a given part of the movement and preferring to see things as far as possible in comparatively static and reasonably optimistic terms, it might appear that the main thing that has happened is that we in the West are at last engaged in the throwing-off once and for all of the undesirable inhibitions which have hog-bound us in the past and crippled our freedoms, and that we are *all* and everywhere finally on the road to a bright and rational new world. But this, alas, is illusion – isolating itself not only in time but in space, ignoring if not altogether forgetting the monstrous crimes continuing to be perpetrated on an extensive scale contemporaneously elsewhere and whose implications for freedom and rationality and for even minimal well-being in a stable and unembittered (I do not care to use the word 'happy') community give no rise whatever, so far as one can see, for optimism. The convinced optimist will no doubt say, "These problems will be overcome", and I can only hope urgently that he may be right, but at the moment there is nothing whatever to show it, and all the lessons of history – history not, surely, at anything like an end, unless it be a bad one – from the remotest known past up to the latest current instant teach us, at the very least, to exercise the extremest caution in our judgement. In any case the idea of a bright new world here and at present in the offing for us is, beyond denial, total and vain illusion.

The day before yesterday we were still not so very far from the reticences of speech and behaviour (and, up to a point, of thought too) which governed the Victorians, and into which it may well appear impossible for us, in our new and – should we not say? – enlightened atmosphere ever to fall back. Yet the fluctuations of time and custom are never so certainly predictable, the direction of events they seem to display to us at a given moment not so unalterable, so irreversible, as we may innocently sometimes think; and meanwhile in the present age our standards for action, so far from continuing an inevitable ascent on a blissful and undeviating upward path, remain inextricably and inexorably muddled, from many aspects self-contradictory. The attitude to reported royal doings is fairly symptomatic, if with characteristics of its own. What is it that the tabloid and tabloid-style gossip-mongers object to – or, rather, that they hold up to their readers for presumed objection? Conduct which they, the writers, would hold as nowadays entirely normal among themselves, hardly worthy of comment, is treated, often on the basis as much of rumour and speculation as of flat and self-evident fact, with exclamation-marks and huge black headlines filling the page, as matters for high disapprobation. This is plainly hypocrisy of the first order – scandal-seeking for the sake of profit, with no other primary motive – but why should it appeal so greatly to the reader? That is the real question.

A part of the story, certainly, must be the popular need – to which I have already drawn attention – to regard the royal family, in their ideal function, as a model for general behaviour, with the consequent mixture of genuine disappointment by some, together with salacious reactions from others, whose interest is evidently less pure, at the spectacle of an apparent fall from grace by the mighty. But the point here is the whole notion, in this context, of a fall from grace, meaning that the concept of permissiveness is not, in this light, to be envisaged as a positive advance into a freer moral sphere ('moral' relating here to sexual activity, if without precise specification), as is frequently maintained, but as a mere falling-back. On this basis Victorian standards are still those we in essence uphold, even if we do not obey them.

I have spoken of popular confusion in these realms but this is 'popular' not in the sense of pertaining solely to the unthinking masses but as an attitude pervasive of the whole of our society. Who can tell us whether our 'moral' standards (whatever we may take this to mean) have risen, or fallen, or simply moved themselves sideways in some remarkable manner? Where can we find an expert voice to give us an accurate indication in this regard? Are we to look to Ministers of the Faith, or of the Law, or possibly of the Government, to guide us? But, then, what particular Faith, what Law, what Government? Are messages from these classes of source single and firm and enlightening? Or do they merely add to our confusion, particularly if we move beyond our own locality and beyond our shores and out to a wider and in many ways darker world, a world rooted, it seems, in never-ending, disheartening, insoluble conflict?

However confidently and frequently we may assure ourselves that we have flung ourselves free from the stifling bonds of Victorian values, it will be clear enough, if we stop to consider the matter without prejudice, that the story is in reality very different. In the first place, as the furore over royal marriages shows very plainly, we may not wish, ourselves, to remain tied within Victorian 'moral' restrictions, but we are prepared to return wholeheartedly to those restrictions for application to others who are felt to be above the everyday level. In the second place the marked Victorian tendency to conflate morality largely with sex has become for us an inheritance we seem unable and even unwilling to throw off. There is, of course, such a thing as sexual morality, as there is moral and immoral behaviour in other fields; but the fact is that when the word 'moral' is used without any qualification, the automatic assumption tends to be that the reference *must* be to sex – to the extent that some seem even to think that there is no such thing as morality unrelated to sex (a thought which, I have to put it to you, is patently absurd).

It is interesting to see how customs in relation to sex and courtship and marriage have developed in Britain over the last half-century or so, and under what main influences. There are, of course, many influences: I wish to select two only, among the most intimate – from our English-speaking neighbours of the 'special relationship' across the Atlantic, and from our nearer neighbours across the Channel, allied with whom and against whom we have fought so many battles in the past, the French. Taking the latter first: sexual freedom, in the way of more or less open consorting with mistresses, has been for a long time a commonplace in France, whereas in England any revelations of such 'affairs' have been a matter for the most deeply shocked comment, efforts at concealment by the parties concerned being felt, rather, to be a point of honour (is 'honour' an odd word in this context?). Correspondingly, I would suggest, with this attitude, in France free-and-easy courtship between young couples, in the form of relatively unrestrained hugging and kissing (no more than this, I have to add) in public places, has been a not unusual phenomenon, and some may remember, after the last War, quite frequently observing such public encounters in Paris, at a time when in London these things were never to be seen or heard of and would have aroused, at the least, considerable amazement. Today such occurrences of advertised self-indulgence would be passed by with as little remark in London as in Paris; and mistresses have long since ceased – in general, that is – to be a subject only for prurient whisperings.

What, then, of the Americans? The American influence on us since the War has been huge, and I will take up some of the wider aspects, too, in a second. But as to sex and marriage and so forth the matter is clear. Once upon a time we read open-mouthed about the multiplicity of Hollywood marriages and divorces, about the female film-stars who had in succession half-a-dozen husbands or more, and about similar goings-on. Now such apparently frenzied activities have crossed the herring-pond in a big way. We no longer have to look to Hollywood, though our own cases may not always be quite so extreme. Victorian 'morals' have, it would appear, been swept away. What, indeed, can we truly say that we mean by 'morals'? We may well ask ourselves. I will come back to this: it is an investigation of some interest.

The American influence has fallen over us in innumerable other ways too. The capitalist philosophy so stridently preached by Lady Thatcher may have theoretical sources in Adam Smith, but in practical terms it derives at large from the United States of America and from the way of life that has been lived by the people of that country since the last century. The aristocracy of America is, it is evident, the aristocracy of wealth: essentially, the Americans know no other. Hereditary titles have no place in this scheme (hereditary wealth is, of course, quite another matter, a point which may sometimes elude popular attention). The system has been imported here, and has implanted itself firmly, to the extent that whereas titles and other official honours continue with great regularity to be awarded, they are now for much the most part limited to lifetime holding, not intended (with very few, specifically Thatcher-family-type exceptions) to be handed down. American fast food has invaded our towns, as also a great many towns elsewhere. The outstanding item in the American civilian uniform (as we may reasonably call it), in the shape of the baseball cap, if not yet so altogether universal here, from top to bottom of the regime, as in its country of origin, is increasingly visible on every side; and even the language has been affected, deliberately, it would seem, so that *The Times* now, of intention, uses 'presently' in the predominant American sense (meaning 'at present', not 'soon'), and, for some quite unclear reason, has adopted the American 'overly' to express what had hitherto been perfectly adequately indicated by other means. What need to go on? I will mention just one further item. The 'happy birthday to you' sing-song, not so very long ago unknown here or at best a slightly discordant curiosity, has now reached the point where it can be chanted without a tinge of embarrassment to the Queen Mother.

I have nothing whatever against the Americans. They are our good friends, 'special relationship' or no, and there are many aspects of their mode of living which are no doubt worthy of judicious imitation; but I confess that the way in which we actually go about such a process of imitation appears to me ham-fisted and largely indiscriminate – I do not know to what extent simply unconscious ('purely imitative'). Certainly, if they are helping in the demolition of our antiquated honours system, this is, I am sure, deserving in principle of much applause – though whether what is now happening here meets the case adequately is a distinctly more open question: it sometimes seems too rough and ready and piecemeal, and still with too many noticeably automatic or semi-automatic elements, to have much serious significance. As to some of the other items, I think a shrug of the shoulders is as suitable a reaction as any.

Twenty-nine
Sex and Royalty

To return to the subject of sex and royalty, a theme, in combination, which we left a moment ago. It is clear, if we consider the matter objectively, throwing off our prejudices (in most people heavily weighted), that all that the 'royals' have been doing is to follow the current trend, adding nothing to it specifically of their own. If we had been wanting to ask them for a 'moral' lead, it has, it is true, not been forthcoming: it is they who have followed the general lead in this respect, not *vice versa*. But have we any right to expect anything different? In themselves the 'royals' are quite obviously ordinary people, whatever they may have been set up symbolically to stand for, and they have been indulging in at root ordinary practices, no better, no worse. Is there, then, something basically wrong about such practices? I offer no quick and easy answers, but I would suggest at least that the practices have both their good and their bad points: that they may be thought good when carried out openly in the right frame of mind but bad when exercised deceitfully for undesirable ends and when driven to extremes by one or the other party involved (or by both). I am sorry if these words throw only a chink of light and need their own interpretation, but I say again that there are no quick and easy answers. In a difficult and highly imperfect world, the situation revealed is a very normal one, with nothing particularly startling about it.

If once we see the situation as it truly is, then instead of demanding from members of the Royal Family that they supply us with some impossible, and historically quite unrealistic, stainless model of what we are pleased to call 'morality', we should, if we feel, as we may, that our own behaviour in this region has been less than adequate, look to ourselves and ourselves alone for improvement. I daresay this is an unpractical precept, we being as we are, but the fact remains that an external model of the type in question, if it could exist, would in any case not be likely to do us much good.

We live in the climate of the day, in an atmosphere these days of what is described as 'sexual freedom'. If the ordinary man thinks that for him, on the whole, this is a good thing, an advance on older, too tightly restrictive systems, then, in accepting the desirability of such freedom for himself, he deprives himself at the same time of the right to deny it to another person, on whatever social level.

Should we require a straiter rigidity of behaviour from our royalty than the ancient Greeks plainly did from their gods? This may seem an astonishing question, but it is not perhaps entirely off the mark, since our attitude to royalty is not so utterly different in all respects from the Greek attitude to their gods. In each case what is involved is, to a degree, the idealisation of human characteristics and personalities; and, since in the Greek case the idealisation was more complete, one would naturally expect the behavioural requirements laid upon the products of the idealisation to be more complete too – though I have to admit, with regret, that to say what I have just said is to attempt to apply rational criteria to what is in essence an irrational situation. In fact, the one chief thing the question undoubtedly does is to throw into relief the irrationalities in which the situation abounds.

In passing, it also raises another matter; introducing, as it does, the religious theme, which is by no means irrelevant. The Greeks worshipped their gods. We do not officially worship our royalty, but we connect them officially with religious worship none the less. Not being a religious-minded man, I do not feel that I should perhaps go too deeply into this matter, but it certainly seems to me, as it has done to others with possibly more right to speak about these things, that the union in one hand of the formal headship of the lay state in this country with that of an established church has little in the way of genuine validity and nothing in the way of necessity. There is no case, in short, for the King or Queen to be also head of an official Church, and if we take the ill-fitting priestly function away from the monarch, in whose lap it rests owing only to a very rusty historical tradition (doubtfully meaningful at the best of times), we can leave the monarchy then to do its own effective work, in which we need it still to engage, operating from its seat quietly (or as quietly as we will allow) remote from us, removed also from the mayhem and clamorous self-seeking of the political battle.

We came to these questions about British royalty via Plato's *Republic* (see page 132 ff.), and I would like at this stage to repeat some of the things I said at that point, but laying fuller and more direct emphasis on the relationship between the two conceptions. Very different in significant ways though the present-day hereditary British monarchy – totally lacking in any 'philosophic' character – is from Plato's exotic notion, yet it has certain elements in it which correspond closely and curiously with essential elements in the other.

1. The 'philosopher-king' is looked up to for his superior wisdom; the British monarch is looked up to simply for his/her hereditary status: the important thing in this connection is that they are both there to be looked up to, on whatever basis.
2. There is no cause to be wary of the actions of the 'philosopher-king', for he is guided at every turn by right reason; there is no cause to be wary of the actions of the British monarch, because he/she has no effective power (as things are these days) to do anyone any serious degree of personal injury.
3. The 'philosopher-king', being a king, has no need to campaign noisily for election or to offer inevitably, as such campaigners do, a host of unfulfillable promises; the British monarch, being hereditary, is equally free from such undesirable constraints.

In brief, what the British monarchy has developed into (and not perhaps purely and simply by chance) is something having just those qualities of most genuine value in the Platonic picture, but without the unreal imaginary qualities and improbable or frankly impossible characteristics which the Platonic picture displays in misleading prominence. I have a feeling that if Plato himself were here to take cognisance of these developments, he might be much readier than some to approve of them, and in my opinion for the very best of reasons.

Public thinking on sex and morals and such-like being, in the way of things, more than a little confused, it is natural, as I quite appreciate, that widely and gleefully publicised marital difficulties among the 'royals' should lead to those calls we have noted, and particularly perhaps from some of the more rationally-minded thinkers, for the abolition of monarchy – already so much reduced in its powers over its 'subjects' – and for its replacement by purely republican instruments; no account being taken of the considerable consequent disadvantages, which completely, in fact, and heavily outweigh the apparent advantages. In these circumstances, 'Leave well enough alone' would be my motto.

Among the marital differences and difficulties in question, those that have eventually arisen at almost the very apex, between the Prince and Princess of Wales, not surprisingly bulk very large. I have no desire to make any great efforts here to probe deeply below the surface – others with possibly less compunction about failing maybe to distinguish adequately between fact and highly-coloured fancy may be left to do their own no doubt satisfying researches in that region – but I cannot forbear to make a few passing comments, if I am allowed.

Of the Princess I wish to say only this: that I cannot help seeing her as an extremely self-willed young woman, with a keen and skilful eye to personal publicity, and determined at all costs to get her own way, whatever the effects on some of those about her – or for that matter on the whole institution of British monarchy, for which I would venture to suggest that she may have at best little care. It may perhaps not be so extraordinary, if obviously undesirable, that her husband, in the circumstances, sought or continued to seek some romantic consolation elsewhere (on conjectures, or more, not unexpected, that she may not, in due course, at least, have been free from such liaisons herself I have no comment to make), and if illicit eavesdroppers, early on, captured on tape, and broadcast world-wide, certain of his more intimate resulting telephone-conversations, that was his misfortune. On this last I do however have some general points to put forward: first of all, supposing, that is, that we assume the tape in question to be fully authentic, it must be said that the really grave offence was evidently that committed by the intruder without leave upon a private conversation, to the end of purely personal profit (the commonest of all motives these days). Profit on the basis, clearly well founded, of the recording's likely appeal to the global public's least admirable instincts. If that offence has not, I am sure, been altogether overlooked, it has too often nevertheless been glossed over and pressed into the background in favour of a mainly prurient concentration by the public, at the receiving end, upon aspects of the tape's content, including – a point worth considering in itself – what have been claimed to be the latter's verbal infelicities.

Note how the public's interest, being, as must be sadly admitted, primarily salacious, has tended very much to concentrate itself upon altogether the wrong things (indeed to an extent upon complete trivialities). The main point to take into account should surely have been that we have, in this surreptitiously obtained recording, apparently a married man communicating sweet telephonic nothings to one who was at the time the wife of another. How far ought we to construe this as a straightforward moral offence, according to the standards of our day? If we are to be perfectly honest with ourselves, if we know how to be, the truth is that, in the end, we cannot be really absolutely sure. The precise emotional and formal relationship of each participant to his or her legal spouse is something beyond our ken (on the Prince's side we do know something about it, but by no means everything of any importance), and this is a matter of more than passing relevance. To that extent it would certainly be reasonable (and rational) on the whole to suspend judgement; but what strikes me here is that, according to Press reports, which I have to confess have been my only source of information, public interest seems to have concerned itself little with such niceties, preferring instead to dwell much more on what are clearly total side-issues – including, as I have noted, on words, on language, on terms of endearment, on tones of voice – which have little enough bearing on matters of any major significance (though, published in this way to an unintended global audience, they do help to damage the dignity of the speakers). They are lapped up nevertheless for the most part with obvious under-the-counter relish or with hypocritical displays of (quite evidently pretended) shock.

I must limit this discussion; but I think I can at least ask: in the matter of language, what on earth could anyone expect to find in an intimate private conversation of this character, not for an instant meant for broadcast circulation or indeed for any kind or shred of notice from outside? Are the speakers to be condemned or scorned because they lapse from the highest ideals of literary excellence? Did those who bubbled over with unthinking and excited laughter as they read the recorded words imagine for a moment how some of their own telephone conversations might seem if subjected to the same close examination in print, or when, having been recorded, they were replayed cold? The fact is that if the recorded conversation were to present itself in what we might consider an acceptable manner when in print or when replayed, it would probably have sounded intolerably stilted at the time of delivery. What fault there is lies not with the speakers, but with those who have intruded upon and (in intention and in effect) misrepresented them. This brings us round again, appropriately enough, to not far from where we started.

Thirty

Sex and the Moral Question in General

Let us leave at this point the moral trials and tribulations of British royalty in our latter day, together with the unhappy perplexities aroused in some of their subjects as a consequence, and pass to a much broader field of moral inquiry but, in its way, a connected one. I have spoken of the close link in the public mind between morality and sex, so that at times it may appear that the two are bound up together quite inextricably and can hardly be conceived of apart. I do not think it should need microscopic consideration to show that such a point of view holds no water: sexual activities may impinge on moral issues in very many regards, but it is surely not altogether impossible to think of them outside such a framework and unrelated to it; and as to moral criteria, certainly they may be applied to sex, as so frequently they are, but they need to be applied just as much and just as emphatically to all sorts of other, wider aspects of our human activities, many of them obviously quite remote from any sexual implications. Why, one must therefore ask, do we tend so readily to conflate the two elements, in our thought and utterance, into one composite and apparently indissoluble unity?

I do not think the answer may actually be so far to seek. If the view I have expressed of what is the ultimate driving force behind all terrestrial endeavour is correct, then the striving to perpetuate the community's existence is at the root of everything we undertake, however blindly and indiscriminately the motivation operates and however sometimes apparently in opposition to its own interests. In these circumstances sex comes automatically to the forefront in our activities, since community perpetuation requires it and would not be possible without it, and, once moral considerations come into play, whatever their origins, sex and morals cannot avoid reacting very strongly on one another in certain leading respects, particularly in view of the great emotional hold which sex naturally has on many or most of us.

But what I am truly concerned with is not sex as such (I hope this will not unduly disappoint some of my readers) but the whole question of morality, of what it really is and how it comes into being in our conceptions and of how and why we look to it, and to the basis on which we may imagine that it stands, to cope with some of our deepest problems and inquiries and hesitations. Behind all this there lies, it would appear, a huge anomaly.

The anomaly is fairly simple to set out. We are descended, at no vast remove comparatively speaking, from beasts of prey, and we continue to share some of their outstanding characteristics. The beast of prey has no knowledge of morality. What it does know, by its instincts, is that it needs to protect and, as far as it absolutely can, provide for the survival of itself and its brood, and by every means at its disposal. The means both of protection and, to an extent, of provision too are limited originally largely to the personal apparatus of tooth and claw, and, on a broader (tactical) basis, to the ambush, but these it uses ruthlessly to attain its ends, the ends which Nature has firmly and without qualification established for it. The chief thing differentiating us in essence, as human beings, from the beast of prey as we have just described it is the development in us of a highly conscious, ratiocinative awareness of what we are about – what we are about in at least (for most of us) immediate terms (the long-sighted are in this respect very few and far between) – combined with the development at the same time of a quite new power of articulate communication immensely facilitating intercourse and making cooperative planning between individuals and groups available in a manner and on a scale as never before: none of this has however necessarily any profound effect on the character of the basic urges, implanted deeply in us by Nature, which stimulate our actions and have done so from the word 'go'. We are still concerned primarily with the business of survival in one way or another, starting from ourselves as individuals as necessary centre, but extending outwards in varying degrees to kin and connections.

In the struggle for survival we make use of all the techniques instinctively natural to the brute beast, but we do so, for the major part, in a considerably more refined and subtle fashion. That is to say that we do not always, for example, have to aim at the physical maiming or destruction of other living beings standing in our way but are able instead frequently to achieve the power and status required for the expansion of our possessions, and promotion of ourselves and our case, by fraud and lying and general manipulation of events without particular consideration for anyone outside us, so as to turn things in our favour – and not always, if we are clever enough, at the cost of any genuine personal risk. These means and methods are publicly well enough known on the whole, and are sometimes frowned on officially when they become too obvious, but they remain a persistent accompaniment of what we have learned to call civilisation and are apparently inseparable from it. Those who indulge in the practices concerned often do so, openly and cheerfully, in a surprisingly big way.

Some of the anomaly should have become already clear from certain of the expressions I have had to employ in describing the situation. I have used the words 'fraud' and 'lying' – pejorative words with plainly moral implications – and I have spoken of the methods and techniques in question being "sometimes frowned on officially when they become too obvious" (see previous paragraph), which evidently brings moral criteria forthrightly into the picture. What we have before us is thus a state of things generally accepted, but containing in itself nevertheless a continuing flow of significant elements in human activity which, while accepted, and to a very large extent openly, are not thought strictly 'acceptable'. We divide things into 'good' and 'bad', but many actions which we are fully prepared to countenance in our ordinary lives (sometimes, it is true enough, under the force of circumstances rather than by positive choice), whether executed by others or by ourselves, are not classifiable by us as 'good' – not, that is, unless we see 'good' as merely an alternative term for 'useful' or 'profitable', which, however, seems immediately to deprive it of any universality, since what is 'useful' or 'profitable' to one person may often be quite the opposite in reality to another. Though 'good' and 'bad', like multitudes of other words, can have wide semantic possibilities of application, the sense I necessarily have in mind here is the fundamental, ethical sense, where absolute (as distinct from relative) and universal values are considered to apply. If now we still wish to equate 'good' with 'useful' or 'profitable' we can only do so (but we can do so) if we think of the two latter as somehow so for *everybody* and in, no doubt, the long run.

The beasts follow Nature's plan for them – 'the law of the jungle' – straightforwardly and freely, without any theoretical moral standards to guide them or to confuse them. We, in practice, live by much the same pattern, but acknowledging at the same time in theory a 'higher' law, the moral law, of which our conscious interpretations may vary a good deal (from person to person, from group to group, from time to time) but whose edicts nevertheless at certain cardinal points seem quite clearly to run counter to the socially accepted procedures of our natural and normal behaviour, causing a severe conflict in us of ideas and ideals, and without solution. Where does this 'higher' law come from? What is its intention? How do we need to adjust ourselves to it, and how shall we be able to make such an adjustment? Some would no doubt deny that the adjustment is really necessary at all, but at least the problem is impossible to ignore.

The source most often claimed for the moral law is the word of God. How can we say that we know the word of God? By Scripture, we are told: "It is written". These inscribed records, in which absolute faith is required, purport to be the actual word of God as transmitted to mankind through the mouths of His terrestrial messengers, the holy Prophets and the super-Prophets, the Messiah or Messiahs. This statement that I have just made is an extremely condensed, but yet I hope fair, representation of a proposition or set of propositions – not peculiar, in this general form, to one particular religion but common ground to a number, attributing to themselves considerable authority – which have in fact provided material for many theologies, developed often at great length. I am sorry, however, that for me (I am not alone, I am sure) this formulation of a solid basis for morality fails at the first test.

Nothing can offer any valid guarantee that such-and-such words are genuinely 'words of God'. It has to be proved, to begin with, that such a being as God exists at all, of which we have nothing remotely amounting to reliable proof, however many inferences may be drawn, at second or third or other hand, from carefully selected events, selected often with some skill, by convinced believers. (The fact that many and many generations of men have indubitably believed firmly in the notion of divinity, whether in the shape of a single divine godhead or as in earlier times of a multiplicity, tells us in effect nothing except that mankind needs, despite lack of serious evidence, to support itself in its fundamental weakness by the assumption of a superior governing superhuman power above it capable of responding to its prayers and affording help in its recurring tribulations.) But, apart from this basic unfulfilled requirement, which we have indeed no way of meeting, how readily are we to accept – assuming, let us suppose, that there is, after all, a God of some kind – the absolute authenticity of some person's claim, in, say, or after a trance, to be inspired by God, from Whom he or she announces the delivery of such-and-such a very special message?

The avowed Prophet himself or herself may be absolutely sincere: that is not the point. The message itself may even, in appropriate circumstances, appeal, perhaps profoundly, to a discriminating intelligence: that is, surely, not necessarily the point either. The point is that if we look to God as a justification, an authority, there is no such justification or authority truly available to us – whether a God is assumed to exist or not. As to the matter of "It is written", we are, I fear, long past the time when the written word was new and strange and somehow magical in quality, and able to inspire unquestioning belief purely on the basis of its written character. (This that I am writing now is, after all, 'written' too, but that proves nothing about its validity, and I cannot see that the fact that certain other written words were written a long time ago adds much in itself to their credibility – it could do the opposite.) And further, as to faith, why should we be expected, at whoever's behest, to set aside our reasoning faculties (also, no doubt, God-given?) in favour of an unsupported declaration in solemn tones from without?

On a completely different tack: why, if God is the all-powerful being He is normally in the monotheistic creed propounded to be, does He, in the guise of Nature, lay down for the animals a set of values which we, as animals, naturally continue to follow, but then lay down for us as reasoning human beings (but still, nevertheless, animals) another more complicated set of values, in opposition in many ways to the first, to confuse the issues; or rather, having laid down the first, apparently immutably, then over an extended period lead us by gradual steps into the second, without even effectively countermanding the first, so that, in the result, we are left floundering between the two, hardly knowing properly at times which is which, or how suitably to defend one against the other?

Thirty-one

Morality and the Community

I think it is time to leave such questions as those of Scripture and divine authority, which evidently throw little direct light on the subject we have in mind, and return to our original thesis, concerning the community and its insistent pressure for survival, to see how far this can provide us with possible clues about the nature of morality. On first sight it appears to provide us with few such clues: if our whole basic purpose is to survive, or to promote survival, then surely the only true morality for us is to use every means at our disposal, without check, to achieve that purpose, which involves employing in principle the methods developed by our brute ancestors but applying to them the highly sophisticated techniques of which, as human beings, we have found ourselves capable. Up to a point there is no doubt that this is just what most people, or at least if they have any practical ability, do, or attempt to do. (There are some significant exceptions which I will look at in due course.) 'Morality', as preached and prescribed, now and then through legal rulings, throws up against these people's material advancement in the world certain prohibitions of a greater or lesser kind which such people clearly do not like, and which they will either ignore, if they can do so with impunity, or do their best to circumvent, by 'fair' means or foul. 'Morality', I have said, as preached and prescribed... but where, then, does this come from? We seem to be no further forward.

Yet is this not too brief and superficial a glance? The essence of the matter lies in our interpretation of the word 'community'. It is a word with no sharp and obvious limits to its meaning: there can be vast communities and there can be tiny ones; but in our usage, if we look at it squarely and objectively, there can be only one eventual meaning which adequately and truly fits the case – no less indeed than the community of mankind, the whole of mankind, for that, without restrictions, must surely be the group whose survival is ultimately in play, whatever may happen, in the course of human development, to the smaller communities which at any moment the great community contains and which constantly rise and fall and rise and fall within it.

Does this throw a gleam of light on the object of our search? I think it evident that it does, but not by any means in such a way that the answer to the fundamental problem becomes immediately self-clarificatory. The situation is a highly complex one – otherwise it would be much more easily understood – and some at least of its involvements require to be pursued and disentangled. In the process I shall have to go over again some of the ground already covered, but it will not be mere repetition.

The community has no existence except through its members: without members it disappears, but this is the prime outcome which it is essential for it to avoid. Lesser communities act, in a variety of ways, as members of more comprehensive communities, but the final descending member of all is the individual, not himself or herself a community but in some measure or another the representative of community at all its stages, and emphatically and in particular of the overriding community of all communities (whatever and wherever that may be).

The community can reproduce itself, which it must constantly do, only through the individual. It is in the individual, therefore, that the reproductive urge necessary for effective propagation has to be implanted – strongly, as we find, in some, less strongly or more waywardly in others, according to the customary methods of Nature, which varies its offspring (if we may so call them) to achieve the widest spread of significant possibilities. But the reproductive urge is by no means the only urge that Nature implants. The individual not only is but must feel himself to be the representative of the community, so as the more vigorously to pursue and promote the community's value and values. This feeling operates in the human individual through what is known as the ego, a driving force which impels him or, on the same principle, if not always in the same way, her to concentrate himself/herself on his/her own needs and personality as the mid-point of his/her world – not merely, perhaps, in all cases as the community's representative but now and then as if he/she were, somehow, the very community itself (an enormous and unhappy exaggeration at all times). As far as mankind is concerned,

Nature's latest addition to the armoury of characteristics supplied by her is the facilitating power of reason, increasing freedom and the field of action by providing the ability to calculate, including, if not only, by strictly mathematical means, on eventually a formidable scale.

The provision of powers is no guarantee whatsoever of their appropriate use. This is the type of statement which, when made, may seem almost a truism; yet it is remarkable how little it appears to be generally understood. How often do we hear, uttered in tones of awe, "He's a very clever man", with the clear implication that his judgement is therefore not open to question. On the contrary: the cleverer he is, the more careful in every way should he and others be about the quality of his judgement and the danger of trusting too confidently in it. Dazzled by his own spectacular brilliance, he is liable, indeed all too likely, to fail to perceive, outside the excellently-lit area of his immediate awareness, a variety of dark pitfalls whose threatening presence a lesser but more cautious man would conceivably be willing to treat with a great deal more respect.

While reason and its accompaniments are able to grant dominion over the brute beasts, who are lacking in any such weapons with which to defend themselves, and while mankind is assured also, by these valuable aids, of the achievement of material success in the subjugation, in course of time, of some of Nature's ultimate elements to his uses and increasing needs over an extensive range, there is one significant area within which the admirable faculties of his intelligence have, in at least their long-drawn initial stages (not yet at an end), too little positive effect, that is, in regard to the mastery of himself and his primitive and unbounded desires, desires developed on the basis of the natural urges deeply implanted in him, as described, and for the ends suggested, but left for him himself to shape and direct and hold under constraint. In bestowing upon man the inestimable gift of reason, Nature, in Nature's way, offers no precise indication of how its gift can be best used; reason, once there, is left to its own devices, to work out its own salvation; and any man has the power, if he so wishes, to turn the gift against another man – which often seems to him as good a thing to do as any other thing, or so it would appear.

The three fields I have here distinguished from each other – relating to the 'lower' animals (together with which we may classify, for greater completeness, insects and plants), the inanimate natural elements, and man himself – and the degree of mankind's undeniable success, within at least a certain range, in coping with and overcoming the pressures and resistances of the first two, while undergoing in the same breath evident failure so far (I fear), in, from some aspects, extreme and threatening form, in his handling of the last, produce, *in toto*, a picture which may not, in the upshot, be too difficult to make sense of in its underlying human causality. The connection binding the three fields, in regard to the human approach, is the concept of power – power, which is perhaps the greatest generalised driving force of all in the human consciousness, and with the widest sphere of applicability in its practical operation – and with this goes the fact that the pursuit of power, through reason, over the unreasoning would appear to have every prospect of a successful and in most ways satisfactory conclusion, whereas the pursuit of power, through reason, over opposing reason has no such obvious and satisfying ultimate end, whatever may be some of its short-term results in one way or another.

Thirty-two
Power and Glory

In building up dominion over his surroundings, man has no hesitation in proceeding to the assault on other men whom he may defeat or by whom he may be defeated according to the fortunes of war. In the process larger and smaller groups and hierarchies form themselves, with, in each, one at the head whose qualities, real or ostensible, give him the power to issue commands which others below must obey, leading to the perpetuation of a system of inbred inequalities such as we know well through experience and through the historical record.

In the event the human ego, arising, in its self-awareness and compulsive need for self-expression and for the imposition of itself upon its environment, in origin from the community and from the community's requirement to make itself known and felt in the only way it can, through its fleshly representative, the individual – the ego when, as may happen, it finds itself in one of the superior positions in the group, and in circumstances where it can spread itself apparently without hindrance, being carried as it is on the shoulders of other individualities subordinate to it and to its aims and desires, when indeed no wind seems for the time being capable of blowing with any effective force against it, runs the danger of unreasonably inflating itself and of behaving as if laws which were fully appropriate for others were of no relevance for itself. Thus, there are, for example, in the purely civilian world of everyday, the tycoons, the men at the head of 'big business', who, as already noted, while pressing their subordinates as hard as they can to accept minimal increases in their pay, regardless of what may be their needs, are prepared when it comes to themselves to demand and receive increases of fifty, sixty or more percent on already enormous salaries, though this has self-evidently nothing whatever to do with needs and is patently intended purely and simply for outward show. (The excuses usually put forward for this sort of behaviour, which its practitioners do from time to time realise requires a modicum of explanation, are, it appears to me, uniformly quite preposterous, and not worthy of any serious consideration. They have everything to do with an insistent, ceaseless vying for top place, and absolutely nothing to do with the needs and down-to-earth necessities of normal, even normally luxurious existence.)

The business world is in its ultimate reality no more, as one may well say, than a second-order world, mimicking closely in some of the principal characteristics it displays the manners and the ethos of the world of warfare, whose activities are the type of what is considered by a great many highly influential persons, following age-old tradition and practice, to be somehow basic to all that goes on, the model of all activity. It may be worthwhile, accordingly, to cast a glance at a frequently repeated incident in past wars which reflects or foreshadows, with transparent clarity, to those at any rate willing to take the point, a significant aspect of business behaviour. While it is true on the one hand that there are accounts, no doubt in many cases entirely authentic, of warrior leaders who have fought with passion and intensity at the head of their troops and, when the battle has gone against them, have perished, still striving valiantly, at the forefront of the fray, there are, on the other hand, many other, fully authenticated accounts, particularly from the more modern times, of those who have watched the battle keenly from afar but, when once the tide has been seen to turn with irretrievable certainty against their battered armies, have had one thought only, to save their own skins from the wrath to come, and have fled like fury, without a glance behind them, from the destruction now in implacable descent upon the heads of their unfortunate defenders. This is the model by which the present-day tycoon guides his passage.

I had better put a little more light and shade into my picture of the varying behaviour of the national leader at a critical moment in time of war. Dying at the head of one's troops is hardly a modern practice: it belongs, in its origins, above all to the days of the tribal chieftain, the ruler and principal administrator in peace and the personal leader in war; and it is his place, which he cannot easily avoid, to take the rough with the smooth in the carrying-out of his functions. In the days of more complex state organisation, overall leadership is separated from leadership in the field, and the latter is delegated to a general or generals, who, indeed, without doubt for the best of reasons, may not even themselves operate anywhere in the vanguard of their troops: it is to this situation that we owe the spectacle of the fleeing leader; and what lies behind his flight and the manner of it we will look into more closely a little later. I should add on the other side of the picture that in the most recent days, with some of the more vicious elements in war, always unquestionably present, now showing up much more clearly, and with deeper offensiveness to tenderer modern susceptibilities, the possibilities of personal escape for a defeated leader – for one thing, no longer so readily granted the respect by his enemies once thought to be his due, even in defeat – have become considerably narrowed down, though this does not apply with anything like such certainty to all his henchmen.

To return to our comparison: the soldiers of the militant leader, the active war-maker, may not be exactly represented by the various staff and the shareholders and so forth of the tycoon's empire, but the parallel is near enough nevertheless for our present purpose (note the common expression 'workforce') – and in any case, as to precise similarity, even different superior authorities in relation to the waging of war itself, and such matters, are unlikely ever to repeat with any measure of preciseness each other's style and organisation. The basic point is that the attitude of the two classes of commanding authority, of what I have called the militant leader, glimpsed at a moment of battle, on the one side, of the commercial and purely civilian ones on the other, to the inferior masses whom they need for their support (as distinct from their attitude to themselves and to their personal survival in the face of strenuous opposition) is essentially the same. The supporting forces are in both cases considered essentially expendable. The militant leader, when things go utterly wrong, is concerned above all for his own safety, if that is in any way achievable (true that in some quite modern periods it may perhaps not have been, which was just his bad luck); the tycoon makes sure above all of his own complete financial protection in all conceivable circumstances: not only does he make certain that his own rewards are always huge in relation to those of his staff and underlings, or at least to the great body of those individuals (some of the higher placed may have learnt the game too well to be so treated), but he sees to it that if things should go against him and he should be forced out of office, at whatever stage and for whatever reason, even demonstrably through his own fault – provided, of course, that there have arisen no awkward complications in law, which may occasionally happen – he will retire from the immediate limelight with a pay-off of very considerable dimensions.

The psychological position is in fact noticeably clearer in the case of the tycoon than in that of the war chief (or wartime head of government), though that does not diminish the comparison; rather it clarifies it, the special problems (and the special hazards and the wider range) of the latter-named tending to obscure the fundamental issue. The tycoon has simply and obviously himself in mind from the start, and pretends to nothing or nothing much more. He is the high-flyer, the achiever, and so forth. The human means outside himself which he uses to attain his ends and ambitions are no more than his pawns – a not inapt figure – and that is really all there is to it. Any apparent outward modifications of such an attitude are as a rule, whatever the impression given, largely for the sake of furthering the original and still, in itself, totally unaltered intention. This attitude can be transferred *in toto* to our picture of the overriding war chief – certainly in the case of aggressive war – on which it throws abundant light, light in its turn reflected back in fullness on the tycoon, whose outlook and inner motivation thus become yet plainer to be seen.

So, oddly enough, the militant leader, flying at speed from the bloody havoc of his army's rout, is not necessarily to be thought of as showing in any primary degree personal cowardice, and perhaps indeed – incredibly – not at all so, since his behaviour in this instance is altogether of a piece with his attitude in general to the mass of his supporters at all relevant times, quite regardless of any specific and perhaps largely automatic accompanying reactions on his part, of the manner of bravery or its opposite, to particular incidents. The fact is that, for him, as for the commercial tycoon, from the beginning and throughout, he himself has been absolutely all that matters. His view of the men in his forces is essentially Napoleonic, in the sense that he sees their whole function as being simply to fight and, where need be, as now, die for him, that it is not his place to die for anything or anybody, and, if he can make good his escape, he will, for that is his proper line of action under these conditions, if only so that he may live to fight again another day. He is in all respects above the fray; his men are merely what has been popularly known, since at least the First World War, as 'cannon fodder'. To him they are not individuals but puppets; they exist on his behalf, he does not exist on theirs, he is not in the least emotionally or spiritually involved with them, his relation to them is only to command them. Their lives, their thoughts, their inner feelings, their families and loved ones, are nothing whatever to him, nothing: in a way, he does not acknowledge that such things are even entirely real, certainly not one small fraction as real as his own needs, his own overpowering and god-like personality.

This class of approach, so described, might seem at first to belong especially to warfare and to those who rule the roost in warfare; but I think I have already shown plainly enough that it is not so at all. And if it is not something peculiar to the state of war, nor is it either some rare phenomenon to be seen only now and then, at the most perilous turning-points of history: on the contrary, it not only apparently emerges of its own accord independently of circumstances of war or peace, but it does so with all frequency, on all sides, in times and places near and far apart, in every kind of culture. It is a commonplace of living, constantly repeating itself, on a large and a small scale, wherever we look – in war, in peace, or occasionally in activities where the two are barely distinguishable from one another except perhaps that actual war has greater persistence and intensity and demands (even if it does not always receive) a greater degree of overall organisation.

We live, all of us, very much in a fantasy world; but the imperious, totally inward-absorbed world of which I speak presents us with fantasy of a profound and formidable kind – destructive delusion, of self and others, pushed to a high and dangerous peak. All that is wanted to bring it into full being on some level of activity or another is for one person, with skill and aggressive drive and good fortune to back him or her (and not necessarily with actually the acutest of intelligence, which is always liable to be something of a hindrance), to set himself or herself up as a superior person, a leader, above the throng, and for others to be prepared to yield up their independence or an important part of it in order it to secure his or her protection, obeying him or her and helping to carry out his or her enterprises, as the led: we see it happening everywhere about us in some shape or another, and unceasingly. It is not in any degree a new phenomenon: it goes back as far as we can trace, though no lessons seem ever to have been learnt from it. But if it is not in itself new, there are these days new weapons at its disposal (and some of them, in some contexts, are extremely dangerous).

Any major players in this game – and there will always be numbers of them about, and an army of apprentices coming up behind them – are not likely to preoccupy themselves overmuch with requirements of morality, however defined, or of legality. In regard to the last, their general view will undoubtedly be that human laws and regulations are for the most part pusillanimous intrusions into the life and freedom of action of the outstanding personality, the entrepreneur or whatever he or she may be. 'Freedom' is a note much sounded by such individuals, if not always with the clearest of reference (and see, of course, 'free market'). The model is the buccaneer, whose standards we have earlier remarked upon, and the relevant vocabulary, relating to the buccaneer and buccaneering, is often used in the context, almost always with unqualified admiration.

So we come back most forcibly to the question which pressed itself upon us – how and why, in the face of a universal system so obviously and indeed overwhelmingly favourable to the unfettered expression of 'individuality', a system governed effectively by no laws other than those we are accustomed to denote 'the laws of the jungle', does there arise nevertheless a strange counter-system, a clear set of principles in many ways explicitly contradictory of the original laws just mentioned and offering us (certainly, it would seem) no superior profits, such as to make these principles in any respect apparently better worth our while to use as basis for the conduct of our affairs? The principles of 'morality', of justice, of equity and so forth – so often in practice, as we are aware, totally ignored – are, still, preached at us daily and laid down as the foundation of what is 'right' and 'good' to guide us in all that we do. What does this mean? Is it merely to be viewed as some wily and elaborate device conceived and concerted among those in charge to keep their subordinates in order – to ensure these latter's continued humble obedience while they themselves proceed freely in whatever way they think fit, without restrictions of any kind on their own behaviour, and in pursuit simply of their own self-satisfaction and personal aggrandisement? Some have thought this to be so, and it is not beyond understanding that they should have done so, seeing as we do what goes on everywhere about us and at all times, with the powerful doing their best to hold the less well-endowed masses under as heavy constraint as possible, while in the same breath doing all they can to keep constraints of any sort off their own shoulders.

This notion, that morality and law are nothing but conspiratorial devices of the powerful to perpetuate their power, is an interesting one but to me unpersuasive. However, before I say briefly why, I feel I should return again for a moment or two to what I had been saying just before, and offer something additional by way of background comment.

Thirty-three

The Nature of the Ego

I had been speaking of the ego and of the dangers thrust by it, in certain of its more sinister manifestations, upon the world about it. I need, I think, to go a little more deeply into the question of the ego and what it is, and of our experience of it. The truth is that our experience of the ego is a totally inward experience, which no one can undergo of any person other than himself or herself. We have no first-hand contact with any ego other than our own. We judge of the existence of other egos by the fact that we are aware of other persons outside ourselves resembling us in general appearance and behaviour and presumably therefore having also inner experiences not unlike ours, particularly as we are able to communicate articulately with them. But, although we can perfectly well see ourselves too from the *outside* by reflection, say in a looking glass, there are no practical means imaginable by which we can see others too from the *inside* as we ordinarily see ourselves. In fact it is necessary to go further: I have said 'we' and 'our' but the ultimate truth is that the only ego of which I personally, the writer, can possibly have any first-hand experience is my own. I know nothing, except by analogy, of yours or of anyone else's.

Philosophic systems have been built up upon this perception. Some thinkers have taken it so much at its face value as to be prepared to reduce the world in its entirety (in thought, if not in everyday practice) to the illusion of a single isolated individual. Others, while basing themselves with full acceptance on the same original viewpoint, which, indeed, it is impossible to contradict, are more optimistic – I mean the word metaphysically, that is to say in relation to the assessment of the possibilities of knowledge – and, starting from a world of apparent illusion, are able nevertheless, by cunning argument, to restore to us, as they assert, the world we thought for a moment to have lost.

"*Cogito ergo sum*", said Descartes, "I think therefore I am". This is often read as being intended to suggest that thought is in some way the cause of being, or at least that it is the chief characteristic of being (or maybe of the completest being). In fact, as it stands, and in its context, it can hardly mean this, whatever may have been in due course faultily deduced from it, by Descartes as well as others. What Descartes was actually saying here was that I may argue everything away, by asserting that nothing exists outside my bare thought – except only that there remains one thing which I cannot argue away, and that is the thought itself. And if my thought is real, then I who think it am real too (though the precise meaning of 'I' here, it must be said, is problematic). I think and, therefore, I am bound to infer that I am. Having satisfactorily demonstrated which, as he feels, he proceeds, by elaborate sleight of hand, to reconstruct, on this base, and to restore to us the whole universe (as then known to him), including and in particular the existence of God – a tall order, as some may think, but carried out with whole-hearted assurance and enthusiasm; and indeed there may even be a good deal in certain of the things that he says, but his preferred interpretation of some of the facts he adduces is frequently and seriously open to question.

I do not know, I must admit, how anyone could ever *prove* the world's existence and what goes with it. We have, as far as I can see, to take it simply on trust: I do not know that we really have much option. If this is so, and the whole of what we are pleased to call reality, save the central ego – apart, at least, from the abstract formulas of mathematics, an exception, perhaps, of some significance – is founded on a huge and unprovable assumption, then what objection can we have, so the religious-minded may well ask, to the requirement, so often pressed by them upon us, of *faith* in religious belief? A good question; but there would seem to me to be some nice points of difference. The religious world is at least one stage further away than the world of sight and touch and sound and smell from the little we can truly be sure of – and if reality itself is after all mostly illusion, then what are we to say of this further-off, unobserved and unsensed world, however much we might desire it to be real – or super-real? I referred, a line or two back, to mathematical truths, which can evidently give us some sort of authentic foothold in the world we know (or think we know); but what relationship can we claim them to bear to the realms of God? And finally, what of the great God himself? Can we believe without faltering in a personal, All-powerful, All-wise, benevolent Creator of a world which, as we know all too well, is so hideous in some of its characteristics and propensities, however charming and attractive in others? In this context the attempt to blame all the evils of the world on man alone is, even with all man's obvious and horrifying imperfections, extraordinarily feeble, denying by implication most of the Creator's alleged fundamental qualities as quoted above, and offering no explanation on His behalf for the sufferings of the innocent. And what of predators and prey in the animal world, or of earthquakes and other such natural disasters? (Or are we to think of a personal God and a personal Devil fighting it out between themselves over the ages?)

It is surely just a trifle more plausible to posit at the foundations of reality some quite impersonal force, unconcerned, whether in one way or the other, about individual suffering, a force whose progress and techniques of operation can be traced and analysed in the things that actually happen all around us (I have reverted now to assuming the world to be as it appears to be, in general terms at least), without calling in aid divine or quasi-divine interferences beyond the scope of our reason to grapple with. Conscious personality as we know it and conceive of it is not something which controls the process described: it is something which emerges from the process. If this is in some respects avowedly difficult to take, it is not half so difficult as the tissue of improbabilities and flat self-contradictions which constitutes (and invalidates) the alternative.

Back again now to the ego and to the problems which its nature creates for it. The ego is a closed-in system, having no access to other egos except through intermediary representations, and with absolutely no possibility of actively experiencing the ego-reality behind any such representations. The fact that no ego, thus, can ever experience any other ego in the way that it experiences itself has some unfortunate results. It tends to lead – it is not hard to see why – to an unbalanced self-emphasis, whether of unreasoned self-magnification or the opposite. The two tendencies can exist together – and without necessarily very visible contradiction, as seen from the outside – in the same person, but one is always more marked than the other, and it is the dangers especially attending the first which require to be dwelt upon, and to which I have devoted some space.

Self-obsession, in the form of self-aggrandisement, accompanied by large (or entire) lack of thought and feeling for others, is no rare thing, and what I have said about the ego may help to explain it. An alien experience, in which one can in no way directly participate, is easy to treat as of no account. On the other hand an isolated and unbridgeable inner experience, which is of and to oneself alone, can easily inflate itself to the apparent status of, as it were, the whole world and universe. In this circumstance the God whom we are so eager to celebrate becomes subsumed into the self. Every man – or woman – then becomes his/her own Messiah, openly or not, with, in extreme cases, the urge and, too frequently, dreadful opportunity to draw all about himself or herself to an envisaged or unenvisaged doom.

The above description is an approach of its own kind – and I believe it should be seen as a very recognisable one – to my basic thesis of what happens when an individual identifies himself too closely with the community of which he is in reality never anything more than a single exceedingly short-term representative. We will all have at one time or another heard the colloquial expression, used of some excessively pompous and conceited person, "He thinks he's everybody", an unanalysed reference to the identification I speak of, an identification wholly overlooking the subject's essential impermanence and severely limited practical effectiveness in favour of what is ultimately a grotesque self-expansion into and, for that matter, beyond all the wastes of space and time. A 'self-made' man indeed!

It is easy to see how and why, in such circumstances, the feeling makes itself strongly evident in not a few minds that morality and moral standards may be appropriate regulators of behaviour for other, lesser fry – but not, or hardly at all, for the great Self, whose duty it is to break as free from all shackles and hindrances as it is able to do (a feeling in patent contrast to a general attitude prevailing on the other hand among the indeterminate mass of those at the opposite end of the scale, who appear to have a positive yearning for external checks and well-defined limits to show them where they are and in which direction they should be pointing their otherwise uncertain steps; though it is to be observed nevertheless that they may not be without their own minor Messianic urges, through the self-powered and self-supporting medium of groups and mobs from time to time). Even so, the theory that I mentioned a little earlier and left temporarily in the air, that the whole idea of moral inhibition was invented purely in order to keep underlings firmly – indeed brutally – in their place, is not in my view a sustainable proposition.

Who, originally, could have deliberately concocted such a scheme, and how and by whom could its long and lasting and developing tradition have been in so cunning a manner coordinated and transmitted across continents and centuries secretly and yet, in a way, openly? True that by a natural enough opportunism those in authority have frequently made use of the notion of the moral code, in one distorted form or another, as a method of control of those subject at the time to their orders (themselves ignoring any such imposition on their activities), but this, as I say, is opportunism, for a specific (and malign) purpose, but it is not in any sense original creation. There is no doubt, in my opinion, that we must look quite elsewhere for the source of what we are discussing – for the source, that is, ultimately, of a concept which lies at the root of all moral codes, however much they may vary in detail from one another, the concept of an absolute moral imperative, of universal application.

Thirty-four

How Do Moral Codes Arise?

The concept of some kind of moral imperative has its origin in the self-illuminating mind of the human race. It has no place in the animal brain: the animal, as such, is governed by instinct, which impels it, on the one hand, to feed – now alone, now in gangs, now by nourishing itself on the earth's produce, now by preying on other animals – and, on the other, to breed and to proliferate, with all that accompanies these activities. It can hardly be thought that the brute beast is capable of conceiving deliberate principles of action, or the idea of them. It is only in man that such developments can become articulate, wherever it may be that they come from. And as we know full well, these developments, while in some ways they operate to extend enormously the range of animal-type activity, in other ways act flatly to countermand such activity.

The moral imperative says nothing in itself about what precisely is or is not to be considered moral – about what ought or ought not to be done, from the purely moral point of view, in particular circumstances. An actual moral code is, of necessity, implied and involved, but its specification is left to be shaped out somehow by the general character of a given period and culture (in the last place also, however, by the individual himself or herself within the period and culture in question). Under these, it can hardly be denied, obscure and far from stable conditions, it is not at all surprising that those individuals and groups who find themselves in a position of power should exercise themselves in every way to shape out a moral code in their own image and to gain from its imposition what support they can for themselves and their own authority. The original, pre-moral urge to dominate at all costs has not by any means disappeared under the force of the moral concept, whose uncertain indications are all too easily overwhelmed by that urge, for at least a time, a time which may continue for ages, with whatever modifications nevertheless to the ordering of things in the long course of events. If, that is, the interests of the ruling classes are not what is responsible for the wholesale creation of moral codes, there is yet little doubt that those interests can radically affect the manner and formation of such codes for an indefinite while.

The result is, however, a developing discord, a conflict of ideas and actions at variance with one another and not to be brought into a common and commonly directed unity. Despite all, there disentangles itself at length from the confusion of disparate elements a body of principles which, though still open to copious distortion, are nevertheless definite in basis and structure and not to be gainsaid, and have their root source elsewhere than in the assertions and claims of the powerful, intent only upon the maintenance of their power.

I referred, just a moment or two ago, to justice, equity and so forth. These ideals – for this is what they are, signposts to guide the way, ends to be aimed at, only reached perhaps with comparative rarity (even, I fear, at the best of times) – have no immediate relationship to the requirements of the rulers, even if they are far from incapable of being misapplied in the rulers' direction, but arise, as it appears, spontaneously; and we are not to be surprised if they find a leading place among the propositions, assurances and commands issuing with dogmatic enthusiasm from the mouths, as we are told, of Prophets who have come forward, when opportunity presented itself, to proclaim and to spread abroad a vigorous message – sometimes, it may be, in a type of language sounding (not merely because of its antiquity) a little peculiarly to us at the present day, partly, I suppose, because the subject is no longer a novel one, but partly also because the fruits of the message, for what they may be worth, are as far from being gathered as ever.

"It's an unfair world", we hear said; but this is itself an acknowledgement, indeed in almost so many words, of the underlying, contrary, unachieved ideal still setting itself unrelentingly before us, whether we all of us like it or not (just as it has been held that hypocrisy is the hypocrite's concession to the ideas of goodness and right behaviour, which he may not deeply care for as guides for his own footsteps but which he cannot easily think away).

Justice, equity, fairness: where, then, do these overriding notions, these pressing demands upon us which we cannot so easily ignore or put away from us, whether or not we permit them actively to affect our customary behaviour – where do they originate? Is it perhaps not inappropriate to see working in them in a fashion, once again, the same unfettered impulse which I have asserted to be somehow at the root of all our endeavours – that is to say the impulse of the community in its urge to self-perpetuation by every means at its disposal? This may or may not be the whole matter, but that it is a foundation-element in the picture is surely undeniable.

Unending conflict among its individual or group offshoots can hardly be the community's aim – if 'aim' is the appropriate word, but I do not know what other word to use. (It may appear just the kind of personalisation I objected to so much a little while back, but in this context I am at a loss to improve upon it.) The group itself, of whatever size and on whatever level, requires some principle of equitable sharing – of community, no less – inchoate or more developed, to maintain it in being, to give it force and effectiveness. In the brute beasts the principle is instinctive; in humanity it becomes a consciously formed concept, emergently ordered and constituted in a variety of ways, but in the long run with the ideal clearly underlying it of 'to each his due', with whatever that, in differing societies, may eventually be taken to signify.

Man differs from the other animals, from the 'lower' forms of life, in being able to express himself, conceptually and verbally, with a remarkable appearance of precision – but, beyond a certain point, this precision is as much appearance as reality. The only true precision of expression open to mankind is through mathematical formulation. This is because mathematics works through 'empty' units of self-evidently universal application. In their universality they are also quite specific. Other modes of human expression, having every air of being much more specific, are actually much less so, and their applicability is fluid and changing, their precision never certain. Words in everyday language have meaning, but that meaning can vary considerably according to context and intention, such intention being as often concealed as explicit, and, in so far as concealed, concealed probably as much from the user's own uppermost mind as from that of the person directly addressed. If some of this seems, as I imagine, less than straightforward, it is because life in general is a good deal less than straightforward.

Concepts and their verbal expression need interpretation: they are nothing, from any practical point of view, without it. Concepts of a non-mathematical nature may often be open to a wide variety of possible interpretations, which means at the same time to misinterpretation, which may take them perhaps well out of line with the circumstances to which they are supposed at a given moment to relate. The more high-sounding a concept when it strikes on the mind (and, let us not forget, on the emotions), from whatever may seem to be the source, the more necessary is interpretation, carried out in an appropriate and clear and logical and impartial manner (I have added 'impartial' because the use by the politician of the well-sounding conceptualisation which he has dug up and reformulated in order to press a case and to overcome an audience's probably justifiable hesitations, is all too frequent.)

The interpretation of 'to each his due' will, naturally enough, incline in favour of whatever happen to be the general theories regarding practical action held by the interpreter, taking into account the background of the interpreter's circumstances of time and place. I will not go any further into this aspect here, since there is a more important and basic matter to consider – that is to say, concerning the concept of 'community' itself. As I have already pointed out – in so far as it is not in fact obvious – the interpretation of 'community' is far from simple. A community can be of any size you like, from the one concentrated extreme when it may even seem momentarily, to some eyes, at least, to be improbably lodged in a single highly self-important individual to the other where it comprehends not merely the whole of mankind but even the whole of everything that is in any sense living. Normally, it is true, one tends not to think of either of these extremes, but rather of some group of human beings to whom one has some evident or apparent relationship in the course of one's activities; nevertheless neither of the extremes mentioned is by any means ruled out, and, according to one's way of thinking, each can have in fact its own peculiar force of attraction – conceivably, however faint and unlikely its apparent significance to the uninvolved, a very powerful force if a person very determinedly points his thought or has his thought (and feelings) pointed in a given direction.

Thirty-five

The Interpretation of 'Community'

The potential variations in the concept of community are very obvious historically. In saying this I do not mean to dwell particularly on the widely different significances which can be attached at any time, without confusion, to the word itself, provided only that a sufficient defining epithet is present (as one might say, for instance, 'the academic community' or 'the child community' or 'the criminal community' or 'the religious community') or provided, at any rate, that the context of ideas, at the moment of utterance, makes the particular intentions behind the word's use at that moment sufficiently clear. While I am not wishing in any measure to deny the importance of this sort of variability of application of the concept in question and of the word which clothes it, a variability indicating plainly enough, as I feel, the central place that word and concept hold together in our conscious and less than conscious approach to reality, nevertheless at this point of the argument what I have in mind, rather, is the major environmental and in some sense or another spiritual community to which the individual acknowledges that he belongs and to which accordingly, in general, he announces his allegiance – I refer, in short, to the political community.

Since I have, in these pages, used the word 'politician' with not entirely approbatory overtones, I had better make it very plain that when I speak here of the 'political' community, I do so without any such implications, and in no way pejoratively. I use the word in an objective sense. It is derived from the ancient Greek *polis*, a word standing for an entity we now name as 'city-state', which was then in Greece the accepted central unit of communal activity. The *polis* itself is in fact an excellent example of what I mean when I speak of historical variability, in respect of this (political) notion. Thus in the Greek age, a period of acknowledged and indubitable high culture and civilised endeavour, the effective model of the community as a centralising factor, for the building-up of groups and the organisation in some more or less appropriate manner of their living arrangements, was not, as far as the Greeks themselves were concerned, the extended nation-state of modern-day theory, covering a considerable area of territory and embracing as many as possible of those persons of (in some sense) common origin, or at least, these days, of, in principle, acknowledged common allegiances, speaking a common tongue, and scattered through numbers of towns and villages and so forth: it was the quite small 'city-state' – hardly bigger maybe by our standards than an out-sized village (limited downwards by the fact that below a certain size it could not be viable or, particularly, defensible), and making no pretence to the sort of national comprehensiveness in terms of which we consider the matter nowadays, yet self-sustaining and probably as fiercely independent as any present-day nation of vastly greater physical extent. The Greeks were, it is true, very conscious as a race of their difference from (and in many respects, as they believed, superiority to) the 'barbarians' beyond them, but their basic political allegiance, and in no uncertain terms, was to the city-state.

The small, self-contained, self-centred city-state was not an invention of the Greeks. If we go back – thousands of years – to the very earliest days of what we call civilisation, five millennia and more ago, we find in Mesopotamia, in what may have been the earliest civilised concentration of all, a series of small semi-fortress communities, each one holding tightly together, and ready apparently, for some conceived advantage, genuine or imaginary, to go ferociously into battle with any of its next-door neighbours regardless of ties of blood or language. This interesting and somewhat bloodthirsty characteristic was no less distinctive of the Greeks, so many years and centuries later, who were ready to tear one another apart on almost any pretext, the major intention being in fact to declare each his own city's supremacy.

The Mesopotamian states came in time under the dominance first of one superior power among them then of another; but meanwhile the contemporary civilisation growing up along the Nile valley pursued a largely different course. The shape which that civilisation took was of a unitary Pharaonic kingdom, a 'double kingdom' of north and south, of Lower and Upper Egypt, under a single god-king – a kingdom subsisting in principle as one entity, one national community, and continuing so through millennia, whatever the multitude of changes to which it was inevitably otherwise subjected. Note that there is no real question here of any gradual general evolution from one lesser manner of state to another, essentially more advanced. The city-state, as such, in one form or another repeats itself through history, reduced at last out of the picture eventually, as much as anything through the development of transport and communication facilities, but in all its forms, while it exists, acting in its own way as an essential cradle of civilising culture, not by any means as a political regression.

This differentiation into two main outward types takes no account of very considerable differences within the types themselves. But it will do as an indication. What it does show, at least, is a development in different ways, along contrasting channels - almost as if two alternative experiments were being tried - of the basic idea of community. For it is clear, in the first place, that if community were to be limited to its representation purely through the individual as such, this would be a not merely quite inadequate but indeed self-contradictory expression of community's nature and dynamics: there must also be some coordination of individuals (seen, as we know, to an extent also, in many differing ways and degrees, through the workings of instinct, among the 'lower' creatures), some cooperation between them for the furtherance of communal purposes, so that we are not to be left with the simply destructive basic formula (from whose bloody restrictions, however modified, we have never in fact more than partially and minimally escaped) of one-against-one. And as a result we see, in the formative stages of human civilisation, the fundamental principle of cooperation and coordination brought well into effect and operating with all visibility, but in two generally different styles, in Mesopotamia and in Egypt, and with differing consequences for the individual - whose individuality remains throughout in both, never in principle or in entirety overcome, but magnified or diminished according to the individual's eventual position in the integrated state hierarchy.

It is community as thus conceived - in particular, in the version manifesting itself in the city-state of the Greek age - which gave and gives rise to the notion of an underlying individual equality, of 'fairness' and personal rights, leading to the demand for distributive justice, formulated as a moral requirement, overriding in theory (too often, it is to be confessed, in theory only) all urges to powerful individual aggrandisement. This may seem a trifle startling as a general proposition, in view of some of the more sensational aspects of the early civilisations as we know them or know of them, and as they are presented to us; and it is only a part of the story; but it is a part that goes deep, however much overshadowed, very frequently indeed, by other, more striking elements. It is also necessary to understand that it is absolutely never the case that some new kind of light on human action, and some new compelling viewpoint respecting obligation and the rights of one human being in relation to another, are enabled, at once on their emergence, by some remarkable and swift transition, through the working of some irresistible inner power, to assert themselves, in practical functioning, without hesitation or obstruction, over previous less analysed, in the long run less communally profitable (though this effect, it is true, may not straight away superficially appear), more direct and personal impulses to activity. In fact, in practice, all motives and motivations operate together, without any pre-arranged harmony, and, rather, with the probability that the prospect of some immediate personal advantage, for oneself and those about one, will take weighty precedence over the idea of any longer-term benefit for one's society at large.

It will be observed that in speaking thus of society at large (an entity or, if you prefer, quasi-entity whose very existence, on whatever plane, the then Mrs Thatcher took it upon herself, for no straightforwardly self-explanatory reason, forthrightly to deny) I have still been prepared to refer to 'profit' and 'benefit', distinguishing simply between the profit and benefit of a single individual or particular narrow group and of the greater community. Is this, then, all that we are to understand by the notion of morality, that it bids us still function in pursuit of gain, but of gain that lies in principle a good way further off than our immediate vicinity and on behalf of a much wider grouping of individuals than of merely oneself alone or of those nearest at hand in some appropriate sense? I might, I suppose, have attempted to avoid this very obvious problem by using other words, but that would actually have solved nothing, since it is just this class of words and ideas which is in common use in the context and, as far as I know, in all languages. It seems to be taken for granted that profit of some sort is the ultimate aim (cf. our 'What shall it profit a man...?' and so forth) – but of what sort? An easy question with, I fear, a far from easy answer.

There are really two questions to be answered here, not one. The question of what species of profit we intend involves also the closely associated question of what precisely is the nature and extent of the community we have in mind; and I think we had better look to the latter question first, since a great deal indeed depends upon it. 'Community', as we have already on more than one occasion remarked, and as is in any case obvious, is quite the most unspecific of words: it can cover any size of grouping, great or small, and can refer in a particular case to almost any manner of context. In respect of what we have here in view, can we ultimately set any real limits to it at all? True, I have in one place above spoken of 'our' society, and this may seem on the face of it to suggest a clear(?) limit of some sort; but any society less, in the end, than that of the totality of humankind leaves inevitably massive room for conflict (do we, in this age of disasters, need any examples?), and the resulting profit must involve also loss, perhaps devastating loss, and if my original principle of community and its central urge to the propagation and perpetuation of life has any ultimate virtue then this continuing battle of the strong must surely come to an end at some time, on whatever basis. If that is so, then the profit, or gain, we so earnestly seek must be on behalf of nothing less than all mankind – but, in truth, we must go further still, for 'life' does not automatically limit itself to the life of man, but is comprehensive.

Why do we have to extend our range so far? Can we not at least draw a conceptual line below humanity, and leave it at that? Logically, this will not quite do. If we are to draw lines between higher and lower types, what is to prevent our doing this, as has in fact frequently been done, within humanity itself? There are undoubtedly those who will still think that perfectly acceptable, but there are others who would, very rightly in my opinion, resist it fiercely, even though I might possibly not find the manner of their resistance always so completely acceptable (but that is by the way).

Thirty-six

Profit in Relation to a World Community – and Competition

The notion of 'profit', under these express conditions, of the widespread promotion of the existence and blossoming of the world community and its constituents on every level, must imply for every individual or conceivable unit or centre of living of all kinds the fullest possible enjoyment of life without impediment and an encouragement at the same time to the onward transmission of life (within reasonable bounds). If this definition is far indeed from specific, that is because the requirements for the fulfilment of so broad, so all-encompassing an aim are extremely variable, as must be plain. Not only are there vast differences between classes of living entity in the respects under consideration, but even within the class, say, of human beings alone, the variations can be enormous. What constitutes enjoyment for one person, or even at one time of life, can offer seemingly inadequate resources in the case of another.

It is, as a matter of fact, inordinately difficult to see how such demands – so many of them being, when pursued and elaborated into precise practical detail, to all appearances in direct conflict with one another – can ever satisfactorily be met. How, in principle, to deal with both the predator and the prey, human or otherwise? I offer no ready solutions: I have said, and repeat, that it is very much easier to pose such questions than to find anything like appropriate answers. The end, whichever way one looks, seems to be a flat self-contradiction. Are we then compelled to stay within the closed circle of the 'get-on-your-bike' philosophy, and of the relentless, ruthless competition so constantly and powerfully preached at us from a significant sector of high authority? If the former of these counsels is unclear in regard to the consummation aimed at, the other part is much more explicit, and points to an inevitably destructive climax: that climax may well however be unexpectedly toned down now and then in actual practice. When two opposing tenders are put forward for a highly important government contract, and one of them is, as it is bound to be, turned down, efforts are liable to be made, with some appearance of urgency, to relieve the resulting problems for a defeated and desperate workforce by the offer of some lesser alternative, as it were a consolation prize. We have seen this done, not so very long ago, not by a Socialist ('soft', 'wet') government but by a Conservative one. What does this prove?

The truth is that what we have here is a simple case of backtrack, with little of serious principle behind it. The original dogma, so firmly laid down, so stoutly maintained, has shown itself flawed when put to a vital test. Like most dogmas, it is riddled with hidden inconsistencies, and if carried through in all circumstances unflinchingly to a finish becomes hardly more than a recipe for confusion. Such a dogma may appear serviceable for quite a while, so long as one is able sufficiently to obscure its less happy side-effects, but in the end, when the results are too shattering and can be no longer ignored, it will break down, and, in the long run, utterly.

So far we have been talking of domestic matters. When it comes to foreign affairs, it might seem that things are totally different. But are they? Take the extreme case, of our relation to what we call the Third World. Here the notion of unrestricted competition is replaced, we find, or at least replaced in important part, by that of aid. To some extent this is, of course, due at bottom to a fear of 'unfair' (!) competition, derived from low labour-costs, but this is not usually the open face of the matter presented to the public eye. Aid means help, and what we are supposed to be doing is giving assistance to the Third World so that those in it may be enabled to raise their standard of living. If, in so doing, that offers us competition which is in our view a little 'fairer', well, that is our just reward for a good deed benevolently accomplished.

In both the above quoted instances, the element of competition is there, sure enough, but in neither in the full and unimpeded form one could be led to expect. In both instances it is heavily modified, in the one so as to avoid too devastating a blow at the life of the community at large through its agency, in the other in such a way as to alter its very appearance and to adulterate it with elements of in significant ways an alien nature. I have quoted extreme cases, but it is not to be thought that they exist, in some remarkable manner, on their own and *in vacuo*. On the contrary, they are essentially indications of a failing at the heart of the theory involved, a failing which cannot conceivably be overcome if the theory is to be pressed to its natural and in fact loudly advertised limits.

Competition in peace is the equivalent (or what is considered the acceptable – the more than acceptable – equivalent) of battle in war. In war one engages aggressively in systematic armed preparation against the enemy, then in bloody battle itself; in peace, accordingly, one is egged on to so-called aggressive competition against all comers. I have been into some wide aspects of this before, but there is no harm in taking it up again, since the idea behind it seems to govern so overwhelming a part of our activities. There is evidently something in man's nature which seems to demand if not always fighting in so many words, at least something as closely resembling it as possible. Sometimes the latter alternative is fenced in by the competing (!) demands of legality – sometimes not. Sometimes the demands of legality are theoretically met but in effect overstepped without much hesitation where opportunity allows – sometimes they are rejected entire.

I do not think it is possible to overemphasise the fact that competition is essentially a double-sided coin (what coin is not?), the question of legality apart; and I am prepared to repeat as many times as need be that where there is competition there is not only success in waiting but also necessarily at the same time failure. (This can assuredly help towards explaining the visible tendency of those involved in such competition often to ignore legality, sometimes even at great personal risk, and to use any means available in order to achieve the success they are after.) At the end of a war there is a victor and a vanquished; equally the eventual conclusion of a given episode of competitive struggle must leave us with a winner and a loser, one who has succeeded and one inevitably who has failed.

So in these circumstances, when defeat (for some, certainly) is every bit as unavoidable as victory, what then becomes of the theory of 'the common good' whatever that may be taken to mean? In what degree are the two aims compatible? Admittedly, 'the common good' is a remarkably vague expression, but, whatever interpretation one wishes to put upon it, there seems no way in which it can be brought seriously into line with the current injunction inspiring us to ruthless competition at all times. If it is said perhaps that we are attempting here to compare incomparables, that such an injunction is essentially short-term in its aim, while 'the common good' is a very long-term ideal indeed, it can only be replied that it is difficult to see how the former can ever conceivably lead to the latter, over the longest term imaginable. The two will always remain, in principle, in irredeemable conflict.

There is nevertheless – still – one method, or so it may seem, for bringing the two apparently quite antagonistic conceptions closer into line, and that is by reducing 'the common good' to the good of 'the best', on the assumption that 'common' relates not to the whole body of individuals in the community, without effective discrimination among them – undeniably, it is true, a very difficult conception to work out in any detail – but to the community itself considered as a single entity, and in relation to its one main purpose, of self-perpetuation and development. On this basis, only those individuals who can most powerfully help fulfil that fundamental purpose need ultimately be taken into account, and in the final picture there is only ever room for winners, losers can be forgotten. 'The common good' is the community's good as an entity, nothing more, nothing less.

But on such a basis one is naturally induced to wonder what can be the precise value of ethical principles in the context, the value of moral or any other laws. There must be a place for laws, it will be clear, but if power and driving force are the key, then the greatest value will lie with laws which help to concentrate power where it is most effective, to produce in the upshot such a situation, for example, as that in which the Mongol hordes of the thirteenth century can be seen to have flourished and secured predominance, when they overran an area of Asia far exceeding the extent of the renowned empire of Alexander the Great, under mighty leaders and using utterly ruthless means, involving mass extermination of those opposing them. Law here is simply the law of the leader and centre of power, in principle nothing else. I do not know whether it really makes sense to talk of any sort or reflection of moral law in such a case at all, even in terms of a *distortion* of moral law. But equally, the kind of law-giving in question (I refer now to no particular period of history) can hardly be thought of as serving in any way as an original model for moral law, except in so far as all law-making is similar in setting limits of some kind to what may and may not be done. Of some kind – it is the kind which makes the difference.

I think there are three chief comments requiring to be made here:

1. There are not very many people who would be likely to endorse wholeheartedly this interpretation of the common good, so baldly stated – an interpretation which, if followed through, could indeed, quite apart from any other consideration, lead us into a forest of self-contradictions.

2. Under this interpretation, morals, it would appear, as we normally understand them, simply go out of the window.

3. The interpretation pays too little attention of the right kind (as I see it) to a significant element in the community purpose which I have noted above for, I think, the first time, but which I have not defined. I spoke, that is to say, of the community's 'one main purpose, of self-perpetuation and development'. Observe that this is one purpose, that the two parts of it are, in my view, impossible to separate but their balance is nevertheless easy to misconceive. Any attempt to divorce the two, or to restrict the item of development in favour of perpetuation of the process of life is not in accordance with the facts, with what actually takes place, with evolution as we have come to know it. We do not know where this development is going, but we cannot abstract from it for an instant – it is an absolutely vital (apt word) part of the picture.

Development as in a society dominated by the competitive ethos is seen primarily in terms of 'growth', that is, of commercial and financial expansion – and, in sum, of the increase of wealth in the hands of those who, by their exercise of appropriate skills, are thought most to merit the ownership of such wealth. In this context 'good' is a concept relating first and foremost to what is called 'the good life', where the epithet, for all its verbal shape, has little enough in reality to do with the same word as appearing in 'the common good'. This is not because it happens to be grammatically different but because it refers to a totally different, in fact opposite, field of ideas, to the field of the inward-turned and the self-centred as against that of the outward-looking and communally-angled. 'The good life' suggests 'good' food (extravagant and highly refined, but not necessarily nourishing) and a variety of aspects of self-display, sometimes on a portentous scale, with magnificent houses (the plural can indeed be taken quite literally) and all the showiest allied appurtenances possible: yachts, helicopters, and anything else guaranteed to make the owner's wealth patent and obvious - for what, after all, is the purpose of wealth which is at all outstanding except to make its existence known to all and sundry? Blatancy, it may be declared, is here the order of the day, and here not least does competition rule, indeed run amok.

Thirty-seven

Competition and 'The Common Good'

From what has been said it appears fairly plain that attempts to combine into a serious and workable unity the ideas of unqualified competition and of the common good have little likelihood of success. Yet there is no denying that they exist somehow together in what we may term the general mind and are frequent enough, both of them and probably equally, in general parlance, without usually any thought of contradiction. They form part, indeed, of a vast stock of ill-analysed conceptions thrown higgledy-piggledy into close contact together without consideration of whether or not they can truly be matched up to one another – of whether, that is, they can possibly be brought so close without danger or severe loss or damage to what in basis they are intended to stand for – but finding their place in the general stock simply on account of some attractive or seemingly attractive characteristic in them of which their brief and bare normally-accepted description is emotionally suggestive. They belong to a class of ill-defined or undefined clichés of thought whose appeal, for whatever (perhaps quite superficial) reason, is evident enough but whose meaning is usually far from clear.

'The common good' is undoubtedly an expression requiring proper elucidation, and I must try to do something towards such elucidation, even though the effort is bound to be very incomplete, since a full investigation is hardly possible in the limited space at disposal; but before I undertake it, I should like to take a momentary look at the question of how the general principle behind it can live at all in company with the relentless competitive principle, on the face of it so drastically opposed to what it stands for. (In the human world, it is worth re-emphasising at this point, principles of action at obvious and maybe extreme variance with one another nevertheless sit constantly side by side together, affecting our beliefs and activities in a multitude of ways and in many degrees.)

In the strange and strangely confused world we live in, it is evident that not everybody is governed at all times by the uncontrolled urge to accumulation of personal wealth and to ostentatious display of the results. There are numbers of people whose aims, perhaps in source often more modest (?), are at any rate to an extent in a different direction, sometimes radically so. Some persons, oddly enough, seem to have an urge in basis within themselves simply to give assistance to their fellow-beings, human or indeed otherwise, in whatever way is open to them; others have an urge for the accumulation not of wealth but of knowledge, for its own sake, and for the assistance of their fellows to the same end; others again have a primary urge to express their own inner feelings in some artistic or near-artistic way, in this case at times perhaps with a strong intention, implicit or explicit, of leaving their imprint on society, if only in the long run, by this means.

I abstract here from the situation of those who merely feel that they are not, within their abilities, capable of joining with any likelihood of success in the main rush to money-making, and so who are prepared to follow minor roads towards affiliated but necessarily more restricted ends. I am thinking, rather, of those whose goals, clearly or not envisaged, may ultimately be of an essentially different nature. Such goals being not always (perhaps I should say, not usually) clearly envisaged, the accompanying motivations can sometimes be remarkably mixed, and there is in the social spectrum a wide field in consequence in which, in practice, a drive to competitive money-making can attach itself to a spirit of more or less genuine underlying altruism to produce utilitarian results not by any means entirely contradictory of the ideal of the common good. I specify the example of the medical profession, where the impulse to formal membership can derive from extremely mixed intentions (including, no doubt, one based on an interest in the fascinating prospect of cutting up bodies, a thing which has nothing much to do in itself with either altruism or money-making but can still in the event serve a useful human purpose) – these are intentions which can relate to one another in varying proportions, now one, now another in the lead, but, in an emergency particularly, can prove in the end of considerable human value, with the notion of personal profit being quite likely demoted for at least a time to a low place.

What does this mean? Does it mean that there is, after all, some profound underlying principle which is able to combine these apparently contrasting modes into a superior unity? I doubt it very much. The modes remain in extreme and irresoluble contradiction, but, in the never-ending struggle for survival, that element in the deeply muddled human spirit which sees somehow beyond itself alone and looks, however obscurely, towards a freer, more unitedly cooperative, more brilliant if, by the nature of the case, largely uncomprehended future, clings, for the protection of its uncertain but compelling vision, to a semblance or more than a semblance of the old aggressive ways which it is unready yet to cast off – but which, in due course, cast off it must at length, if the vision, for whatever it may be worth, is to be genuinely realised at the distant end.

What interpretation, then, can we reasonably put upon 'the common good'? If all persons were innately of high moral quality and of more or less equivalent ability, the problem in purely practical terms, though still complex, would be limited at least to ensuring that all were offered equal opportunity to exploit their potentialities to the full. But 'high moral quality' is itself a quite uncertain description, not interpretable by everyone in the same or even approximately the same sense, and in any case, whatever the truly appropriate interpretation, it is perfectly obvious that not all persons by any means will satisfy the requirements, and a considerable number will fall far behind; while, as to ability (ability, we may well ask, in what respects and to what ultimate end?), not only are individuals quite evidently not equivalently endowed, but, as we very well know, the differences can be vast. Furthermore, the two requirements cannot successfully be separated: high ability allied to low morality (not a totally unusual conjunction), whatever the terms can be taken precisely to signify, form plainly the worst combination of all.

Again – and this is no novel problem in our context – what is to be considered here the coverage of 'common'? Does it in essence cover all life, of whatever kind? Or all human life? Or possibly the life of an individual nation? Or of any smaller, more intimately related group? Actually, the answer is surely quite simple. If the notion seriously means anything, and assuming that it rests fundamentally on an internally non-exclusive basis, then its outward extension must have no limits. It must cover everything. This is so obvious, it should really need no stressing; it is pretty much a truism; but it is also one of those things easily declared yet extraordinarily difficult to put in any effective way into action, and it is at the same time strikingly difficult even to succeed in getting most people properly to understand it.

It may seem that one can perfectly well talk realistically of 'the common good' of even one quite small sector of society, paying no regard at that moment to any other sectors, yet the truth is that one cannot even talk realistically of 'the common good' of an entire nation – bound up together closely by history and language and tradition over centuries – but without reference to the requirements of other nations, since the inevitable outcome, as all the records plainly and irresistibly show, is for one nation then (and the closer bound the members are, the more likely the outcome) to face another, sooner or later, whatever the published grounds, on the grisly field of blood and of grease – and what becomes at the last, in these circumstances, of the fundamental 'common good' of which we have heard so much? Curiously, indeed, and in qualification of what I have just said, it is often considerably easier to pass, in the mind and in action, from the concept of one of the smaller (sub-national) communities to that of the widest and most comprehensive of all, and to subsume the one under the other, than it is to do something of the same kind when starting from the fully-blown concept of a nation, as we understand it, in its entirety. That is probably because the latter type of entity, which, when all is said and done, is still only ever a partial community, pretends to much too much: it has too many characteristics too closely resembling those of the grossly swollen ego of some self-centred and portentous individual as I have described the phenomenon (and as it is all too frequently encountered).

Whatever the appropriate definition of 'the common good' – a definition, as we have seen, far from easy to discover – there can be no doubt that the most outstanding sins against it have visibly arisen from the unwarrantable and forcible oppression of one group by another. In consequence, it is natural to feel, and to feel very strongly, that when at long last such a particular oppressed group has been torn away successfully out of the clutches of its oppressor, a new day is about to dawn and the world at large, too, is ready to breathe more freely and will surely continue to do so. This is, on the whole, I am much afraid, a severe delusion. It is not the way human beings work. I recall an old Marx Brothers film in which Groucho addresses a burly man seen harassing Groucho's smallest (and often unruliest) brother, who is attempting to resist him. "You big bully!" cries Groucho. "Stop bullying that little bully!" In its deliberately eccentric way this joke reflects a truth we can all immediately recognise though it may not previously have struck us quite so powerfully (and though, I regretfully must add, it may not remain for too long in our active consciousness). The fact is that the ousting of an oppressor is not at all necessarily the beginning of freedom – certainly not, I fear, of freedom for mankind, which is likely to continue on its boulder-strewn course regardless; but not even, I am sorry to say, for the original oppressed group, where it is just as likely that the signal has been merely for one oppressor or species of oppressor to be succeeded by another; or, alternatively, the signal may even have been for an oppressed group as such (having had opportunity, from its own bitter experience, to observe intimately, from without, the advantages accruing for a longer or shorter time to an oppressor), to become, in a crude kind of compensation for its previous suffering, an oppressor group in its turn. This is hardly a move to greater general freedom, or even to understanding: the understanding I speak of is founded in part on a realisation that all empires fall, that no oppressive regime lasts for ever, and that the best way forward in the long term (how long a term? – I do not know) is not to imitate vice but, if one somehow can, to make and take a better, more universally helpful path.

We are back, with this observation, to where we started. 'Universally helpful' equates itself, fairly obviously, with 'the common good'. But how universal is 'universal'? 'Helpful' may help us. If we are really being helpful, we should try to help everybody, without restriction, and that means that those who do not meet our standards should be helped, in any way possible, to reach up to our standards. I do not deny the difficulty in this, as in most sectors of the argument, but however great the difficulty, and in some respects it is a truly formidable one, it is there somehow to be overcome. Behind all this, behind 'the common good', there is, it is evident, the basic assumption of a common standard.

Thirty-eight

The Common Good and Common Standards

This is the fundamental problem, the formulation of a standard of behaviour by all which will be good for all – a 'good for all' which cannot be conceived in terms of 'the good life', the latter being something neither achievable by all (a part of its very essence is that its possessor shall stand out above the crowd) nor even desired by all. Not all desire the same or the same degree of material satisfaction, if that sort of field is what tends to preoccupy us at the moment, so that a definition in simple terms of material satisfaction, or at all events material satisfaction primarily, would itself in consequence seem out of court. Not, however, that material needs can be ignored: we live in a material world and have at all times material needs which require to be coped with, and which cannot be overlooked, and Aristotle was to that extent undoubtedly right in specifying for his ideal philosophising individual a situation where such a man has a sufficiency of material goods for living purposes and need not concern himself about such essentially mundane and lowly matters. But this was all Aristotle asked. Though he nowhere objects to great riches, if suitably acquired and appropriately used (in particular for the public benefit), he certainly did not demand, in the special and significant case in question, an overflow of material goods. Our major concerns these days are, it must appear, extraordinarily different: we not only ask at large for plenty, but for a surfeit of plenty, and are not satisfied (if we are ever satisfied) unless we have more, preferably much more, and visibly much more, than the next man, and however acquired.

At the same time I must say that not everybody who diverges notably, on the surface at least, from the 'entrepreneurial' ethos, and who may be able indeed to draw after him bands, small or large, of enthusiastic – even hysterically enthusiastic – followers, does so, sad to say, and as we are surely in general well aware, from the purest and most unblemished of motives. There are, there have always been, hosts of false prophets, and in every conceivable field. They come and they go – and their relative impermanence, the evanescence of their doctrines in the longer term, are among the signs of their falsity. But such signs, which may display themselves, unhappily, too late for a number of us who are too readily impressionable, are, on their own, unquestionably not enough. It is necessary to be able to discriminate, to be capable of distinguishing at short range what will eventually be recognised by the great majority as patently false, of distinguishing it with sufficient clarity from what is at least honestly struggling towards the truth. How, then, can one do this? I must make no attempt to set out criteria for detecting the false message as such, and in so many words – a complex task, in all conscience; but what may be worthwhile instead, I think, is, starting at the other end, and not going into too nice detail, to set out a small body of criteria, not in themselves too grotesquely complicated, which can help towards determining what may be a reasonable and credible approach to a true message.

In the first place an acceptable system must be built on rational foundations: a grounding of any kind in the appeal to emotional urges is unspeakably dangerous; and for that matter a mere rationalisation of preconceptions, themselves based on emotion and on unanalysed or half-analysed impulses is no whit less dangerous.

In the second place, the doctrine must be of genuinely universal applicability. We have already seen that, in connection with standards of behaviour, which are here our primary concern, this is a very difficult principle indeed to pursue, but it is a principle none the less which has to be perpetually borne in the forefront of the mind and perpetually active. No group, no individual, must be treated as of no account. If there are those among them whose actions are, or are likely to be, damaging to others, then all steps must be taken to prevent that – the police forces of civilised states at the present day represent this aspect in concrete shape, if perhaps not in every way adequately – and, in preventing that, to try to gain understanding of what leads them to behave as they do, an understanding which will indubitably be of utmost assistance for one's future efforts. This itself – the question of damage to others – is a point of basic importance. If freedom of action is to be available in theory to all and sundry it must be a freedom that is not, as such, in theory damaging to anybody (so far, when put into practice, as is humanly possible in an as yet distinctly imperfect world), a freedom for the one that does not impinge on the freedom of any other.

How this will work itself out in practice is complicated to determine. Since there are the widest variations in ability, mental and physical, between people, and also in modes of behaviour and outlook, there can be no question of treating all alike. Apart from the differences in ability (and however one judges that quality), individuals, as I must emphasise, vary very much – on all levels of ability – in their approach to things, whether in reference to particular items or in generality, and such variability is indeed absolutely fundamental for the necessary all-round development and increasing well-being, as one would hope, of mankind. So it is not possible or desirable to think in terms of treating all alike: multifarious distinctions of one kind and another there will be, and they will continue as vital elements in the whole; and even hierarchies of a number of kinds and of differing extents will be quite unavoidable. But if all are decidedly not equal in these important senses, there is yet one sense in which they *are* to be so considered – in the sense of their value as individuals. Value is the key word.

The value of an individual is not merely his value to the community. It is that, certainly, but it is also his value in himself, as a living and self-conscious being, with his own inner thoughts and ideas and feelings and needs. When the community creates, as we may say, the individual, it creates, in effect, a fleeting and incomplete version of itself and of that towards which its aim is bent – whatever, in the last resort, that may turn out to be – and if the individual tends too often overweeningly to treat himself as though he were nothing less than the entire community and supercommunity rendered singly real, that is because such self-identification *in some minor degree* is indeed a natural result of his mode of origin, and if, as happens a great deal too frequently, the result overbalances itself, leading the particular individual and with him others astray, that is just our bad luck. It cannot be too much stressed that the community at large, the great Community, is not to be thought of as a benign and all-seeing super-being, adjusting every little item of existence specifically and consciously and deliberately in the direction it requires – though at the same time leaving to its animated creations a curiously inconsistent freedom, a freedom mainly, it would appear, to go awry. But, rather, it is an unending and unreflecting *process*, rolling on irrevocably and irresistibly without pause, and showing no apparent sign of any particular individual attention to its individual creations, whatever their fortune. Yet in each and every one of these individual creations it somehow embodies an aspect of its own self, in its very essence, even though only obscurely, and only for a brief and passing moment; and it is not an unreasonable demand that, if we ever respect anything at all, we should respect the eternal spirit so evident in each passing being, though its meaning may be very far from clear to us.

I have spoken of the inevitability of hierarchies in the organisation even of the ideal community: this must be self-evident, in view of the immense and, as I have said, essential and necessary variability of mankind in its capacities and interests; but the theory and energising force behind such ideal hierarchies will be considerably different from those attached to many or most actual hierarchies today. The notion of a master-and-man relationship will be in principle alien to the whole conception, and will be superseded by a notion of cooperation, at various rungs of the ladder according to personal ability combined with developed skills through appropriate training, for a common and worthwhile cause. The governing atmosphere will be one of friendly working-together, with some persons specifically under the charge of others for good and recognised functional reasons.

In certain quarters of certain of the most advanced civilised societies today we are in fact able to observe movements in the direction I indicate, movements, it is true, very partial only and, at best, exceedingly incomplete, and all too resistible and counteractable, as is made clear enough frequently enough; yet, if we take, as it were, an overhead historical view, we are bound to become aware of distinct improvements, as seen from our angle of approach, in some of the ruling attitudes across the last couple of centuries – even if they continue to be accompanied by an apparently totally contradictory set of phenomena, still very much in evidence at the present hour (the intervention, into all types of event, of apparently flatly contradictory types of phenomena being normal enough in all regions of human experience), characterised by bloodshed, by brutal and indiscriminate slaughter, and by violence on a monumental scale, such as no previous age can possibly outdo or, probably, even match.

Some of the improvements are undoubtedly due at least as much to an increase in the material and mechanical-type facilities that have become growingly available to us, with accelerating swiftness, for the performance of the more menial and subordinate tasks, as they are to a lifting, simply and from within, of our moral sights. The two aspects, it is plain, go very much hand in hand. It could be that the increase in facilities leaves us room in our lives for the emergence and expansion of certain better feelings already present in us in potentiality but tending, otherwise, to be suppressed. At any rate, and however that may be, the fact is that the physical need in anything like the normal household for bodies of servants has been vastly reduced during the period named, and especially the last part of that period, and that not only do we not now acknowledge human slavery, to take the extreme example, as an acceptable method for coping with particular classes of work and of individual, but we have, in practicality, no need of it. Our slaves these days are machines. What we must look forward to now is a time eventually when not only have we abandoned totally the exercise of such an unsavoury practice as the actual and officially recognised enslaving of one human being by another but when we look with horror and contempt at the perpetuation of any system (anywhere in the world) in which the subservience of individual to individual in anything remotely resembling the relationship of slave to master is not heartily condemned. As I hope I have shown, this is in no way to suggest that the whole concept of management, of the control of larger by smaller groups or by competent individuals, is thereby lost to us.

I have purposely avoided references here to 'leaders' and 'led' since, although these terms are common form at highly significant points in the sort of general context we have under discussion, they present, in my opinion, just the wrong image, arousing the notion of masterly men followed by docile dogs of subordinates who trot obediently in their train and respond without resistance to every command descending upon them from above. That this is by no means a serious exaggeration of what is implied and what is intended to be subliminally conveyed is demonstrated fairly adequately by the fact that both Mussolini and subsequently Hitler almost automatically chose in each case to be known popularly as 'the Leader', any more official denomination being allowed to be for the most part overshadowed by that ringing title. The relationship I have in mind is in basis very different indeed, being rooted in conscious agreement, agreement made and remade at every feasible moment.

If I do not use the word 'consensus', which I might have preferred, it is because that has in recent years acquired certain nuances of meaning in certain circumstances which could conceivably, in some respects, confuse or obscure the issue: this is, as one need perhaps hardly say, the regular way with words – their meaning is subject to constant modification, not infrequently to what may even, as some might think, be justifiably described as distortion, with usage.

Thirty-nine

Leadership and Democracy

It is, of course, precisely, it must be said, upon this principle of wholesale agreement that the theory of modern democracy is founded – upon a freely elected and, so, directly empowered representation for the taking of appropriate action (after the fullest discussion); upon freedom of thought and speech at all times and at all levels both among the elected representatives and outside their limits, without restriction. Since we already have this conception, and in mighty operation, do we really need to look any further? Is not this the answer to our problems? I am afraid it is not.

For the conception is also heavily involved with that other conception of leaders and led, and the two approaches, though obviously thought to complement one another, in fact mix very badly. The elected representatives are considered to be 'leaders' (politically speaking) of those who have elected them, and they in their turn (the elected) elect their own group-leader, who has for a given period supreme and in theory unfettered power. The supreme leader may do in principle whatever he or she pleases, appointing at will men and women to sit about his/her feet for counsel and subsidiary action, and, by the wave of an imperious hand (or handbag), abolishing old, long-standing institutions when they appear to stand in the way, and creating new ones, or not, as desired. The possibility that this might perhaps induce a certain loss of sense of proportion in the supreme leader has not escaped notice, but it has been felt that freedom of expression in the country, combined with certain powers left to junior leaders to oust their supreme commander from office if it came to the point, would serve to counterbalance this. The background thought, plainly, is that action at the top must be as unhampered as possible, subject only to certain necessary national checks in the name of popular freedom: the result is what may well be described (as has been recognised) as delegated dictatorship.

The truth is, however, that (1) there are many respects in which the system is at odds with itself (I have already previously denoted it a makeshift), and (2) delegated dictatorship, if one does not take the greatest care, is liable to become true dictatorship. With regard to (1), for example, election by majority vote, as is the custom, must leave a minority – and it may be a very sizeable minority – unrepresented; also, note that election is for a party, with a party policy, a policy invariably at many points singularly ill-defined, and that any group policy of the kind is bound in any case to contain disparate elements. Not all of these are likely to be fully acceptable to every party voter, who simply in the end has to make the best of it. As to (2), it is surely not necessary to search for examples, of which there are far too many and too ready to hand, and if, in certain instances – in the case of our own country, let us say – it is not perhaps very likely that such an extreme should indeed be reached, there are nevertheless many intermediate moments even in these instances – even, undoubtedly, with ourselves – when highly dubious steps will be taken, in favour, it may well be, of nobody very much in the long run, with little practical interference at the time beyond an unhappy and ineffectual public moan.

Why should problems of this nature arise? If all concerned had it perpetually in the forefront of their minds and efforts to promote their community's interest, the situation would be transformed, and many of the difficulties listed would sink into the background or even not arise at all. Great problems would still undeniably remain, but mostly of a quite different (perhaps, *in toto*, a good deal less formidable) kind. This is, however, to ask for a world having little relationship to the world we actually inhabit at the present time and have done for as long as we are able to look back. Those who rise to power in our present world do so because power as such is what they are after, and not much is done to conceal the fact (why should it be? – in most eyes it is admired as a virtue, even if the end result is hardly likely to be to everyone's taste or benefit). There is much talk of carrying out policies which will be for the country's good, but the supporters of such talk usually lend themselves to it because they see behind it some material advantage to themselves, not, I fear, because they are genuinely anxious for the country's good. Meantime the true intention of all this talk is, as we have seen, and transparently enough, to elevate the talker to a superior position from which he can dominate the lesser fry and feel himself not so much to represent his community as, in a wonderful way, to *be* that community individually and in person.

Let us not be too entirely pessimistic. If hypocrisy is the hypocrite's tribute to the truth, then possibly the rhetoric so commonly and freely bandied about concerning the national interest and so forth can be given a not dissimilar reference, and, un-heartfelt though it may in normal circumstances be, can give us nevertheless a glimpse, or more, of what should ultimately be – of a real goal to be aimed at and, by some at least, and not always by the naïve and insignificant alone, felt seriously to be so, and to be worthy of being held in constant view on that basis (the faint chink of light – according to a ready and well-known image – barely visible at the remote end of a long, dark, previously seemingly unending corridor, offering us promise of a relief which in our more hesitant moments we may fear to be illusory but on which our hopes remain bent).

War, slaughter and all manner of violence, every shape and style of callous and indiscriminate mayhem, these irresistible concepts and related imaginations and impulses lie deep at the roots of a major part of our thinking, they throng through our ideas, even those ideas claiming to fall into a spiritual category ("Onward Christian soldiers..."), they build themselves into our fantasies, and it is not surprising that so much of cinema and television drama should look to them for easy support. They represent – do they not? – the darker side of human nature; but we have continued to repeat to ourselves, often and noisily, and refusing desperately to see them for what they truly are, that they are essential to us, that we cannot do without them, that the whole of our virility is bound up with them, that without them we descend into insignificance and are overwhelmed. It is not for nothing that our figures of speech so overflow with notions belonging to them.

If 'national interest' is to be anything more than a rhetorical cover for, in reality, intense personal ambition and striving after power, then it is obvious that attitudes must change, and change to a huge extent, of which there has so far been little enough sign – in many respects it would appear quite the contrary. Yet in the same breath it must be said that there is one respect in which a countervailing tendency to the main trend does force itself in a singular way upon the view: this is not a matter of a genuine change in attitude; there is in fact hardly an inkling of such a thing in itself; but the development of man's powers of destruction has seemed suddenly to turn against him and to compel him, much against his will, to think again. The warrior is suddenly found to be making war, in a grotesque and intimidating way, against himself.

At the end of the Second World War the victors-to-be discovered the ability, after much secret experimentation and, happily for themselves and for the world, in advance of their enemies, to produce a spectacular new type of bomb having the power to destroy a whole city at a single stroke. Their victory was thus finally assured. But secrets of the kind involved, secrets of such weight and magnitude, do not as a rule remain secret for long; and since that time understanding of the requisite technology has spread across the globe, and those with the expertise to apply that technology and, in the appropriate (or probably inappropriate) case, to sell themselves and their practical knowledge to the highest bidder without compunction – compunction being apparently a feebly operative restraint when material wealth in any quantity is set up against it – have multiplied considerably. In the situation arising from this sequence of events any participants in a large-scale war now run the patent risk of flattening one another and all that they possess to the ground almost before hostilities have properly begun, and, as if that were not enough, of leaving behind them a vast mass of wreckage capable of poisoning the atmosphere and those inhaling it for unknown years to come. Under the possible threat, accordingly, of immediate mutual devastation such as has been hitherto hardly envisaged, it is perhaps not entirely surprising that 'statesmen' who might previously have sent their troops without too much forethought into battle (as in 1914) now, with immense show of caution, openly resisting provocation and enticement, hold themselves determinedly back from the brink.

This they do, not for the greater good, but out of fear and uncertainty in regard to themselves and their own futures. It is the lowering physical menace which haunts them and presses them back, not any lofty aspiration from within. Yet this is surely a good thing, however outward the cause? Well, that may be so, but if so, it is so only up to a point. In the absence of powerful external intervention, 'little' wars find themselves with freedom to burst out and to persist, and to create their own fine degree of havoc, with cruelty and violence uninhibited and unlimited and unending. And meanwhile on the home front, among the nations under restraint, the vigorous and in many respects it seems unmanageable destructive urge so appallingly evident in the complex human make-up has freedom now in individuals to make itself felt, without excessive hindrance and without divergence as in the past into routine great wars waged in claimed defence of the homeland. So, a scourge of 'little' wars, and elsewhere regularly increasing domestic violence, have their day.

Forty

The Need for our Threatened Society to Change its Colours, and Rapidly

No, really nothing will do short of a thoroughgoing change of heart and attitude: anything less leaves room open, wide open for chaos without foreseeable bounds and without cessation. Drawing back by the governments of the major powers in a hesitant and confused effort at self-protection, out of fear lest the worst befall, can only lead to what we have seen, to a series of breakdowns in every direction on lesser levels, both without and within.

And yet – might not the withdrawal itself, superficial in its intentions though it may be, induce, over a period, just the very change in attitude required, through compelling a deep reconsideration of the facts and all that is at issue? I must, I think, agree that this could be more than a purely fanciful supposition and I would not deny its theoretical possibility in the long run. Such things *can* happen. But what is the long run? Any such result is not likely to take effect quickly: a fundamental turn-about of the kind we have here in view, involving so radical a transformation in ideas, has nothing less than the status of an evolutionary development, and demands, like all evolutionary developments, more than a moment of time in which to establish itself, not perhaps, it is true, anything resembling (even remotely) the enormously long periods in past ages needed as background for the physical evolutionary developments in terms of which, since Darwin, we have accustomed ourselves to think, but nevertheless demanding a full stretch of time, even if on a greatly smaller scale, for the overcoming of all the innumerable obstacles left inevitably by human history thornily in the way: the perpetual and continuing strife of personalities (actually held out very frequently as a glorious ideal), the innate drive to conflict of man against man, of tribe and nation against tribe and nation – and, with it all, the sheer incredible charlatanry visibly present behind almost every item of genuinely conscious human behaviour on every level, not only, certainly, but certainly not least, on the level of those we see preening themselves ecstatically at every instant in the seats of power. Will such a stretch of time be indeed granted us, before those very advances in technology so remarkable to the innocent eye, such objects to us hitherto of pride and admiration, have caused the world in which we exist to collapse, in total and final ruin, about our ears?

The truth is that we are not really in any position to sit patiently and wait for some helpful evolutionary or quasi-evolutionary development to take place and change our attitudes for us: the problem is too urgent for such passive tactics, and requires instead that we take some conscious, rational, more immediate action to cope with the menaces hanging so thunderously over us – that we make indeed an active and intentional effort to change our own attitudes effectively from within. Is this a serious possibility? Have we any even minimal guide to point us on the way?

Curiously, there *is* such a guide, and it is more than minimal, too much more perhaps for the confused mind of man, under a host of conflicting pressures and held back by the constraints of its ancient heritage, even, it appears, to see it clearly in its proper light, let alone to follow it. What we are searching for lies embedded in the common religion continuing to be professed by most of the western world today, and has done so for something approaching two millennia. It lies partly concealed under the cover of various layers of the miraculous and the ritualistic and by alien elements of every manner of kind incorporated into its surrounding canon from antecedent religious beliefs, sufficing too easily to obscure its message; but it is there, and still clear – too clear, it may seem, to be understood.

I confess I have little use for religion as such. It is fanciful and obsessive, a frequent occasion of unreasoning and often seemingly ineradicable prejudice, both communal and personal, and historically indeed the recorded cause – with time and the developing fixation of certain narrowly defined systems of implanted beliefs – of persecution and atrocity committed, in bloodthirsty, hardly spiritual fashion, explicitly in its name.

Despite all this – despite the army of evidently (to the unclouded view) immoral accompaniments which religion seems always in one way or another to carry in its train (and the more so, as one may well think, the more concentrated and specific the religious beliefs involved) – nevertheless it is very much in the context of religion and religious ideas that the plainest moral codes habitually make their appearance, endowed as they then are to believers with the loftiest and least questionable authority by their assertedly divine derivation. The customarily brief wording of such codes cannot possibly, by its nature, cover every eventuality, and it remains open to expounding and interpretation; and from time to time a new light may be shone upon it from an unfamiliar angle, with the effect of subtly changing the hue of the general picture it portrays, if without radical remodelling. How far actual practice is affected by any of this is, in general, quite another matter. In the main religious environment it is more likely that the darker, potentially more violent and destructive aspects of the religious drive should maintain the upper hand, leaving the pursuit of moral excellence, in whatever exact terms conceived, to look after itself as best it may.

It is not difficult to see how this description can be fitted to what has been happening in the Christian religion over its approximately two thousand years; and it is precisely in the scriptures of the Christian religion that the moral guidance to which I have referred, in the context of our current needs, finds an outspoken place. It is in what is known to us as the Sermon on the Mount (Matt. 5 and 6). There is nothing hidden about the words in which that sermon is expressed, nor are Christian worshippers ignorant of them. They are, on the contrary, very well known and frequently quoted, but the fact still stands that the course of moral action they urge upon the hearer – and they do so in the most forthright and unqualified manner – is one that remains very far indeed not only, perhaps understandably, from the common practice of individuals but also from the oft-repeated counsels of the vast majority of those exercising human authority over us and, most assuredly too, from the declared or for that matter underlying policies of governments. It is a notable thing that the numerous expected references to God which the Sermon contains are in terms of divine grace rather than of disciplinarian fury; while its exhortations to the individual are strikingly different from what is the mode today. Nothing, for example, could be further from the strident calls upon us of the frantic public-relations world in which we live, and from the persistent pressures upon us to be 'aggressive' and competitive, than the tone and implications of "Blessed are the meek for they shall inherit the earth".

There is, let us be in no doubt, a severe practical problem, impossible to overlook, which provides an inescapable cause for this vital clash, and which, at the most critical moments, faces with an intolerable dilemma those who might wish to carry into straightforward operation the teachings of the Sermon on the Mount. What are such persons to do when presented directly with the diabolical battalions of a Hitler or his like advancing mesmerically and with huge destructive force against them? How, when opposed at short range by a hostile fire-breathing monster or its human counterpart (or worse), does one offer the other cheek? What purpose would such an action serve? It seems clear enough that there are horrendously dangerous occasions, too many as things are, when the only half-satisfactory defence against the invading powers of darkness is by those powers' own hideous types of weapon, the inevitable dire consequences notwithstanding – when anything less will obviously fail, will simply lead to ruin, to irreparable devastation. What is one to say to this?

What one can say is, at least, as follows. The world in which we live is a remarkably inadequate one, overloaded with blatant self-contradictions up to the point, apparently, at the present stage, of imminent self-destruction, in view of the immense forces now potentially under its command (or under the command of some of the least responsible among its members). If that world is permitted to continue unchecked and unaltered along the main course it has been in general pursuing from as far back as one is able to observe, its end could be, indeed is more or less bound to be a bad one. It is essential, in such circumstances, to bring about some radical alteration in the behaviour of the world's inhabitants towards one another, not so as miraculously to turn human beings somehow into angelic creatures living in an atmosphere of permanent goodwill – clearly an impossibility – but so as to modify their emotional reactions to events in a way that induces them, instead of concentrating upon personal interests and the self-gratifying idea of personal gain, to try to achieve a genuine and continuing insight into the feelings and needs of others, and to set some store by them. If I have emphasised 'emotional' it is because intellectual recognition of the situation is decidedly not enough – quite apart from the fact that intellectual capacity alone, isolated from proper emotional sensitivity, is always likely to constitute itself, rather than a help, a threatening, perhaps the most threatening of menaces.

This is the beginning of what one might say. Let me go on. The endeavour to achieve such ends as I have outlined involves an extended and intense and painful and perhaps desperate communal effort; but once those with some real influence over the mental and instinctive tendencies ruling at large among individuals in the more civilised nations have succeeded in making a serious impact in the direction required – and it is evident that the first overwhelming necessity here is for the mood at the top itself to change – then every means will need to be put to work to spread the message as far and wide over the earth as modern communications make possible. This is not, I repeat, a matter of attempting to turn men and women somehow into saints and angels but of inducing in them, against all opposing forces, conscious and unconscious, a truly enlightened approach to life's problems and to the human and natural *contretemps* which will indubitably continue to face them; which will face them in principle no less now than before, and at times, I am sure, so overbearingly that the strains of trying to overcome such problems may well at first seem quite intolerable. In our new kind of world most of the aspects of human frailty which we know so well will still in their essence remain, but our methods of dealing with them will have become different: this is the meaning of the counsel to turn the other cheek – not that the speaker envisages a state of things from which violence and ill-will have magically been banished once and for all, but that when they recur, as inevitably they still must, the general atmosphere in which they do so will be such that a quiet reaction from the offended party will be sufficient to bring disagreement to an end, with no attempt being made at retaliation or at repayment of abuse with equal or greater abuse.

Forty-one

And the Nature of the Change

For a situation of this kind to be conceivable, what is demanded, and this is the deep problem, is a thoroughgoing change of heart on all sides, not only on the side of the offended party in any particular instance, but, essentially, of the offender too. The offender, that is, must have, as we say, a heart which can be touched, a capacity for a degree of shame, otherwise there is certainly no prospect of success for the course recommended – and in our present-day world the probability that one will find this to be so is, for too great a part, slim indeed. We have only to think of trying to appeal along these lines to the better nature of a Hitler or a Saddam Hussein, or for that matter of a ferocious lynch-mob out for Negro blood in, say the America of the 1930s, to be convinced of the absurdity of the proposition. What we have to aim at, therefore, is not just a change, however profound, in the behaviour of uncoordinated individuals, who are likely to earn little but further blows in return for their modesty and for many of their acts of self-denial, even if the effects of such acts may in the longer term not be entirely unrewarding, but a coordinated and concerted change in the attitudes of society as a whole, in which, instead of receiving perpetual exhortations from the highest quarters to gird one's loins for battle or its equivalent, one would receive frequent and positive encouragement to cooperation, with the aim thus not only of self-help but of help for others less fortunate or less well-placed. Persons must be encouraged to united striving for the good of all, on the broadest scale – such encouragement being not hypocritical and concealing probably motives of intense personal ambition, as one might reasonably enough suspect if so addressed at the present day, but sincere, and backed by official action demonstrating its sincerity and helping to produce concrete results accordingly.

Many may find all this perfectly ridiculous, an example, no doubt, of 'the higher nonsense' or of the 'bleeding heart' syndrome or perhaps of 'suburban sensibility'. But, first of all, I would ask those among the objectors who consider themselves in some degree devout Christians why it is that they are so ready to profess the dogmas and carry out in some measure of detail ceremonies and rituals which, to persons not so fully indoctrinated, may seem to belong more in the strangest realms of fairy-tale fantasy than in any of rational belief and activity – while at the same time totally ignoring some of the most direct and plainest and most pressing moral precepts ever delivered, reported as from the mouth of the Prophet himself. Certainly, they are precepts which are singularly difficult to follow, at least without very considerable and wide preparation of the ground on some such basis as I have suggested, and it is true that no indication whatever of the need for such preparation is declared in the original; but then it is the way with precepts of the kind, so delivered, to be uttered simply and barely and without qualification, leaving it to the hearer to work out for himself or herself the conditions under which they can be brought into proper effect. Is the working-out itself so inordinately difficult, even in this case? Is it not, rather, all too obvious, even if it requires by implication a huge readjustment in the human spirit? And, without it, what do we face – what night of appalling and consuming darkness, of whose impending horrors we have far too much advance experience already?

I speak of readjustment – not in any way of an entire remaking from source. No minor readjustment, without a doubt; still, readjustment, among elements already in distinct measure observably in place, if often, in great degree and perhaps deliberately, suppressed. I have previously drawn passing attention to a fact which calls to be re-emphasised here and expanded upon – to the fact that, even now in our present unregenerate days, amid all the tumultuous, elbow-jostling pursuit of riches in abundance and superabundance, of huge and obstreperous power and of noisy ostentation, there are a few persons, noticeably, here and there, whose inclinations seem to be on a different tack; who lean, indeed, eccentrically, outwards from themselves, towards a species of apparent altruism rather than inwards to an intense and other-excluding self-concern. Or again, their desire may appear to be less for the rapid acquisition in vast quantity of this world's crude goods than perhaps for the more painful, less materially rewarding, piecemeal achievement, in some manifestation or another, of the beginnings of wisdom, in so far as humanly attainable – or for the construction, perhaps, of what they feel, with intuitive compulsion, to be intrinsically worthwhile artefacts, or something similar. These characteristics, rare as they may be in anything approaching true purity, yet far from altogether unknown, represent in their essence some of the seeds of the readjustment I speak of, the seeds, I would go so far as to say, of a world portrayed by the Sermon on the Mount as already approaching full flower, a world therefore patently built upon the conception that within the human mind and heart there are not only monstrous black devils waiting only in impatience to burst out and engulf all about them, but also feelings *inter alia* of at least potential friendliness and warmth and commencing comprehension in respect to other unrelated individuals on a quite broad front, and perhaps even in respect to other forms of life. Mankind does not therefore have to remake itself entirely in order to avoid self-destruction; what it has to do is to give its better feelings a great deal fuller rein and not allow them to be overcome by the worse.

To other than professing Christians, of whom I am not one, I would wish to make a point in connection with what I have already said about a certain apparent softening in approach among us, in some parts of the world, at least, during the last few centuries or so, towards things and persons of whom or of which we may happen to disapprove. Here you must read some modification of my remarks a little earlier (perhaps written too much in momentary despair), to the effect that there was hardly an inkling noticeable of any genuine change for the better, in modern times, in the general human attitude, apart from certain changes finally brutally forced upon us by some of the horrid events of the present century, now coming at last to its inglorious end. The truth is that, while prevailing official tendencies are still much what they have always been (and to that extent the impression of little change is undoubtedly justified), nevertheless what underlies them is by no means so rock-firm as it once seemed – and this is not only due to the shattering effects of two world wars.

It is a fact that, if we look just within our own country, over the last three hundred years or so, we can observe the progress and increase of not unimportant tendencies, considerably accelerated (by reaction, no doubt) in the current century, with its dreadful calendar of horrors – tendencies, side by side with the repellent and continuing main theme, towards perceptibly greater general compassion (now showing itself more unashamedly than has been hitherto customary); towards a sharper feeling of antagonism against cruelty and carnage; and towards a reduced readiness to give wanton offence to alien groups and persons. Such tendencies I do not see as merely a part of the mental phenomena to which I have made previous reference, whereby we are enabled, for example, to dispense with the idea of human slavery because we now have trustworthy, often more trustworthy mechanical slaves available. These tendencies, for what they may be worth, and though sometimes no doubt humanly exaggerated in their expression (when they lend themselves to caricature by opponents under the head, now commonly thought of as entirely pejorative, of 'politically correct') are far indeed from universal, and incline, it is true enough, to be balanced or even outbalanced by opposing factors, such as a surge in what is known as 'fundamentalism', a species of semi-murderous fanaticism, with all the profound intolerance of which that is unhappily capable; yet, incoherent and ill-organised though such movements of thought and sentiment may be, they are, if undoubtedly not new in the sense of being without precedent of any kind in human behaviour (in which its seeds have always visibly been present for those with eyes to see), at least appearing to announce a new step in the human development in the sense of being spread more widely, if unevenly, than in previous ages, and not limited to small specialised or in some way doctrinally isolated sectors.

Could this not be in potentiality a fruitful sign of what we are, in essence, in search of, of something deep in the human heart struggling to emerge and to make itself felt, if only we will allow it and will give it actively a helping land – and to show itself superior, in the long run (not, we must hope, the too long run) to the powerful and destructive forces of darkness, threatening otherwise to bring us all down at short notice into an unbroken and infernal night?

Some of the more recent among the novel-seeming movements in mass outlook I describe are, of course, in some ways directly attributable, as noted, to the frightfulness of the experiences undergone in this century; causing such a reaction of stunned shock across the community at large that numbers of us – sadly, not all – have revolted with an unprecedented openness and vigour, in a confusion of heavily battered emotions, against everything that such experiences appear to stand for: the revulsion has never before been quite so plainly and popularly expressed. This is, it seems to me, what may justly be regarded as a species of mass twentieth-century shell-shock (the notion is both more and less than a metaphor); and it is not to be got rid of, in the manner not unusual in the First World War, by the brutal shooting-down of the sufferers, if only because there are now far too many of them and they are too widely scattered and not, for the most part so readily amenable to military-type discipline.

Perhaps, indeed, we needed some terrible sequence of disasters of the kind to bring us in a measure to our senses, if we have them – though one can hardly imagine any superior organising intelligence (which some might wish to presuppose) so exceedingly harsh in vision and feeling as to plan things deliberately in such a way; and though also the current political signs are hardly such as to suggest that we have yet positively learnt anything which might be truly significant from our experiences. Even so, it is a fact that we have been stunned, some few of us at least and in however ill-adjusted a fashion, into the realisation that there must be better roads to the suitable fulfilment of human wants, on whatever reasonable level, than those we have traditionally been travelling so recklessly and unthinkingly (and unfeelingly) hitherto; that the unadulterated evil of certain types of man-instituted regime, which we have defeated for a moment, but which are threatening always to rise again in all their hideousness (since malign forces defeated in battle are very rarely to be thought of as dispelled for ever – it is not in set-piece battle, ultimately, that one is able finally to overcome them) must be resisted at all costs and at all times; and that we have something in the depths of our hearts which is contrary to and can gain the upper hand of our lower natures and which must be brought, with whatever effort, to the fore.

In sum: it is our own lower natures which have thus in essence to be overcome, not anything or anybody outside us. It may seem often otherwise; and when two parties go to war against each other, for whatever surface reason, each normally is concerned to represent the other as the embodiment of all that is evil, while they themselves are the party of all that is pure and good; yet this is not the true way of things in general: it is only in the most extreme case (with the Nazis, in particular, we have, all too recently, suffered the grimmest of examples) that it has any veracity at all, and then only in respect of the one side, never, from the point of view of 'goodness' and 'purity', of the other. One side may, in such an extreme encounter, be black, but the other is never white, never more than a dull and blotchy grey. If it were not so, the side that is painted black could never, in that form, have been permitted to emerge. History at large is portrayed as the battle of civilisation against the barbarian; but the barbarians are not, in the end, specifically a group or groups of men – they dwell deep in the soul of mankind. We will only overcome the barbarians when we have overcome ourselves.

That there is a source in us which can be tapped for this purpose, provided that we have the will and clear-sightedness to turn to it with determination, is clear. That we need no bolstering-up in this from the myths and rituals of organised or any other kind of religion is to me at least equally clear: the fact is that too deep an attachment to the beliefs and practices of a religion, and too close an adherence to the demands that such things make upon us, with consequent exclusion of those persons with any differing religious (or non-religious) observances from the tightly-guarded fold, can work disastrously in precisely the opposite direction. Religious wars, as is well-enough known, have been some of the worst in history. (That there are, nevertheless, certain fundamental moral truths which have come down to us wrapped in religious garb is, again, clear to me, and it is for us to set them in relief as they deserve, but without self-contradictory persecution of any who have failed to understand them and so to carry out their behests.)

Forty-two

So How Do We See Things Now?

That there has in the present century been in certain respects, and in certain not (potentially) uninfluential quarters, a fairly striking modification of previous attitudes is apparent if one reads some of the things written by highly regarded historians at the very beginning of the century – I speak, at the moment, of British writers in particular, but the mood goes in essence a good deal further – and compares them with some of the things said by historians of approximately the same standing in the last decade or two. It is not merely that the superb and over-confident assurance of the old imperialist tone is nowadays largely absent, a development one might, I suppose, have reasonably anticipated now that the empire itself has vanished into the past, has gone to add itself ineluctably to the procession of old empires that have, one and then another, risen and fallen, that were once living and mighty, never conceivably to die, are now in being no longer – it is, rather, that from certain significant aspects the whole perspective seems subtly to have altered, that with reference, for example, to the 'great' men of other times and whatever nationality, whereas, earlier, many historians appear to have largely or wholly disregarded Lord Acton's warning (which, it will be recalled, equated 'great' all too often with 'bad'), the general mood has now become at the least considerably more cautious, ready to take other things into account than splendour and glory and the deckings and devices and heaven-aspiring monuments of self-proud magnificence.

The truth is we all of us, not just that body of us out of the greater world-community who find ourselves looking back with mixed emotional reactions on the receding memory of a departed empire, but all of us, as members of a vastly more extended grouping, who have undergone and remain battered and dazed by this century's monstrous and repeated kicks and blows, we all are now immensely more uncertain of ourselves and of the world we are in some manner aware of outside ourselves. This outer world we once perhaps may have imagined was for the most part well within the range of our normal comprehension, without too heavy a mental effort, but we now see it overhung by shadows of doubt in all directions: we see such an outer world now with a great leaden question-mark over it, not only the world of today (of tomorrow we are likely to have at best only the most confused conception) but, by a sort of huge backward reflection, of the past too, for those of us at least with some limited capacity to envisage that past and put some degree of interpretation upon it, who find such a capacity now troubled by the need for the widest possible realignment of ideas. Ideas once thought stable and unshakeable for all foreseeable time, now seen to be at best mightily arguable, at worst false and perhaps drastically so.

What are we to make of all this? Do we give up the ghost and confess ourselves defeated? Or do we pretend, as many in fact obviously do, that nothing has really radically changed, that we can go on in much the old way as before, that somehow all will be well if we close our eyes to the more unpleasant alternatives facing us? The emphatic 'every man for himself' philosophy is a not unnatural outcome of this latter approach, where men and women live in a spiritually blind and breathless world, in which everyone vies endlessly with everyone else, and in which, in that world's upper reaches, there is a perpetual battle (I speak figuratively, of course, not of war and physical violence, whose menaces, never in fact wholly remote, can remain temporarily obscured) aimed at the piling-up with all rapidity of untold masses of wealth, by fair means or foul, at the accumulation of 'directorships' or the equivalent, in impressive numbers (with the contractual provision that if one is too obviously unsuccessful in any such post one shall be shown the door with what is expressively known as a 'golden handshake'), and ignoring absolutely anything but one's own, strictly one's own, though including possibly in that conception certain of one's kin's, material interests – in a world which, seen from a long and uninvolved way off, might appear to the astonished eye to resemble nothing so much as a grotesquely speeded-up silent film having in it multitudes of little humanoid figures scurrying aimlessly hither and thither in a frenzied and meaningless rush. If all too many of the evidently less fortunate among these figures are seen being trodden relentlessly under foot at every moment, well, that is the way of it, one will be told, and without noticeable regret.

Somewhere at the heart of this confusion of activity, and of considerable significance in the making of it, is a root element in man's nature, one we know well and easily recognise, the element of unappeasable desire for colour and excitement, for risk, for adventure, with often little apparent care for the outcome, even though at the extreme it may involve the possibility of total self-annihilation – an element existing in some human measure in all of us, in some of us more, in some less, but vital. This element is not, in itself, to be thought of as either virtuous or vicious, even if such a comment may seem on first sight strange, seeing that in the popular conception the characteristic in question is held, on the whole, to display itself very much among the virtues.

The point is that there are several of our most basic characteristics, and this is one, which, taken away, would leave us in a state of obvious spiritual (perhaps sometimes even physical) deprivation but which, notwithstanding, are in themselves neither good nor bad but become the one or the other according to the direction in which they are steered. They are, however, so essential in their way to the full working of our human natures as individuals, that without them we feel pressingly that we would be much less, in potentiality, than we are. We tend to laud and sanctify them for themselves, to look upon them as though they needed no steering to appropriate ends but were competent on their own somehow to guide us, to take us wherever, as it were, the winds should blow them and, with them, us. We have to be warned: the desire for excitement and so forth – describable also as the gambler's instinct, to put the matter from one aspect at its plainest – is not, as such, rationally defined and, so, self-limiting, but impulsive and, as I say, instinctive, and urgent for satisfaction by whatever means unless limited and given direction by some moral and reasoning pressure from some quite other part of the human spirit, from somewhere more firmly based to envisage with a degree of lucidity an action's or course of action's end results.

The buccaneer; the ferocious highway robber; the old mercenary fighting-man, ignorant or careless of the cause for which he hired himself, his interest being not in a cause but in adventure and loot; the reckless and consistent womaniser and lecher of all eras; the unscrupulous tycoon; the gun-toting Westerner; the ruthless conqueror

– all these and others of the same basic ilk, on a larger or a smaller scale, have in their time won unrestrained admiration, and do not cease to do so, for their freedom from regulation and their readiness to give fullest rein to their wildest urges. They are untamed, ungoverned, miracles of excess and of self-drivenness beyond all bounds showing no regard for any persons or circumstances outside their immediate circuit: they have become all too easily objects of secret or open envy, their numerous less appealing characteristics falling well into the background, concealed from us by our normal tendency to see only what we wish to see, or even metamorphosed by a trick of thought or presentation into something positively, in appearance, to be desired.

There is, of course, also the aspect of power, of power unconfined, to captivate the hearer or viewer or other recipient of the accounts, duly romanticised, of exploits, real or fictional (largely fictionalised, without any doubt, even when in basis in some measure or other real) of the kind under consideration. There are two opposite sides to this process of captivation, working together – the one affecting those who fancy themselves in the full role of the central character portrayed, and eager to emulate him, the other affecting those, and they are inevitably many more, who have no ultimate illusions about their own ability to play such a part, but who are fascinated by the spectacle of a superior, heavily idealised and glamorised figure, of a type they could imagine themselves following as a God-given 'leader' – someone to spur them on and to inspire them with his magnificent and charismatic self-confidence, to compensate them so for their own hesitations and profound uncertainties in the face of an intractable world. I am far, necessarily, from claiming that everyone belongs strictly in one or other of these two classes – but I am afraid that too many do.

We have at the same time to remember, in view of the army of difficulties thus obviously setting itself up against the hopes of anyone seeking to find some genuine path of order and of universal long-term benefit capable of being traced out of so ill-regulated, so near-chaotic (even so frankly hostile) a field, that there are already in existence a number of types of example of human pursuit of excitement and adventure that have managed to free themselves from the worst of the failings to which I have pointed. They have either developed themselves in a direction of which, at the very least, it is hard to find good ground to speak in unfavourable terms (though some may occasionally have been tempted for ill-based reasons to do so) or, going further, have even enrolled themselves positively in the ranks of those offering service to the community. In the first of these categories are evidently the mountain-climbers and the explorers; in the second, those choosing to work in, say, policing and defence forces, of which areas of communal activity neither is ever likely to become dispensable, though their forms, and the purposes to which they are directed, may need to undergo considerable modification in the future. In a middle, perhaps less obvious category but of the very greatest significance, are to be found those persons whose idea of excitement is not in terms of strenuous physical exertion but of intellectual-spiritual exploration, and whose aims may not in the first place be clearly set towards any species of avowed community service, but which, nevertheless, may provide ultimately huge communal benefits.

Forty-three

The Task to be Faced

It is clear that the seeds, the elements necessary for the creation, potentially, of a more productive future for the human race are already in being, in place on all sides, demanding only to be recognised fully for what they are or can be, and to be given conscious and organic direction. It is true that we have lately been very badly shaken, and we need urgently to see things illumined in their proper light and to take action accordingly. But in doing this there is no reason why we should deny our basic instincts as I have painted them and endeavour with impossible effort to suppress them. They are a part of us, and need to be employed usefully, not suppressed. We must learn to detect where their appropriate goal or (more properly) goals truly lie. Where, for instance, competition is in question we have to learn to compete not ferociously and without restraint or pity against one another as individuals or institutions or nations but together towards the attainment of an ideal held in common, some of us working in one field or in one way, some in another, according to our individual constitutions and capacities as made known to us through our own growing knowledge of ourselves and of the underlying motivations that drive us, and by means of a chart of possibilities set out for us in principle, one would hope and expect, by the society in which we live, for us freely to follow in one or another unforced but adequately indicated manner: that society at its controlling levels not being governed everywhere, as at present, by fierce personal ambition never more than pretending to take note of the needs of those subordinated to its authority, but actually and actively involved deeply in the day-to-day interests and requirements of all about it and all for whom it is in the remotest degree responsible.

The Sermon on the Mount preaches meekness. The besetting sin of mankind, it will be evident, is the direct contrary of meekness, pride, on an overweening and indeed terrifying scale, counterbalanced for the most part rather by fear than by anything more positive or valuable. This is confusedly reflected in the God-figure built up over our heads by religious myth in general, which tends to portray the Supreme Being mostly as 'proud' and 'jealous' and requiring absolute submissiveness if we are not to find ourselves subjected to the direst penalties. This is without apparently taking into consideration that if God is to be seen as a model, the highest of all possible models, for human beings to shape themselves upon, then such a model as this is not merely a hardly suitable one but plainly self-contradictory, for how can one be both proud and submissive at one and the same time? To which there is, of course, a good Jesuitical-type answer, to the effect that it depends which way one happens to be facing: to God one must be entirely submissive at all times, and so, no doubt also, to anybody in agreed higher authority, but to those over whom one can establish any kind of claim to superiority one can presumably be as proud as one likes (as proud as the Devil?). What we have here is, in essence, a magnificent recipe for all the conflicts, all the irrepressible violence which have hounded mankind in the past and look fit to destroy it in the future.

The situation thus depicted is one which has persisted historically in one form or another over many parts of the world and over very lengthy periods of time (we know it at its clearest, perhaps, as 'feudal') and from the oppressive rigidity of whose self-freezing attitudes we have been attempting constantly to free ourselves, but blindly and with the utmost difficulty, and never with more than incomplete success, since, when demolished in one form, usually through internal violence, always an inappropriate method, it tends to reconstruct itself in another, less obvious but equally constricting. What we have to do is, if we can, to rid ourselves of its bonds by rational and well-ordered means, so that it has little power to return.

I have quoted 'meek' from the traditional version of the Bible in English, but it is not in fact the most suitable translation of the Greek word in the original. One of the best New Testament dictionaries available, probably the best (University of Chicago/Cambridge UP 1957), gives the following list of meanings: '*gentle*, *humble*, *considerate*, *meek* in the older, favourable sense... *unassuming*'; and the *New English Bible* of 1970 abandoned 'meek' for 'of a gentle spirit'. It is as well not to run the risk of being misled by the use of an old English word which has somewhat changed its implications since its first appearance in the context. The essence of the meaning is 'gentle and considerate', suggesting an innate feeling for others and an accompanying readiness not invariably to seek priority for oneself and one's own personal interests. This is, of course, the exact opposite of what remains the prevailing approach today – prevailing (particularly in ruling quarters) if not quite universal.

The current mood and its excesses are well displayed in the eagerness with which ex-premiers and ex-Cabinet-ministers turn and rend one another when they have lost office. Edward Heath turns on Mrs Thatcher; Lady Thatcher (now ennobled) rounds furiously on her old colleagues, whom she accuses of 'conspiracy' and of 'treachery'; Norman Lamont comments unflatteringly on John Major and his policies; and so on and so forth. Mutual vilification (no whit less between members of the same political party than between official political opponents) has become the order of the day. The brittle veneer of community spirit holding a party together would appear to have been all too clearly shattered.

I doubt incidentally whether the principle of scoring as many points as possible, by whatever verbal means, over one's political opponents – and I mean now even very specifically those of another party – is in any case a sound basis for Parliamentary debate. Such debate ought to have set out, one would have all too innocently imagined, to discuss with serious intent the problems facing the nation, many of them in all conscience formidable, and the best means of dealing with them. The present practice smells far too much of the boxing ring or (not unreasonably, I suppose?) the market-place. Would-be witty rhetoric is the enemy, one feels, of serious discussion and rational analysis; as it is of true criticism in the review columns of certain newspapers and periodicals, where one feels often that the writer is struggling much too hard for the achievement of some fought-over journalistic crown, it may be at the risk of near-unintelligibility to the passing reader, and it may be also with hardly more than glancing relevance to what was in theory the true object of the exercise.

I have spoken of the desirability of reshaping, and of learning to develop in a right direction, man's innate faculties and natural impulses, rather than of attempting crudely (and almost certainly ineffectually) to suppress them. So far as society's institutions at large are concerned, the principle is equally true, that a diversion into more worthwhile channels does not have to mean the flat rejection of every present category and its replacement by novel inventions but, rather, an appreciation of where humanity's ends in reality lie and of how, by understanding and appropriate handling, current categories can be so rendered as to service those ends in particular, and as effectively and fruitfully as possible. I have no wish to go into all the conceivable elaborations of this thought, but there is one field in especial to which attention should undoubtedly be drawn in this regard, that of public defence. The nations have at present their ministriea of defence, in which the name, where it exists as such, is likely to be as much a mere euphemism for war-making pure and simple as with any genuine significance of some more self-limiting qualification. That name does, however, seem to imply very clearly, whether deeply felt or not, a recognition, for what it is worth, of the tremendous explosive perils of a tinder-box world - on reflection, maybe, a less than adequate metaphor - with unexampled and unpredictable destructive potentialities, and of the intense desirability of steering clear of these latter, of protecting oneself against them by all available means and also of taking care at the same time not unnecessarily to provoke them.

I have no vision of a future world in which the aspect of large-scale defence against hostile forces is no longer relevant, any more than I see a world without efficient local policing - nor do I see a world from which those inner drives urging us to seek risk and excitement and physical and other adventure into the unknown have been banished, no longer need satisfaction, for it is in those very drives that the core of our humanity rests, though they must be properly governed and directed. But as to the concept of defence, I certainly do not envisage a state of things in which men and women, in their intense desire for unity and their rejection of aggression, have allowed themselves to sink as a general body into such a condition of spiritual and physical softness that they lay themselves open all too easily to attack from some sudden and unexpected quarter (whatever that quarter might turn out to be). On the contrary, the price of any future worth having is unending vigilance, and the building-up and maintenance of defending forces (truly defending, not with any hidden aggressive intention) capable, as far as human foresight can determine, of repelling any vicious enemy who might arise.

These future possibilities may seem pretty nebulous but they are in any case a very long way off: I do not see a better world as just around the corner, and I think it would be extraordinarily unwise to imagine us overcoming our present troubles and emerging somehow on to a new and elevated plane of being without long ages of struggle and torment and a multitude of grotesque set-backs and near-disasters. Much of what has quite recently happened should be sufficient to teach us, though I fear mankind is not a quick or ready learner. The (I fear) false dawn of the collapse of the Soviet Union from irresistible internal pressures, leading in the upshot to fragmentation and gruesome potential or actual conflict and in some ways to an actual increase in global instability, is a lesson needing to be taken to heart.

Forty-four

Good and Bad; Right and Wrong

A great line of argument proffered by apologists for current regimes is on the basis of "It's always been like this, and only the quite naïve can think it can ever be any different". But the fact, in so far as it is a fact, that it has always been like this, is no proof whatever that this is how it should be (that that is clearly not so is, I suggest, painfully obvious), nor even that this is how it must always be, the direst of forecasts if it were so, in view of humanity's present predicament. If we are on the brink of self-annihilation, it is essential that we drag ourselves well away from the brink, and surely that should be evident: are we to say that it can't be done? Why? We have seen that there are elements in us which say the opposite, and which offer us at least the opportunity of redemption, an opportunity calling urgently to be grasped before it is too late and we are quite undone.

We have the concepts of good and bad, right and wrong, but what do we mean by them? They are without precision and lay themselves open to interpretation by individuals in the latter's own preferred way. There are those, for example, who will in all normal circumstances be perfectly prepared to interpret 'good' in terms primarily of what is to their own personal (mainly material) advantage on the short view, and 'bad' of whatever may militate against this. If it is proposed that such a state of mind, so described, is an extreme and rare one, I would hesitate for a long while before attempting to make a considered response, though the degree of intensity of such a state may, it is true, vary greatly. But it is not, after all, so very rare to find cases of persons whose attitude towards obligation is, in principle, that the individual concerned is owed a variety of obligations by the outer world but owes nothing at all, not even adherence to a promise, in return. This attitude is a good deal more common than may at first be thought, and in pointing to it I am very far indeed from wishing to make some crude kind of political-type attack on, for example, unmarried mothers dependent on state benefit, but am thinking of people who can easily be a good deal higher up in the social scale. I am thinking not in terms of their possible dependence on state support but of their relationship to other individuals of their own or (particularly) of a lower social or moneyed class. It is only the extension of this attitude beyond certain norms regularly accepted, for good or ill, by any particular local community at large, extension into a wider field – and so likely, among other things, to interfere with big plutocratic interests – that produces instances of openly-accused fraud and public misdemeanour. It is all too common, in fact, and implemented very often by persons of high intellectual ability and a reasoning faculty which it is regrettable to see devoted to such, in final effect, miserable and lowly ends. It is an attitude seeming in some persons to be quite deeply ingrained, and, in extreme cases, and where the intellectual power is not high or coherent, diagnosable as a form of illness. (I would hold it in fact always to be – metaphorically, if you like – a form of illness.)

If there are no simple absolutes of 'good' and 'bad' such that their transparent significance can be registered at a glance, we may feel at least that the categories of 'right' and 'wrong' offer a more solid basis of objectivity against which to test them. Up to a point this is perhaps so, but it does not take us all that far, since these are categories which can easily he misused by those having overruling power to 'lay down the law' and can be applied to categories on the other level just referred to, which not only explicitly contradict them in an immediate sense so that what is 'right' may be equated with what is evidently from a personal aspect 'bad' a clash of interests which may be unavoidable, but, much less helpfully, may prove in the long run to be bad in a much more general and conclusive sense. The fact is that the only truly valid test is a genuinely long-run test, in which the conflict of categories will ultimately be ironed out, but which, it must be confessed, is extremely difficult for *homo sapiens*, with his at present extremely limited capacity for foresight (and all too frequently with even less willingness, through short-run motives of selfishness and greed) to apply.

Where do these concepts come from? We cannot possibly have anything resembling a direct idea, since to suggest otherwise would be to propose that we have some inconceivable ability to project our awareness outside itself so as to survey its workings from an external point of view, taking in at the same time factors foreign to it but able to operate upon it. This is not perhaps the whole story inasmuch as it is also true that the rational faculties present in us have, by their nature, powers of analysis and inference taking us by abstract theory and speculation some way beyond our narrower human limits; but it is wise not to expect too much of such powers, or at least not too much in the relatively short term. To expect too much is certainly to court disappointment (probably far too mild a word); and the best we can readily assert at the moment is that our moral concepts, like the groundwork of our perceptions – of shapes, colours, forms, sounds and tangible and palpable images – are an integral part of our interior human make-up and not able to be thought away. We can be immoral, therefore, but we, as conscious human individuals, taken all in all, cannot be unmoral, whatever may be said of particular human faculties or propensities seen on their own (such as the urge for excitement, of which I have spoken), which may be able in effect to be turned either way.

I naturally do not mean to imply that there is no part of our activities which can be viewed as without a moral bearing: very many of our minor actions at least have little to do in any obvious way with morality, though they may quite often have a pseudo-moral gloss put upon them in the context of whether or not they are considered, in a particular time and place, to be socially acceptable. What I do mean, however, is that we cannot free ourselves, in our total personalities, from the concept of morality, and that once the moral category is seen to be applicable in any observable degree to a specific mode of behaviour, there can be for us no genuine middle way, and that '*a*moral', as frequently seen, is on the face of it strictly a meaningless word perching itself on an implausible or to tell the truth impossible fence, in reality to be viewed invariably as a euphemistic cover for a species of avowedly immoral activity of which the speaker wishes by implication to declare his personal readiness to approve, if behind the hand.

And I do not mean to say that there are not also innumerable occasions, some of huge and awful significance, when we may find ourselves forced into a moral corner and compelled to choose between courses of action all of which are to a greater or lesser extent bad and immoral but of which it is permissible to assert that one, by the nature of its probable consequences, is more likely to have at least a partially good outcome than the other or the others. Most of our moral choices, in this sad and imperfect world, appear of this kind.

We have come back again to the (competing) notions of 'good' and 'bad'. The easiest way to think of these is obviously in terms of profit and loss, and if it is asked, "profit and loss for whom?", by far the easiest answer, coming all too readily to the mind, is "for myself". Hence the race (the 'rat race') to accumulate worldly goods, in vast quantity, for oneself and one's heirs, and the readiness to be growlingly aggressive to others, to kick them (metaphorically or otherwise) violently in the teeth or the crutch if they stand for a moment in our way, and to let the rest of the community go hang. As for other communities outside the limited one we envisage as our own, on this basis they do not count for us at all, except in so far as they may pose some real or imagined threat to our personal profits or, alternatively, in so far as they may offer us some perceived and realistic-seeming opportunity for our own betterment (that is, on this interpretation, for our own greater material gain).

Yes, indeed, we have earlier been into all this, and have seen how little of genuine reasoned argument is really necessary to throw into high relief all the cracks and crevices in this basically instinctive but essentially flawed approach, widespread though it is at the present day – practically universal, it would seem, at the moment of writing – and apparently ineradicable from the global mentality. If life and the promotion and perpetuation and wide and fruitful opening-out of the living community in all its forms is truly the root of all, as seems to me the most rational possibility, then the tiny self-enclosed world of grab-for-myself and bugger-the-customers is a world only, in the end, of pain and illusion and mighty but fundamentally self-defeating effort, overhung by the sinister, growingly menacing clouds of an irrepressible, apparently unstoppably self-developing technology devised by mankind for nothing more likely, it must appear, than mankind's own ultimate destruction.

We spoke of profit and loss; but are these really suitable words, in the wider connection, whether they come easily to the mind or not? What the word 'profit' will most readily suggest to most hearers is some kind of short-term, over-the-counter, money-type benefit as earned by a tradesman (or 'entrepreneur' in Thatcher-speak), or, in the slightly longer term, but tending to be limited to the span of a human lifetime or a very few such lifetimes, an accumulation of precisely such benefits but on an unrestrictedly greater scale, earned by a tycoon, that is, by essentially a super-tradesman, above handling anything of the nature of counter-work himself but delegating all such basic or near-basic or semi-basic operations to a highly-organised army of understudies – at the head of a commercial empire of size and importance offering in the course of its growth opportunities for agents and shareholders and hosts of similar hangers-on to line their pockets with minimal personal effort but hopefully maximum result.

This seems hardly an appropriate conception to apply to the aims, if one may so describe them, of the ultimate community – the overriding community of all communities – in its fundamental, long-term aspect. Profit and loss, as so understood, are surely hardly more than a degraded representation of, in so far as it reveals itself to us, an unquestionable superior reality; than a reduction to material, earthy, fragmented terms of a transcendent, originating, life-giving, comprehensive force essentially above such piecemeal crudities and wanting much more than they can possibly provide. If in the past such a force has succeeded in working somehow through these markedly inferior instruments, the requirement, at this highly critical present moment, and with an urgency indeed not hitherto known, is for inferior instruments of the kind to be abandoned forthwith, to be trodden aside once for all, in favour of something loftier and more effective and longer-lasting – that is, if we have any true desire to see any sort of valid future before us at all.

Forty-five

A Discussion of Terminology

I am aware of the inadequacy of normal terminology in this context, and the fact is not surprising, since we are attempting here to stretch our concepts beyond the normal sphere and into unexplored, in great part unknown territory. I think it necessary, accordingly, to examine with some care one or two at least of the words I have just used, have in a way been more or less compelled to use, for lack of practical alternatives, but which I recognise nevertheless as evidently unsatisfactory. I have talked for example of a superior reality: in what sense can I justifiably say that I view the envisaged reality as 'superior'? Frankly, I can only answer such a pointed but unavoidable question by negatives and by exclusion: for reasons which I hope may be obvious I can offer nothing positive.

The reality I propose is clearly not on our own familiar level; nor, just as clearly, is it on any lower level; therefore, all that is left is that it must be superior. What this involves is nevertheless far from clear, and I do not know how it could well be otherwise; for if it were describable in to some extent familiar terms this could only be because it had certain familiar characteristics, and this could only be if to that extent it belonged in fact to our familiar world, which almost by definition and as I have already indicated it can hardly do. There is however at least one thing which without a doubt our superior reality can firmly and with full confidence be asserted *not* to be, for reasons touched on sufficiently in earlier pages – it is *not*, that is, some manner of personalised super-Being, accountable to no one, in minute and intimate and overweening control of everything that takes place: now, it would appear, as we are frequently told, condescendingly benevolent to its creatures (for such we are assumed to be), now by contrast wantonly fierce and cruel and with little observable trace of pity or sympathy.

If the superior reality is not personal, it must be impersonal, and it is indeed as impersonal process that I see it – process in the same way as evolution is process, working itself out according to its own inward and unconscious methods and formulae over time, through years and millennia, with unrelenting persistence, towards ends unseen, which we could not possibly forecast in any specific terms. But we can still surely say that such a process has full potentiality to be creative and unifying rather than destructive, rather than, that is to say, perpetually tending to set person against person, group against group, with thus the looming conclusion at length, appearing dangerously near and drawing constantly and rapidly nearer, in view now of our enormously increased and increasing technical powers, so recently so much enlarged, of mass destruction on a frightful and vast and irresistible scale, so as to leave at the last a world unrecognisable, in poisoned ruins.

Since the superior reality is not personal, it cannot have personal 'aims' and 'purposes'; and all such terminology that I have employed derives simply from the fact that this is the nearest thing available to me, along the lines of our ordinary verbal usage, to what I am trying to say, even though it seems to imply, according to that usage, something which is absent from and foreign to my actual meaning. We cannot normally conceive of purpose except as a matter of personal intention; but how, then, can the supra-personal have purpose? I think the answer that must be given is that we have to call it 'purpose' because we have no higher concept to which to relate it, but that it is in fact as superior to the ordinary idea of purpose as the supra-personal is superior to personality. Personality is individual, partial, a dying fragment of a greater undying whole; the supra-personal *is* that greater whole, on a level unknown to us except by glimpses. Its relation to us can perhaps be compared, in a quite inexact way, if obvious in the principle embodied, to the human relationship to the 'lower' animals: we have perhaps as little real idea of it as a cat or a dog may have of what goes on in the mind of a human being.

But I have also used the word 'unconscious' of the method by which the superior reality unrolls itself and its purposes (if I may be allowed that word again). It must be plain at this stage that I cannot mean by 'unconscious' something *below* the level of ordinary consciousness. It cannot be in that sense *sub*conscious; it must be, in some valid sense or another, *supra*conscious. Do not ask me to explain what I mean by this. I do not see that I can be expected to know, except – and this is, in fact, an exception of some considerable moment – in as far as I believe that in all modes of life, on whatever main level conceived to exist, there are somewhere and in some degree (even if perhaps minimally) the seeds of all other life from lowest to highest. This is not by any means a totally unbiased belief. We are aware in ourselves, through our emotions and our instincts, of an intimate kinship with all kinds of life which we are accustomed at most times to regard as inferior to human life; and at the same time, if we pause to set our minds for a short while in another direction of thought, we can, I think, all of us, whoever we are, catch at least a momentary ray from a sphere out of our ordinary field of vision but not entirely and in all respects and always beyond our eventual reach.

Do I, then, think that even in a tree or, if you prefer, an insect, there can be in some way some slight hint of human rationality, or indeed of some mode of cognition on a loftier plane? Yes, I suppose that I do, though I am not proposing here to investigate the notion.

Mankind – we have seen – shows itself very largely at the mercy of a narrow and at the same time ill-coordinated mass of primitive drives, of instinctive impulses and desires, operating as they do at short, often extremely short range and with no apparent object other than as instant as possible fulfilment, animal satisfaction or little more, though the elements of half-rational thinking superimposed upon the picture may be able to build up on such a base a momentarily adequate-seeming structure for the subject's satisfied contemplation (but essentially a house of cards). As our knowledge and our skills in a variety of practical fields extend themselves immeasurably, and ever more swiftly, our ability to implement the desires acting upon us increases also naturally at a great pace, and with that there comes the necessity, felt pressingly by a few, if by too many ignored, to set severe limits to the initiating desires, in order to avoid interest-clashes. Experience teaches us that such clashes are otherwise assured beyond doubt; and though once, maybe, they were not impossible to settle at what was then thought to be a bearable (if admittedly to many, in many circumstances, disagreeable) cost, they now, unchecked, face us with probable consequences of a plainly catastrophic nature, and on a major scale.

So much in sum. We need, emphatically, to call in the principles of morality, on the widest, most comprehensive basis, to resolve the problems so powerfully threatening us, and I have done my best to present these principles as deriving from strictly rational grounds, which is entirely the way I see them. The attribution to them of divine origin, as not-to-be-questioned commands of God, appears to me not to strengthen but enfeeble them. Yet I have to accept a blatant seeming paradox (life, as I have previously remarked, is full of such paradoxes, and to overflowing) in the shape of a fact I have already made a point of noting, that explicit moral formulae descend to us in the first place in religious dress, in the form of dogma dictated from on high. How far does this interfere with the straightforward rationality I have claimed for such ideas? To what extent may it be said to invalidate my arguments? I answer, not at all; unless, of course, we are wishing to try somehow to get rid of reason altogether from our world picture.

Partly, it is true, there is no necessary conflict, because, for the upholder of Heaven's dictates, there is no fundamental case for setting up the analyses of reasoned thought and the ordinances of Heaven in flat opposition to one another. In theory, on the contrary, the two approaches can well be expected to support one another, and any apparently insoluble clash between them can readily be treated by the seasoned defender of Heaven's prescriptions not as indicating the failure of reason at large but as demonstrating incontrovertibly the inadequacy of the particular piece of reasoning put forward. On the other hand, however, the believer simply in reason need have no inhibitions in the face of alleged divine commands; while he may be prepared to welcome correspondence between the two sides in purely general terms, he has no need whatever to cling to individual detailed prescriptions professedly laid down by God, if reason finds good case to contradict them.

The reality of the matter, behind all these things, is that *all* rational truth which comes to us, in all its multiple aspects, emerges originally to our minds out of the dark wood of religion and ritual and magic, and there is no exception of which I am aware. Even the purest mode of reasoning we know and use, the mathematical, emerges to us at the source from the shadowy embrace of number-magic. From that embrace we have stripped it as clean as we know how. We need to do the same for morals. What we have at present is the prescription of an authentic vision of reality, but cloaking itself still in garments of superstitious belief, which it has, as yet, been unable to cast off.

Forty-six

Morals and Religion

There is nothing at all strange about the view, confirmable to a very considerable extent by data, that rational thought of all kinds arises directly out of a generally sub-rational feeling-and-thought context. It is natural enough, if one stops to think, that in man's first properly conscious encounters with an untamed and potentially unlimitedly hostile world all about him his initial reactions should be of awe, incomprehension, fear and wonderment, and that he should be more concerned to appease the spirits he imagines to encompass him, to ward them off or conceivably, if he can, to invite them to his protection, than to penetrate his surrounding world more actively and profoundly through the encouragement in himself of an incipient, still very dim understanding. Yet the growth of that understanding cannot in the long run be gainsaid or in essence resisted.

If, then, we remain still in basis incapable of detaching the general conception of moral law from the overshadowing conception of a dominating religious world, in whose absolute context such law is absolutely laid down – 'Ask not why, it is God's command' – that, I suggest, is because we continue to find it extremely difficult to divorce the idea of moral requirements from our instinctive imagined need to guard ourselves perpetually against irresistible (though not deemed entirely unappeasable) pressures and encroachments from an obscurely conceived spiritual world felt to be enclosing us on every side.

Much of the religious atmosphere, it is true, has in these latest years fallen away, if, certainly, by no means from all of us, at any rate from a considerable number, particularly in the West, and it is not hard to see why this should have happened, since the assumed power of religious belief to preserve us from harm has shown itself so pitifully and painfully unavailing over so long a time and over so broad an expense of human territory. The total result, however, of this weakening of the religious hold tends, in view of the close connection envisaged as existing between the fields, to relax also the ties of moral obligation in regard to us – this is not so much a 'decline in moral values', in the way that some might wish to put it, as the automatic consequence of conventional ideas of morality (being unsupported in rational thinking to any adequate degree) having at length nothing much left to hold them effectively together.

We need to free the ideas of morality in our minds not partly and half-heartedly, as in the past, but entirely from the religious and quasi-religious presuppositions which have hitherto hugged man's heels as he strives to go forward, and by which his actions have been continually and desperately interfered with and bedevilled (I am sorry in a way to use the word, but do so, I feel, advisedly) – to free them entirely and with the aid of every determined effort from ill-founded, unreasoned religious dogma, from obscurely symbolic but at root unmeaning and valueless ritual, from magical rites and blind obsessive practices which few of us pretend to see into in any way rationally. But we carry on and repeat them interminably with a greater or lesser measure of fervency simply or largely because this is what our fathers and forefathers did and so this is how things are and must be, and we must defend it all to the bitter death, and woe be to anyone who does not accept every item of it and in detail!

If the basic moral code or codes towards which we consider ourselves to owe theoretical fealty are not to be thought of simply or at any rate primarily as enjoined on us by the dictates of divine ordinance, dictates thus appearing beyond our right to question but founded in reality on a pre-rational (indeed anti-rational) feeling of our being in the hands of invisible circumscribing powers with which it is our business to come to terms without too close investigation – if that is so, then on what basis do those codes arise? Where do they come from? The answer is, to my mind, straightforward and indubitable: they emanate from precisely the same source as the elementary drives which have governed and inspired our existences always, and which we share fundamentally with all other living things, the drives to growth and self-preservation and procreation, and to whatever kind of general development is open to us even at a relatively early stage; except only that they, the concepts and codes of morality, operate at a more fully developed level, available only to consciously articulate personalities having ideas capable of being made rational and coherent, and of formulating a clearer picture of what is ultimately behind the original drives and what gives those drives a genuine meaning beyond themselves even though impossible of achievement except in some way through them.

If the ground 'aim' (I have no better word) of existence is life and the perpetuation of life, then it is very easy to see how the elementary drives, in principle, fit in with this aim and vigorously promote it; they appear very nearly to constitute its essence. Yet it is also true and clear that, left to themselves, in their primitive and unorganised state, they are at least as likely by their effects to contradict that aim, to set up impassable barriers against its fulfilment, to lead in the end to directly contrary results, as to carry it through. There is little need, I am sure, to expand upon this highly significant point at the present juncture; I have already said quite enough to throw all the light that is necessary on the matter – in so far as it does not largely clarify itself, to the concentrated and impartial gaze, without special explanation.

Notions of moral obligation, in however inchoate a fashion – however much misunderstood and misinterpreted, however much in the event mistargeted or even flatly resisted – have been present to the human mind from the beginning, since the conditions for their reception are at hand in the human intellect in all potentiality from the word go. The function of these notions and what they carry with them is to coordinate the primitive and instinctive drives and so organise them that the otherwise ill-directed forces of such drives are prevented from clashing with one another and from militating in the longer run in practice against the very ends which they are plainly out in principle to serve. The instincts, and the conscious urges and impulses so obviously and clearly related to them, are, as such, blind, or at best but rudimentarily aware of what lies at more than a tiny distance ahead of their fulfilment; the moral laws are in such fashion devised or derived as to bring all actions so based into a much wider pattern of activity and of associated events, so as to compensate for lack of human foresight and of will to look ahead by the provision of strong and positively-lit rational guidelines to show the way, and to inhibit excess in all its disastrous modes and with all its terrifying and brutal, self-implementing fancies.

I have again, in the preceding paragraphs, and I am perfectly conscious of the fact, made use of expressions which give every appearance of characterising the impersonal life-process at the root of our affairs as if it were a personal being. How can an impersonal process be truly said to have aims or purposes, and how can it be claimed to 'devise' moral laws? To this I must in the first place answer, and you may accept the notion or reject it, that the impersonality which I allege for the process is not, as I see it, something less than personality but, if anything, something more. That does not, however, return it to the fold of conceived divine beings, since it is not a being, but a process, and, as such, no more divine than the Darwinian process of evolution, which I do not believe anybody has yet offered to worship, and to which no temples, as far as I know, have been set up.

The concept of divinity derives from an attempt to draw within the narrow circle of rudimentary human comprehension matters which are in some way or another beyond that circle and difficult to relate to it but too strongly suspected to affect human affairs to be ignored. In this attempt human feelings and emotions, and significant abstractions of all kinds (usually with strongly physical connections) – e.g. love and war – have historically found themselves, in many societies, personalised and among the gods; and when, in due course, the hugger-mugger of individual and competing deities is overtaken by a larger concept, by that of one all-encompassing unity, there emerges inevitably the concept of the One God. This is still, however, clothed in much of the old garb, heavily personalised, thoroughly anthropomorphic (with both the best and the worst of human qualities inextricably intermingled), and seen as the supreme director, in every minute detail, of the whole extended universe of which we have eventually proved to be so incredibly tiny a part.

Once, however, a sequence of events, through accurate and rational observation, has been effectively recognised as a process, working along specific lines, it cannot easily be appropriated into a divine scheme, as just described: a process is, of its nature, impersonal and free from associated human-personal characteristics – and, being free from human characteristics, it is also necessarily free from divine ones. If this last point appears on first view possibly a trifle paradoxical, it may appear less so when one reflects that divinity, or divinisation, rests to an inordinate degree on magnified humanisation, and that if one removes the human-type element, the divine quality thereupon, having little or no genuine content left to it, collapses inevitably out of sight.

As communities are of all kinds and all sizes, from the largest – who can say how large? – to the smallest, so too with processes, which may differ very markedly from one another and may be great or small; but the Darwinian process of evolution and the major process of which I speak are not different processes; they are in essence one and the same.

Forty-seven

The Life-Process

The great, sweeping, all-embracing life-process travels its own definitive course, operating essentially, as we plainly perceive, through the devices, as we see them, of trial and error – all this describable by us only in terms suitable to the level of our conceptions, beyond which, by the manifest nature of the case, it cannot be expected that we should be able to reach. Our conceptions are bound to interpret a progression of the sort we thus witness as a progression to an 'end', even though this may well seem to imply some kind of personal agency directing the operation, by personally contrived 'devices', under some sort of continuous personal control. With a process, properly understood, this cannot be: personal control involves necessarily the possibility of personal interference, of a progression subject at all points to alteration in mid-course according to changes in the controlling viewpoint and will; and, if it be imagined that the All-High must be above such changes, then this is only to portray the progression, once set on foot, as fundamentally unalterable, as once more in the guise of a self-determining or at least self-developing process.

Most processes we know of, apart from the single great overall process and what are clearly its lesser participants, are seen to act under some species of personal human control or control apparently by some other kind of living being. It is not unnatural accordingly that we should assume, by analogy, that the overall process itself is governed by a personal – superhuman, therefore – controller. But this is pure analogy, and in itself has no value as evidence. In my preceding paragraph I have set out the problem facing us if we make the assumption of an All-High governor in control of the overall process. Either we assume, without any genuine evidence, that the controlling power can and does interfere at will, for reasons singularly inexactly conceived to us, with the process, that from time to time he performs what we deem to be miracles – in which case the process can hardly be any longer thought of as a process in the true and complete sense – or he or it, having given the process an initial push, as it were, to get it going, exercises no further influence over it, and, as far as we are concerned, might just as well no longer be there. The truth is that in the latter case there is no real reason to believe that he was ever there in the first place.

From our human point of view, given that we are aware of an authentic overall process of the kind stated, operating in its own right and strictly analysable in its own right, we have absolutely no need to posit a personal power behind it on which it somehow depends (and on which we are supposed ourselves to depend, too). You may, of course, continue, if you wish, to worship a supreme personality sitting above it, and to offer up prayers and (if you are so minded) sacrifices to such an imagined dominant being: there is nothing to stop you; but the truth is that all the intense emotion and vigorous (even violent) effort involved in such practices must now surely amount to nothing, for such an imagined being is quite beyond our reach. He may, for all we know, if he exists (which we cannot possibly know), hear our invocations and supplications, but there is no chance of his responding to them in any active way, since the process runs irresistibly and impassably and, as far as anyone can conceivably tell, perpetually between us.

Those readers who have some acquaintance with mediaeval philosophy will recall William of Occam and his so-named 'razor', according to which the instruction is clearly given and has never since been forgotten that, in the elaboration of a system, theoretical entities should not be multiplied beyond need. God is such a theoretical entity indubitably beyond need.

It is, I think, worth considering and comparing the demands placed upon us by the two, by the (theoretical) divine being and by the process, respectively – for they both do place considerable demands on us, though this may be obvious only in the case of the divine being. The latter, being a personal entity, makes personal demands: he, she or it demands primarily worship, that we bow down and surrender ourselves entirely to it (and woe betide us if we do not); moral requirements which arise here do so only secondarily, however strongly in due course felt, at least by some of us. The process (and I speak here specifically of the great major process), being impersonal, makes no personal demands, but in the first place drives us imperatively from within, making us conform to it in general and to the direction in which it is moving, without our conscious acquiescence; its basic requirement is that we follow out its ends – seeing that we are indeed a fundamental part of it, and inseparable from it, so that we are bound to that extent to further its progress. I say 'to that extent' – but the extent, so long as our actions are blind, will be limited and quite uncertain, and in order for the function we are fulfilling within the process to be fulfilled effectively, it is essential, ultimately, that we attain to some articulate understanding of what the process is and of what lies ahead of it and of us, or do our best to do so. Thus, in the course of its and (in it) our development, we are made to turn actively towards it and to examine it as closely as we can, and to make all efforts to understand its significance, in itself and to us. God does not ask essentially to be understood (indeed, He is said to be 'beyond all understanding'), only to be unquestioningly obeyed; but the process requires categorically and unequivocally to be understood, by whatever means, not necessarily always basically and purely intellectual, at our disposal.

We interpret 'ends' in the sense of personal purposes; it does not occur to us in the ordinary way that personal purposes can actually derive from larger and, as such, impersonal ends: being ourselves personal entities we cannot conceive of such impersonal ends other than in terms equivalent to personal purposes, but I suggest that in origin things are, as I have just indicated, the other way about.

Let not the fact that I have set God and the process side by side for comparison be allowed to suggest for even an instant that they can be taken as in any measure authentically parallel, as genuine alternative aspects of one and the same thing. The only reality rests with the process. The gods, or God, are artificial constructs preceding our full recognition of the reality; they are mental projections out of the process, substantiated figments offering some apparent centres or Centre of stability or quasi-stability for us to cling to while we, in fact, are led to research, in whatever ways are open to us, into the process and its meaning – though we may indeed, for a long while, have no more than a quite rudimentary awareness of what our research is effectively in aid of.

Codes of morals are formulations from within the process adapted for intended conscious acceptance and, by degrees, comprehension by the human mind. The concept of divine personality, plural initially, then monotheistic, having meantime formed itself also in us, presenting itself as an unseen source of our being, and so, naturally – or should one not rather say, supernaturally – compelling from us awe and implicit obedience, the moral codes, in these circumstances, are shown to us in the first place as emanations from the divine source, transmitted of necessity through human agency, there being, as is evident, no other agency available. Or at least, there is no other strictly *personal* agency available, and it is a strictly personal agency which is required, in the current state of our human awareness. This is not, however, the end of the business.

The process itself does not, in its own right, press upon us orders demanding to be carried out without question, commands which are to be obeyed without any inquiry by us into why or wherefore. Whys and wherefores are the heart and soul of the process. It is nothing, if not rationally questioned and inquired into, and, in as far as the power is in us, understood. Hence the drive – for it too is essentially and undeniably a drive, like other drives, though in its nature to be defined as spiritual in origin not simply physical, we being human, and growingly articulate, and with conscious thoughts stirring in us – to investigate, to analyse, to ask in increasing detail how and why, from what beginnings and to what conceivable end, and to create elaborate, well-rounded fictions to fill the great gaps in our incomplete comprehension. Myth, history, science, philosophy are some of the more self-evident daughters of this drive, this compelling urge to explore and to know, to make conscious contact with the process in and through which and as an integral element of which we maintain our little existences even if we may have, at bottom, no more than perhaps the most tentative idea of what precisely it is that we are doing in this way. Art, romance, explicit dramatisation are also vital offshoots from the same fundamental source; they attempt to *understand*, imaginatively, by their own particular means – if entangled with and, in the result, almost inevitably to a greater or lesser degree likely to be adulterated by the effects, extremely difficult often for an individual even halfway to resist, of persistent pressure upon us by our material environing world, never ceasing to hem us in, always projecting before us in deceptive radiance the illusory goal of gains to be got, personal ambitions to be relentlessly fulfilled, whatever the cost.

It is very difficult to get away from the idea of 'gain' or 'profit' as a suitable end of activity, even though I have written off short-term personal gain of a material nature as any sort of genuine rational aim for a thinking human being capable of seeing a fraction beyond his or her immediate needs and circle. Strictly speaking, in fact, nobody ever does have such an aim – in the sense that it is absolutely common form for people to have in view the idea of 'making a name' for themselves, that is to say of establishing for themselves some longer-term theoretical prolongation of their relatively short-term physical existence to give them some specious semblance of immortality; and as to 'personal', this also is regularly subjugated, or, should one say, extended to cover a person's kin or close friends or associates, with much the same sort of motive. How about 'material'? This is the most complex concept. It certainly involves something more than the simply physical: as we have plainly enough seen, accumulations of goods, of worldly riches, are not normally made for their own sake, or, for that matter, for any purely physical pleasure (whatever that might be conceived to be), that might somehow accrue from the possession of those goods and riches, since it is common practice to continue an accumulation of the kind well beyond any such basic and indeed quite narrow limits and to do so, rather, out of what appears to be a burning desire to be ahead, to be 'better' than one's neighbours, however that is to be interpreted. This is very much material desire; and yet at the same time it is a good deal more than material, it signifies somehow a blind groping towards something beyond and above and somehow always out of reach.

Forty-eight

In Sum and in Conclusion

So what of 'gain' and 'profit'? If I have written off short-term personal material gain as a suitable human end, it is evident that actually I am far from the only person alive to do this, even though most people may not do so quite so explicitly as I have done. Have the terms 'gain' and 'profit' value for us outside their patent shopkeepers' meaning? Even the shopkeeper's profits, it has to be said, really do look as though they stand for something in the shopkeeper's mind that is a good deal more than they themselves seem to be on the surface. I have said what I myself take to be behind it all: the constant unending pressure by the life force – presenting itself to us outwardly and palpably in the great comprehensive community of all life – for self-perpetuation and development, through and with the aid and cooperation of every one of its individual living representatives, from what we take to be the humblest to the highest, mortal every one over a longer or a shorter span, but every one bearing the banner, in its piecemeal and fragmented way, of the fundamental and undying whole. It is, of course, too easy and tempting to think of such an overwhelming operation in what are essentially human terms, as necessarily under the governance of a superior personal Being looking down upon us from a great height and controlling all our petty movements; but this – very obviously if we are prepared to stop for long enough to consider the matter rationally – cannot be the way of it. The operation is a totally impersonal process, working itself out from within, to an end we on our level are unable to foresee.

It is impersonal, and can have no conceivable personal regard for us as individuals. We may be said to be under its control, in the sense that we are evidently a good deal less than it is and are under its perpetual regime; we are in a sense its tools; yet, just as evidently, it needs us as much as we need it – for without us where can it possibly go? But we, nevertheless, without it are nothing. The truth is that we are indissolubly bound up with it; we are no less than an integral part of it and we stand or fall together.

The problem is that the process has, to all appearance, no means of realising itself except, immediately, and in the short term, through the individual; and the individual – I refer here specifically to the human individual (of creatures undoubtedly the most distinct and individual) – then, as a result, shows a powerful tendency, in its own less than far-seeing way, to present itself to itself, despite the inevitable short term of its existence, which it readily overlooks, as if it were the totality of the process itself. (It identifies itself, that is to say, with the process – as indeed, in principle, it should – doing so, however, in an extreme and highly exaggerated manner.) Considered coolly and rationally, this is an obvious absurdity, but coolness and rationality are only partial characteristics of the human mind, which is dominated far too easily by the excitable and irrational underlying drives and compulsions which, however limited and limiting, have been in their indubitably forceful manner responsible for the existence and temporary maintenance of the individual being in the first place. It is necessary for the individual to break free from such domination, to learn, not to deny, nor altogether – in whatever way that might be done – to suppress its fundamental energies, but to redirect them into appropriate channels for the benefit of the whole – of the process itself in the long run. It is this redirection to an end, this notion of genuine and ultimate purpose, which we can imagine the process as setting before us, through the instilling somehow of moral principles which we are intended effectively to follow. The gain, then, the profit, are not in the shape of material gain and profit for the individual, but of unseen benefit and value for the whole: benefit which in the upshot is, I have to believe, something more than simple self-preservation (hence 'unseen') even though that is undoubtedly the aspect under which it first presses itself upon us... As for 'value' – I readily acknowledge that I have used such a confessedly imprecise term with a degree of conscious and deliberate intent. How could it indeed be much otherwise? How could I, earthbound, scouting the remote heavens, possibly claim to do more than fleetingly to descry, in a brief and distant and inevitably clouded glimpse, some small indefinite hint – no more – of what might conceivably await us if only we were able effectively to curb our most destructive inclinations?

We strive, all of us, each under the aegis of his (or her) personal and conscious ego, for what is no less than a species of immortality; but if we remain content to strive as individuals, or as self-absorbed individual groupings, one against another, the end most be a contradiction of our patently unfulfillable aims. The great central process running over and through us all has lately provided us as human beings with reason, so that we may be able eventually to understand the nature of the process in itself, and so endeavour, within our powers, to carry it forward; but a too facile application of the reasoning faculty has its own immense dangers – if we do not learn, that is to say, to free it from the lure of immediate self-satisfaction, from the heavy taint of material short-term advantage on behalf of the limited, self-regarding centre-point of personal activity.

I have, then, only this, in briefest conclusion, to add: that the choice for us in the end must be between two fairly direct opposites (extremely opposite in their final implications), between on the one side genuinely listening and genuinely paying attention to and doing everything in our human power to promote and act upon the quietly voiced and rationally based proposals (difficult though they may indeed be for us to come to terms with in our unregenerate state) of the Carpenter's son– not, however, at all for reasons of dogma, but for their own sake and for the reason of reason itself – and, alternatively, on the other side, driven by appetite and the craving for glory, unreflectingly obeying the peremptory, hectoring and strident calls to action of (as she has been called, and as she seems pleased enough to call herself) the Grocer's daughter.

Our Tony Blair
Has lots of flair.
He meant above all to get *there*.
His idol's Thatcher.
He will match her.
Donnerwetter!
He'll do better.
He's the leader, he's the king,
He's the lord of everything.
So come, you chaps, be on your toes.
Tony the Great knows what he knows.
With one smart blow he'll crush his foes.
Make no mistake – what he says *goes!*

Index

A

Abyssinia, 124
Acton, Lord, 25, 211
actors and acting, 104, 105
Africa and Africans, 13, 74
Alexander the Great, 181
America and Americans, 24, 43, 68, 102, 105, 139, 140, 205
anarchy, 129
animals, 16, 35, 39, 113, 152, 155, 166, 169, 171, 227, 228
anthropomorphism, 78, 114, 234
Aristotle, 35, 67, 68, 77, 78, 79, 104, 112, 113, 189
Athena (goddess), 116
Athenian Democracy, The (Hansen), 78
Athens and the Athenian democracy, 78, 79, 83, 84
Augustus, 106
authoritarianism, 54, 55, 86, 107, 109, 135

B

barbarians, 174, 210
Barrie, Sir James, 48
BBC (British Broadcasting Company), 74
Bible, The, 217
black men and white men, 13
Boots Ltd, 73
British Empire, 35, 66, 87
British Government, 35, 61
buccaneer(s), 34, 36, 37, 38, 162, 213
Business in the Community, 72, 73

C

Cadburys, 73
capitalism and capitalists, 67, 68, 69, 70, 71, 72, 74, 75, 79, 80, 82, 86, 140
capitalism and capitalists, 54, 55, 60, 61, 62, 63, 64, 65, 66, 67
Carpenter's son, the, 243
Chancellor(s) of the Exchequer, 116, 118
Chicago Tribune, 44
Church/churches, 33, 143
Churchill, Sir Winston, 46
CIA (Central Intelligence Agency), 102
city-state(s), 29, 79, 173, 174, 175
Civil War, American (1861–5), 68
civilisation, 68, 88, 89, 95, 97, 99, 150, 174, 175, 176, 210
Cold War, 102, 103
communism and communists, 54, 55, 57, 60, 82
communities, 13, 14, 16, 17, 18, 19, 20, 22, 24, 25, 31, 32, 39, 40, 41, 42, 43, 54, 69, 72, 73, 94, 109, 113, 119, 137, 153, 154, 157, 167, 171, 172, 173,

174, 175, 176, 177, 178, 179, 181, 187, 191, 197, 208, 211, 215, 222, 224, 225, 235, 241
Community Tax, 14

D

Darwin, Charles, 78, 200, 234, 235
democracy, 47, 78, 79, 81, 82, 83, 84, 86, 112, 116, 117, 123, 132, 195
demos, 132
Descartes, 165
dictatorships, 54, 81, 82, 86, 107, 113, 123, 124, 196

E

East, the, 77, 80, 102
Egypt, 174, 175
empires, 66, 87, 124, 181, 188, 211, 225
ethics, 28, 29, 33, 36, 73, 74, 82, 107, 150, 181
European Commission/ Community/ Union, 61
evolution, 28, 175, 182, 227, 234, 235
Exchange Rate Mechanism, 115
ex-Nazis, 102

F

film-stars, 139
First World War, 136, 160, 209
Ford, Henry, 43, 44
free market, the, 55, 75, 129
freedom, 13, 40, 43, 46, 55, 61, 75, 82, 83, 129, 130, 136, 137, 139, 143, 155, 162, 188, 191, 192, 195, 196, 198, 199, 214
French, the, 116, 139
Freud, Sigmund, 108, 109
fundamentalism, 208

G

Georges, the, 135
God, 105, 109, 114, 123, 151, 152, 165, 166, 167, 202, 214, 217, 229, 231, 234, 237, 238
gods, Greek, 78, 79, 80, 113, 116, 143
Golden Age, 89
government, 25, 35, 41, 42, 55, 70, 78, 79, 82, 84, 85, 116, 119, 128, 129, 130, 132, 138, 160, 179, 200, 202
great men, 25, 45, 211
Greece, 28, 95, 129, 132, 173
Greek annual magistracies, 79, 80, 83
Greek democracy, 78, 79, 82, 83, 84, 132
Greek tragedy, 77, 78

H

Hansen, 78
Heath, Edward, 218
Hegel, 45, 54
Henry V, 29
Henry VIII, 135
Heraclitus, 50
history, 12, 29, 34, 37, 43, 44, 45, 46, 47, 49, 53, 57, 78, 87, 89, 96, 99, 119, 133, 137, 161, 175, 181, 187, 200, 210, 239
  remark of Henry Ford, 43
Hitler, Adolf, 55, 123, 124, 126, 193, 203, 205
Hollywood, 126, 139
Homer, 28
Hussein, Saddam, 29, 100, 205

I

immortality, 21, 25, 90, 240, 243
inferiority complex, 108
inflation, 118, 119, 120
instinct, 12, 13, 24, 33, 70, 86, 145, 149, 169, 175, 213, 216, 228, 233
IRA (Irish Republican Army), 35, 36

K

KGB (Russian), 102
kings and kingship, 25, 132, 143, 144, 174
Kuwait, 29

L

Labour Party, 85
  New Labour, 85
language and linguistics, 27, 49, 50, 51, 53, 140, 146, 170, 171, 174, 176, 187
leaders and led, 25, 37, 55, 59, 65, 81, 108, 109, 123, 158, 159, 160, 161, 181, 193, 195, 214
life, 13, 19, 20, 21, 23, 24, 32, 40, 43, 48, 49, 50, 61, 63, 65, 66, 68, 77, 85, 88, 97, 103, 104, 108, 112, 113, 115, 120, 140, 162, 171, 177, 178, 179, 182, 186, 204, 207, 224, 228, 229, 233, 241
  'the good life', 24, 182, 189
life-process, the, 233, 236–40
Little Bluebell, the Fairy Schoolgirl, 48, 49
London, 139
lots, casting of, 15, 78, 79, 80, 83
Louis XIV, 25, 135
  L'état c'est moi, 135
Lowry, L. S., 86

M

Maastricht Treaty
  French referendum on, 116
magic, 116, 152, 204, 229, 232
Major, John, 134, 218
market, the, 55, 56, 75, 79, 80, 129, 162
Marx Brothers, 188
Marx, Groucho, 188
Marx, Karl, 54, 56, 60, 76
Maxims (Rochefoucauld, de), 32
McCarthyism, 102
media, the, 107, 134
meekness, 217
  Sermon on the Mount, 217
Mesopotamia, 174, 175
monarchy, 83, 133, 135, 143, 144, 145
Mongols, 181
moral(s), 33, 34, 46, 54, 71, 72, 74, 83, 102, 103, 129, 135, 138, 139, 142, 144, 146, 148, 149, 150, 151, 167, 168, 169, 170, 175, 181, 182, 186, 193, 201, 202, 206, 210, 213, 223, 224, 229, 231, 232, 233, 234, 237, 239, 242
Mussolini, Benito, 124, 193
myth and legend, 34, 77, 89, 114, 210, 217, 239

N

nanny state, 55
Napoleon (Napoléon Bonaparte), 116
Nazis, 102, 209
New English Bible, The, 218
New Testament dictionaries, 217
Nile, the, 174

Northern Ireland, 35

O

oligarchy, 83, 84
On the Heavens (Aristotle), 77

P

Paris, 139
Parliament, 127, 133, 218
Pericles, 83
Peter Pan, 48
pharaohs, 174
philosopher-king, 132, 144
philosophy, 26, 45, 68, 95, 140, 144, 164, 178, 189, 212, 237, 239
Plato, 84, 114, 132, 144
  Republic, 132, 144
police, 190
politically correct, 208
prehistory, 89
president, 134
presidents of USA, 105
  Bush ("read my lips"), 85
Presocratics, 28, 50
prime minister, 61, 118, 128
Prince and Princess of Wales, 145
process. *See* life-process, the
prophets, 114
public relations, 17, 39, 85, 104, 125, 202
Pythagoreans, 28

Q

Quakers, 73, 74
quantum theory, 114
Queen, 143
Queen Mother, 140

R

Reagan, Ronald, 83, 105
reason and rationality, 13, 26, 42, 112, 124, 144, 146, 152, 155, 156, 159, 166, 229, 243
referendum, 15, 117, 128
  on Maastricht, 116
religion(s), 33, 72, 151, 201, 202, 210, 229
religious community(ies), 54, 173
religious wars, 210
Robin Hood, 34
Rochefoucauld, de, 32, 33
Rowntrees, 73
royalty, 133, 134, 136, 142, 143, 144, 148
Russians, 102

S

Sally, 9, 10, 11, 12, 13
Saussure, Ferdinand de, 49, 50, 51
science, 28, 239
Second World War, 102, 136, 198
Sermon on the Mount, 202, 203, 207
  meekness, 217
sex
  and gender, 12, 13, 29, 138, 139, 143, 148, 149
  and marriage, 139
  and morals, 144, 148, 149
  and royalty, 142
Shakespeare, William, 29, 104
Sicily, 132
Sixties, the, 136
slavery, 68, 83, 193, 208
Smith, Adam, 140
Social Chapter (European Union), 61
society, 14, 17, 33, 34, 54, 57, 61, 68, 72, 75, 81, 86, 89, 95, 97,

105, 116, 119, 138, 176, 177, 182, 185, 187, 205, 216, 219
remark by Margaret Thatcher, 14, 116
Soviet Union, 43, 46, 47, 54, 57, 59, 66, 100, 220
Spartans, 54
Stalinism, 59
Supreme One/Being, 21, 217

T

Thatcher, Lady (Mrs Margaret Thatcher), 10, 11, 12, 13, 14, 17, 55, 61, 63, 86, 104, 105, 116, 121, 140, 176, 218
the Grocer's daughter, 243
Thatcher, Sir Dennis, 10
Thatcherite theory of government, 129
The Times, 43, 74, 133, 140
Third World, the, 179
Tiny Tim's Weekly, 48
Tories, 85
and the 1992 General Election, 85
tyranny, 81, 83, 86, 129

U

United Nations, 29
University Boat Race, 87
USA, 47, 105, 140
Utopia, 47, 93

V

values, 13, 14, 32, 45, 54, 62, 69, 138, 150, 152, 154, 232
Van Gogh, Vincent, 62, 67
Victorian firms – provision of free housing and education, 73
Victorians and Victorian values, 137, 138, 139

W

West, the, 54, 80, 91, 136, 231
Western films, 77, 126
Western Powers, 102